BALANCING LOCAL CONTROL AND STATE RESPONSIBILITY FOR K–12 EDUCATION

2000 YEARBOOK OF THE AMERICAN EDUCATION FINANCE ASSOCIATION

Edited by

Neil D. Theobald
Indiana University

and

Betty Malen
University of Maryland

Routledge
Taylor & Francis Group

LONDON AND NEW YORK

First published 2000 by Eye on Education

Published 2013 by Routledge
2 Park Square, Milton Park, Abingdon, Oxon OX14 4RN
711 Third Avenue, New York, NY, 10017, USA

Routledge is an imprint of the Taylor & Francis Group, an informa business

Library of Congress Cataloging-in-Publication Data
    Balancing local control and state responsibility for K-12 education / edited by Neil D. Theobald and Betty Malen.
    p. cm. — (Yearbook of the American Education Finance Association ; 21)
    Includes bibliographical references and index.
    ISBN 1-883001-96-X
    1. Education and state—United States. 2. Public schools—United States—Finance. 3. Public schools—Decentralization—United States. I. Theobald, Neil D. (Neil David). II. Malen, Betty. III. Annual yearbook of the American Education Finance Association; 21st.
    LC89 .B35 2000
    379.73—dc21

                                                                    00-024910

ISBN 13: 978-1-883-00196-4 (hbk)

Cover design by Carolyn H. Edlund
Editorial and production services provided by Richard H. Adin Freelance Editorial Services

This book is dedicated to our fathers, Milo W. Theobald and Harold M. Malen, who gave us our core values and provided the critical foundations of our educations.

ABOUT THE EDITORS AND CONTRIBUTORS

Neil D. Theobald is Associate Professor of Education in the School of Education at Indiana University. His specialty in research and teaching is economics of education and education finance. He has been a visiting professor in the Department of Economics at the University of Edinburgh (Scotland) and is the 1995 winner of the Jack A. Culbertson Award in Educational Administration as the professor who, in the first seven years of his or her career, has made the most outstanding contribution to the profession. Prior to going to Indiana in 1993, Dr. Theobald taught at the University of Washington. His Ph.D. dissertation received the 1990 Jean Flanigan Award from the American Educational Finance Association.

Betty Malen is Professor of Education in the College of Education at the University of Maryland. Her specialty in research and teaching is politics of education and educational reform. She has published numerous articles in professional journals and dozens of book chapters and policy reports around issues of decentralization, choice, and the professionalization of teaching. Prior to going to Maryland in 1994, Dr. Malen taught at the Universities of Utah and Washington. She received her Ph.D. from the University of Minnesota, winning the American Educational Finance Association's Jean Flanigan Award for the outstanding dissertation in the study of educational finance in 1985.

Michael Addonizio is an associate professor in the College of Education at Wayne State University.

Jeffrey Bardzell is a Ph.D. candidate in comparative literature at Indiana University.

Nancy Beadie is an associate professor in the College of Education at the University of Washington.

Barry Bull is Associate Dean of the School of Education at Indiana University.

John Dayton is an associate professor in the School of Leadership and Lifelong Learning at the University of Georgia.

Frances Fowler is an associate professor in the School of Education and Allied Professions at Miami University in Ohio.

Patrick Galvin is an associate professor in the School of Education at the University of Utah.

Tim Mazzoni is a professor in the College of Education at the University of Minnesota.

Donna Muncey is a research associate in the Department of Educational Policy and Planning at the University of Maryland.

TABLE OF CONTENTS

PART I

INTRODUCTION

1

INTRODUCTION AND OVERVIEW: BALANCING LOCAL CONTROL AND STATE RESPONSIBILITY FOR K–12 EDUCATION

Neil D. Theobald
and
Jeffrey Bardzell
Indiana University

The United States ratified a federal constitution in 1789 that, by omitting mention of public education, left responsibility "to the states or to the people" (U.S. Constitution, Tenth Amendment). States moved immediately to recognize this responsibility—of the original thirteen states only Rhode Island had no constitutional or statutory provision for public education (Cubberley and Elliott 1915). Yet, for much of our nation's history, states delegated all executive power and even many legislative powers (e.g., the power to tax property) to local school boards.

The last two decades, though, mark a major change in this general pattern of limited state involvement in schools. In the years since 1980, "state after state, usually led by their governors, enacted significant legislative reforms to their public schools" (Bull 1998, p. 194). This shift in initiative—away from local school boards and towards state-level institutions—has been particularly stark in the school finance arena.

The nexus between state responsibility and local control is the focus of the 21st Annual Yearbook of the American Educational Finance Association. The purpose of this edition of the Yearbook is to analyze the evolving balance between state responsibility for funding K–12 education and local autonomy in operating these schools. The goals of this analysis are twofold. First, the book seeks to characterize how this relationship has changed, both in terms of the policy initiatives undertaken (e.g., charter schools) and the resources committed. More importantly, the book seeks to explain why the intersection between the states' role and local prerogative has shifted so rapidly in the last two decades.

BACKGROUND

For most of our country's history, the balance between state responsibility and local control tilted heavily towards the latter. In retrospect, observers often cite financial considerations as one of the major forces in explaining this tilt. Until the twentieth century, local sources provided all or nearly all school revenue. As late as the 1929–30 school year, local taxes accounted for 83 percent of total public school revenue (National Center for Education Statistics (NCES) 1999, p. 169). In such an environment, it is easy to see how a strong tradition of local control of schools would naturally develop.

It is unclear, though, whether high levels of local funding forged the preference for local control or whether high levels of local funding were simply a manifestation of America's long-standing and deeply embedded fear of large government. Our non-centralized, federal system of government is based on the

Founding Fathers' unwillingness to trust central government with the supervision of the people's liberties. In a like fashion, a non-centralized, local system of school funding could find its basis in Americans' unwillingness to trust central government with the supervision of their children's education. Local people clearly believed they knew the community and its children the best. High levels of local funding for schools kept locals—and not the state—as the primary decisionmakers with regard to their children's education.

Contemporary observers, though, did not cast local control strictly as a matter of "those who pay the piper call the tune." Philosophers justified the practice by appealing either to John Locke's view that legitimate governmental concerns were limited to the protection of life, liberty, and property, or to the principle of subsidiarity which holds that it is unjust "to assign to a greater and higher association what lesser and subordinate associations can do" (Messner 1951, p. 103). According to both of these dominant views, the state should not interfere in public education as long as local school boards can adequately carry out these duties. Thus, even as state funding of public education increased at five times the rate that local funding increased— surpassing local revenue as the primary source of funding by 1980 (NCES, p. 169)—state action remained "intentionally peripheral" (Alexander 1990, p. 307).

Classical economic theory provided ongoing support for the ideology of local control of schools. According to influential eighteenth-century economists such as Adam Smith and Jeremy Bentham, decentralized control over the discretionary activities of public entities (such as schools) allows these entities to best produce efficiency, while also providing these services at minimum cost. Such free market reasoning is still widely used by "efficiency-oriented policymakers [who] traditionally have advocated decentralization of revenue decisions on the grounds that local school districts would remain more responsive to the values and interests of diverse constituencies" (Mitchell and Encarnation 1984, p. 8).

The free marketers were not alone within the economics profession in providing ideological support to the principles underlying local control of schools. According to Tresch (1981), the principle of consumer sovereignty (i.e., individuals know best their own self-interests) underlies the normative theory of public finance with the implication "that the government should serve society primarily as an agent acting in direct response to the preferences of citizens" (p. 13). To the extent that educational decisionmaking on major issues shifts away from local school boards to the state level, though, it becomes more difficult for government to respond directly to the preferences of citizens. Observers of the school finance scene at the time that state governments began to limit the scope of decisions available to local school boards expressed a fear that "escalating state power [constrains] the ability of local officials to respond to constituent preferences [and thus diminishes] liberty—and probably efficiency" (Garms, Guthrie, and Pierce 1978, p. 34).

Organizational theorists joined in the support of local control by contending that the practice allowed schools to adapt to the diverse conditions they faced in the communities in which they were located. According to this view "a large measure of local control is necessary if the public school system is to fulfill its function in a dynamic society" (Holmstedt 1940, p. 45). The primary value of this organizational structure was that it permitted variety and flexibility in school systems. "There must be freedom in the school system to experiment, invent, and adapt, and these are possible only when external restraints are absent" (Holmstedt, p. 46).

Over the last two decades, though, the initiative in deciding educational policy has shifted away from local school boards to the state level. A host of factors contributed to this move by states to take on a more aggressive role in the governance of public schools. One was the new federalism of the 1970s that pushed much of the educational responsibility that the federal government had collected in the 1960s back to the states.

At the same time, a second factor was landmark school finance litigation, such as *Serrano v. Priest* and *Robinson v. Cahill*, which sought to narrow or eliminate existing disparities in spending across school districts. The judicial response to cases such as these promised to push states towards providing a larger share of public school revenues. This change in the revenue stream created clear implications for state regulatory prerogatives: "these forces, along with ever-expanding budgets for both public education and higher education, require that governors and legislators scrutinize programs in education with greater care than ever before" (Campbell and Mazzoni 1976, p. v).

A third factor driving state activism was the Reagan administration's highly effective rhetorical efforts to create popular demand for educational change. The administration's 1983 report, *A Nation at Risk*, "connected the American public's worries about the nation's economic future to the performance of its schools" (Bull, in press). As a result, state governors and their legislatures, driven by this widely perceived linkage between high-quality schooling and a state's economic growth, became "involved in educational policy-making in an unprecedented way" (Boyd and Kerchner 1988, p. 1).

Throughout the United States, state governments in the last two decades have moved into new terrain by limiting local taxation, mandating high-stakes testing of students and more stringent certification of teachers, and by creating charter schools. The intensity and persistence of this effort is likely to continue into the next century—and could even accelerate and expand to the federal level. "A logical implication of federal goals is some type of nationwide base education spending, adjusted by state and regional cost-of-education differences, that would allow each district and school to meet the nation's bold and ambitious education goals" (Odden and Kim 1992, p. 294).

These assertive actions are more than incremental adjustments of long-standing policies. They are creating, or have the potential to create, entirely different sets of state and local relationships. These new sets of relationships will determine who controls educational resources—both financial and administrative—and how these resources will be allocated between state and local institutions.

What legal and political constraints will states attach to the use of school resources? What effect will these requirements have on schools? What are the costs, both intended and unintended, of these new state policies (e.g., high-stakes testing), including the costs of local responses to them? How are the costs (and benefits) distributed? These are among the critical questions confronting the educational finance research community. The models researchers create to measure the adequacy and equity of school resource allocation should reflect the constraints that states place on how local schools may use resources. Are these resources tied to tightly structured state mandates or are schools allowed—or even encouraged—to stamp their own imprint on the programs in order to reflect local values, interests, and preferences? Is the state assuming a regulatory or assistance-oriented role? The constraints attached to resources are intended to ensure consistent and universal minimal adequacy across localities in the state. They also, though, can profoundly dampen local initiative, which may translate into less efficient use of these resources.

Clearly, any full understanding of K–12 resource allocation must include a detailed knowledge of what is happening to state and local relationships and how these new arrangements influence the evolving balance between state responsibility and local autonomy. This 21st Yearbook of the American Education Finance Association focuses on how these relationships have changed and why the balance between state responsibility and local autonomy has shifted so rapidly in the last two decades.

TAXONOMY OF STATE SCHOOL FUNDING ACTIVISM

To facilitate a more systematic analysis of the evolving balance between state responsibility and local license, Table 1.1 provides an empirical taxonomy of the different forms that state activism in the school finance arena has taken since 1980. The columns of this typology categorize state activism on the basis of the social values it embodies. This approach follows the lead of Garms, Guthrie, and Pierce (1978), Boyd (1984), and Monk (1990) in treating equity, efficiency, and liberty "as the basic and fundamental goals that societies pursue when resources are allocated for education" (Monk, p. xvi).

TABLE 1.1. A TAXONOMY OF DIFFERENT
FORMS OF STATE ACTIVISM IN SCHOOL FINANCE

Approach	Value		
	Equity	Efficiency	Liberty
Financial Incentive	Categorical funding for targeted populations	Guaranteed tax base/yield	Vouchers/tax credits
Persuasion	Opportunity-to-learn standards	Public dissemination of each district's state test results	Charter schools within a public school district
Mandate	Elimination of, or strict limitations on, the power of local schools to tax	High-stakes testing of students	Access to school district services by private school students

These values are held in constant tension in state legislatures, though, with "a strong historical tendency for states to pursue only one goal at a time, neglecting or suppressing the others" (Mitchell and Encarnation, p. 9). One way to distinguish between different forms of state activism, therefore, is to see them as implicit endorsements of one of these three competing values.

The rows of Table 1.1 further differentiate state activism by dividing it into three separate approaches that the state can take in convincing local school districts to modify their policies: financial incentives, persuasion, and mandates. McDonnell and McLaughlin (1982) argue that it is necessary to consider the form or "focus" of state-level action as well as its "nature" in distinguishing among policy options. "[The state's] role can be either regulatory or assistance-oriented in its focus: A strong state role does not necessarily mean strong state control" (McDonnell and McLaughlin, p. 7).

Table 1.1 follows McDonnell (1994) and supplements McDonnell and McLaughlin's model by adding "persuasive" policies as a third approach. Clearly, policies implemented in pursuit of nominally identical school funding goals may have very different effects depending on whether they use an assistance-oriented approach (i.e., financial incentives), a persuasive approach (i.e., the bully pulpit), or a regulatory approach (i.e., mandates).

SOCIAL VALUES PURSUED THROUGH STATE ACTIVISM

EQUITY-ENHANCING INITIATIVES

Equity-enhancing school finance reforms initially emanated from legal challenges of state responsibility. The first state initiatives in this regard took the form of categorical funding for targeted populations, such as special education. Later court decisions calling for fiscal neutrality across school corporations led states to eliminate, or strictly limit, the power of local school boards to tax. In more recent years, systemic reformers have developed "opportunity-to-learn standards" that call for the school resources to be tied to outcome and curriculum standards.

EFFICIENCY-ENHANCING INITIATIVES

Efficiency-enhancing policy issues, on the other hand, have most often been debated in economic terms, possibly because "if economists have a comparative advantage in talking about any of these social goals, that advantage lies in the analysis of efficiency" (Monk, pp. 1–2). The focus in enhancing efficiency has traditionally been on maintaining local control of taxation. Thus, efficiency-oriented initiatives such as guaranteed tax base plans and site-based budget councils seek to minimize the shift of decisionmaking power to the state level. More recent efficiency-oriented state programs would include state-mandated universal graduation standards to which all students are accountable.

LIBERTY-ENHANCING INITIATIVES

Liberty-enhancing proposals fall most often in the province of political philosophy, where liberty serves as one of the most fundamental of the classical liberal values. States seek to enhance liberty by issuing vouchers, or granting tuition tax credits, that allow parents who send their children to private or church-related schools to recover all or part of the tuition paid. In recent years, the charter school movement has sought to "swap rules and regulations for freedom and results" (Manno et al. 1998, p. 490). In the last few years, public schools have also been required to allow home-schooled children access to extracurricular activities such as music and sports.

APPROACHES TO STATE ACTIVISM

ASSISTANCE-ORIENTED APPROACHES

"Assistance-oriented" policies seek to encourage school districts to revise their policies and practices to conform with the overriding goals and policies of the state. For example, states may provide a funding system to encourage grade schools to lower the pupil/teacher ratio in kindergarten through third grade. Key components of assistance-oriented approaches are (a) that they are voluntary—school districts are not required to participate, and (b) that a *quid pro quo* exists—in return for participating the district will receive state support.

Clearly, assistance-oriented approaches are appropriate only in pursuit of optional state goals. They allow school districts to overcome any disparities between the tax base of the district and the expenditures needed to implement the policy. In addition, given the combination of voluntary compliance and existence of a *quid pro quo*, assistance-oriented approaches are useful in convincing school districts to implement broad education reform proposals that, at least initially, lack sufficiently strong local support for districts to implement them without such support.

PERSUASIVE APPROACHES

"Persuasive" policies fall into the continuum between assistance-oriented and regulatory-oriented approaches. In a manner similar to assistance-oriented approaches, "persuasive" policies seek to encourage school districts to revise their policies and practices without requiring them to do so. However, while assistance-oriented approaches imply that the state will aid districts in making these changes, "persuasive" policies are more symbolic and contain no commitment of state funds or personnel.

For example, in its pursuit of equity a state can subsidize funding for targeted populations in order to encourage school districts to provide the services needed to treat these students fairly. Alternatively, a state can develop opportunity-to-learn standards that seek to encourage districts to provide such services. The former requires the state to commit resources to the effort; the latter does not.

Like assistance-oriented approaches, persuasive approaches are appropriate only in pursuit of optional state goals. However, since there exists no *quid pro quo*, persuasive approaches are likely to be effective only for those issues that are important to groups to whom schools are likely to be responsive (e.g., business community, special needs parents). Success in convincing school districts to pursue these issues hinges on being able to marshal the forces whose interests would be served by the education reform proposals being advanced.

REGULATORY APPROACHES

"Regulatory" policies are similar to persuasion in that neither approach transfers resources from state to district coffers. The approaches differ, though, in how the state conceives its role. Persuasion is primarily rhetorical, with the state attempting to cooperate with schools in a partnership. Mandates carry the weight of the central government's authority with the state forcing schools to do something that they would not have done at all on their own or would have done inadequately.

Regulatory approaches are used to pursue mandatory state goals. Therefore, they are useful in convincing school districts to uniformly implement education programs that local districts otherwise would be unwilling to pay for, or alternatively, reform proposals that districts otherwise would not want to comply with.

OVERVIEW OF THE YEARBOOK

This Introduction has attempted to set out the central themes around the interplay between local control and state activism. The taxonomy of state activism developed in this chapter provides one way to characterize forms of state activism on the basis of both the fundamental social values they reflect and the approach used to implement them.

Part 1 of this Yearbook, "Framework for Understanding Local Control of Schools," comprises three chapters that examine the wide variety of philosophical, historical, legal, and political forces that have been responsible for the shift from local to state initiative. Part 2, "State Activism in the Late Twentieth Century," provides first a broad national and international perspective, and then a state-level look, at the major ideas shaping the policy choices being made. The final section, "Local Autonomy in the Late Twentieth Century," analyzes local control of schools in three chapters addressing the perspectives of the school building and the local school district and the impact of changes in the state-local power balance on educational resources. The book concludes with a chapter presenting a conceptual synthesis that reflects the contents of the book.

In the opening essay, "Political Philosophy and the Balance between Central and Local Control of Schools," Barry Bull introduces the shift from local to state authority over education, outlining several different historical influences that have led to this shift. He then considers the implications of this shift in light of three major political values: liberty, equality of opportunity, and democracy. Bull argues not only that these political values are often in tension with one another, but also that each value in some ways lends support to both centralized and decentralized political authority. Bull's analysis sheds light on much current political discourse, including and especially the argument in favor of systemic school reform. The chapter concludes with a vision of the legitimate roles of central and local authorities in light of these three major political ideals.

In Chapter 3, "The Limits of Standardization and the Importance of Constituencies," Nancy Beadie provides a historical overview of the relationships between local and state authority over education, ranging from the colonial period through the post–World War II era. Her chapter demonstrates that the relationship has been dynamic throughout American history, and it has surfaced in a varied array of issues. These include segregation and racial exclusion, the emergence of standards, school finance, conflicts between urban and rural constituencies, teacher unions, school reform efforts, and accreditation, among others. Although the tension between local and central authority has been a powerful force in American education since the colonial era, Beadie's history reveals that conflicts over authority in education have been shaped by particular social conditions and contexts. Arguments for and proponents of each seat of authority are historically dependent, changing with the times and issues.

In Chapter 4, "Recent Litigation and Its Impact on the State-Local Power Balance," John Dayton focuses on the tension between the competing ideals of liberty and equality as it has played out in the courts. Starting with an overview of American constitutional democracy, Dayton argues that local control over school funding—enabled by many state legislatures' traditional abdication of educational responsibilities—resulted in extreme funding inequities across districts. The courts became the last source of redress for funding equity advocates. This chapter explores the resulting legal cases, including ones that threw out existing school funding formulas, and explores many of the standards the courts used (and/or imposed) to determine how and where the state should draw the line between local liberty and statewide equity.

Chapter 5, "Converging Forces: Understanding the Growth of State Authority over Education," by Frances C. Fowler, explores the broad national and international institutional forces influencing recent state activism. Beginning with the legal fact that states have always had authority over schools, even if they have until recently largely abdicated it, this chapter traces recent historical and political developments that have led to increased state invocation of its authority over education. These developments include reform in all branches of state government, changes in the electorate, decreased local authority due to a long-term fiscal crisis, economic globalization, and the growth of an intergovernmental lobby. With all these forces simultaneously converging and intensifying since the 1950s, a shift in power to the state is, the author writes, "overdetermined" and likely to continue.

In Chapter 6, "State Politics and School Reform," Tim L. Mazzoni examines from a state perspective—and a political-influence perspective—the causes, processes, and consequences of the "education excellence" movement. America in the early 1980s became seriously dissatisfied with public education, particularly through media coverage of such reports as *A Nation at Risk*. The article asserts that whatever the merits of these reports, or the validity of popular dissatisfaction with public education, these forces created a demand for widespread education reform. Exploring three "waves" of the education excellence movement between 1983 and 1993, the article discusses reforms originating in the South and California, the political and economic conditions that enabled their spread across other regions of the country, increased activism at the level of the state, the involvement of big business and professional associations, and coalition-building between disparate sets of actors. From a political science perspective, the article tracks several key trends, including the increased nationalization of education policy through interstate coalitions that variously included businesses, governors, professional associations and teacher unions, and so forth.

Chapter 7, "Creating 'A New Set of Givens'? The Impact of State Activism on School Autonomy," by Betty Malen and Donna Muncey, examines how the changing state-local relationship affects decisionmaking at the building level. Specifically, the article questions the prominent view that in spite of the state's efforts to enact policies and initiatives, schools, in multiple ways, continue to operate under their own authority. Drawing largely on case studies of policy implementation and evidence regarding the impact of decentralization ventures and accountability measures, the authors argue that state power may restrict local discretion subtly, yet pervasively. The state may circumscribe local discretion through a number of means, including, among others, control over the reform agenda, constraints on resources, and the imposition of curriculum mandates, standards, assessments, and related sanctions.

In Chapter 8, "Salvaging Fiscal Control: New Sources of Local Revenue for Public Schools," Michael F. Addonizio reviews the emerging development of locally controlled revenue sources such as local foundations, business partnerships, in-kind donations, and cooperative partnerships with other governmental agencies and community-based social service providers. His exploration of sources of nontraditional funding, especially in Michigan, reveals that although nontraditional funding tends to have disequalizing effects, with wealthier schools getting more of these funds than others, these funds (and their disequalizing effects) remain very modest in comparison to traditional sources of funding.

In Chapter 9, "Organizational Boundaries, Authority, and School District Organization," Patrick Galvin provides an alternative to the present critique of school districts as intransigent bureaucracies. By exploring the economic assumptions of those reformers who would move policymaking authority out of school districts to either individual sites, states, or both, Galvin reveals the limitations of these foundational assumptions. He then proposes an alternative economic model, New Institutional Economics, to argue that there is at least a theoretical justification for school districts as forces for efficiency and productivity in education. The article concludes with preliminary evidence that suggests that school districts have in fact been forces for efficiency and productivity, consistent with the economic model outlined in the paper.

The Conclusion seeks to better understand if—and how— state activism encroaches on local control of K–12 education. "Achieving a 'Just Balance' Between Local Control of Schools and State Responsibility for K–12 Education: Summary Observations and Research Agendas," co-authored by Betty Malen, Neil Theobald, and Jeffery Bardzell, reflects on the contents of this volume and pulls together several recurring themes. These include the historical insight that the balance between state responsibility and local control is perpetually contested terrain, and the more contemporary recognition that the current balance favors the state and that state activism may well be here to stay.

In addition, the conclusion also discusses a possible research agenda that follows from the chapters in the book. This proposed agenda includes closer consideration of the relationship between state activism and social values, and closer examinations of the consequences of state activism, the financial contours of state activism, and the notion of breaking education's "natural monopoly." Finally, the conclusion reviews the changing relationships among several major actors in school governance at different levels and the values they variously represent, asking whether and how equality has lost some of its priority.

REFERENCES

Alexander, K. (1990). Equitable financing, local control, and self-interest. In J. K. Underwood and D. A. Verstegen (Eds.), *The impacts of litigation and legislation on public school finance: Adequacy, equity, and excellence* (pp. 293–309). New York: Ballinger.

Boyd, W. L. (1984). Competing values in educational policy and governance: Australian and American developments. *Educational Administration Review, 2,* 4–24.

Boyd, W. L., and Kerchner, C. T. (1988). Introduction and overview: Education and the politics of excellence and choice. In W. L. Boyd and C. T. Kerchner (Eds.), *The politics of excellence and choice in education* (pp. 1–11). Philadelphia: Falmer Press.

Bull, B. (1998). School reform in Indiana since 1980. In W. J. Reese (Ed.), *Hoosier schools: Past and present* (pp. 194–217). Bloomington, IN: Indiana University Press.

Bull, B. (in press). National standards in local context: A philosophical and policy analysis. In B. Jones (Ed.), *Educational leadership: Policy dimensions in the 21st century.* Stamford, CT: Ablex.

Campbell, R. F., and Mazzoni, T. L. (1976). *State policy making for the public schools: A comparative analysis of policy making for the public schools in twelve states and a treatment of state governance models.* Berkeley, CA: McCutchan.

Cubberley, E. P., and Elliott, E. C. (1915). *State and county school administration.* New York: Macmillan.

Garms, W. I., Guthrie, J. W., and Pierce, L. C. (1978). *School finance: The economics and politics of public education.* Englewood Cliffs, NJ: Prentice-Hall.

Holmstedt, R. W. (1940). *State control of public school finance.* Bloomington, IN: Indiana University Bureau of Cooperative Research.

McDonnell, L. M. (1994). Assessment policy as persuasion and regulation. *American Journal of Education, 102,* 391–420.

McDonnell, L. M., and McLaughlin, M. W. (1982). *Education policy and the role of the states.* Santa Monica, CA: Rand.

Manno, B. V., Finn, C. E., Bierlein, L. A., and Vanourek, G. (1998). How charter schools are different: Lessons and implications from a national study. *Phi Delta Kappan, 79,* 488–498.

Messner, J. (1951). Freedom as a principle of social order. *The Modern Schoolman, 28*(2), 97–110.

Mitchell, D. E., and Encarnation, D. J. (1984). Alternative state policy mechanisms for influencing school performance. *Educational Researcher, 13*(5), 4–11.

Monk, D. H. (1990). *Educational finance: An economic approach.* New York: McGraw-Hill.

National Center for Education Statistics. (1999). Digest of education statistics, 1998. Washington, DC: U. S. Department of Education.

Odden, A. R., and Kim, L. (1992). Reducing disparities across the states: A new federal role in school finance. In A. R. Odden (Ed.), *Rethinking school finance.* San Francisco: Jossey-Bass.

Tresch, R. W. (1981). *Public finance: A normative theory.* Plano, TX: Business Publications.

United States. (1787). *The Constitution of the United States of America.* Microform.

PART II

FRAMEWORK FOR UNDERSTANDING LOCAL CONTROL OF SCHOOLS

2

POLITICAL PHILOSOPHY AND THE BALANCE BETWEEN CENTRAL AND LOCAL CONTROL OF SCHOOLS

Barry Bull
Indiana University

As the introduction to this volume makes clear, the governance of education in the United States has seen constant, even revolutionary change over the past several decades. In this essay, I will briefly consider the scope of this change and some of the apparent empirical reasons for it. Most centrally, however, I will consider what several common political values imply about central and local roles in school governance and about the extent to which this change and the rationale for it are justified by those values.

THE SCOPE OF CHANGE IN SCHOOL GOVERNANCE

Although the primary theme of this volume is the financing of elementary and secondary education, the modification of school funding mechanisms is hardly the only form that state centralization of authority over education has taken in the recent past. To be sure, since World War II states have consistently replaced school revenue collected at the local level with that collected at the state level. Concomitantly, they have limited localities' authority to establish their own levels of school funding. But just as important, they have simultaneously restricted the purposes for which the school funds available to localities are to be used and the educational means by which those purposes are to be pursued.

Most of these latter restrictions have not been represented as fiscal controls at all, although they end up having clear fiscal ramifications. Rather, they have been represented as reforms in the operation and outcomes of schooling. Included in these reforms have been expanded state specifications of

1. who is to be educated, for example, students with disabilities;

2. what curriculum is to be offered, through, for example, curriculum frameworks for existing subjects and mandates of new subjects such as drug and alcohol education;

3. when and for how long students are to be educated, through, for example, mandates for longer school years and incentives for year-round education;

4. which skills and abilities students are to demonstrate, enforced, for example, through state graduation tests and school accreditation.

In fact, some of these changes have often been enacted with little attention to their fiscal consequences, as local school boards and district administrators have been quick to point out. Faced with such "unfunded mandates," localities find themselves not only with less control over the amount and sources of their funds but also with the clear necessity to spend those funds on purposes and activities specified by the state instead of those determined by the local community.

Although states have been the primary agents of this increased centralization, the original inspiration has often come from national sources. A variety of federal legislative initiatives have sought to provide incentives for states to adopt uniform policies and programs on a variety of subjects—including advanced high school curricula in the 1950s, education of the disadvantaged in the 1960s, education of children with disabilities in the 1970s, student and teacher testing in the 1980s, and curriculum and student performance standards and charter schools in the 1990s. Federal court mandates have also stimulated uniformity across states in several arenas, such as desegregation, bilingual education, and special education. Sometimes as part of federal initiatives and sometimes on their own, a variety of national organizations have also sought to persuade states to adopt particular policies—for instance, the National Education Association, the National Governors Association, and a large number of national commissions such as the National Commission for Excellence in Education, which issued *A Nation At Risk* in 1983. The uniformity in policies and programs that these national efforts have engendered has contributed considerably to the degree and specificity of state control over schooling at the expense of local autonomy in the determination of educational and fiscal policy.

POSSIBLE INFLUENCES ON THE CHANGE IN SCHOOL GOVERNANCE

One might speculate that a number of demographic, social, and economic changes during the past several decades have made this increased state control over education acceptable to our political leaders and their constituencies. First, some of these changes seem to have directly produced a demand for greater uniformity among the nation's public schools. For example, increased mobility for families may have created an expectation that their children would receive a comparable education no matter where they happen to attend school. At the very least, such mobility undoubtedly discouraged dramatic differences among communities' schools—such as different languages of instruction—that would require students to lose a significant amount of instructional time when they move from one part of the country or the state to another. Similarly, global economic competition has apparently produced a heightened belief in the predictable economic consequences of education or at least a worry that a lack of competitiveness may be caused by an inadequate education. This worry, in turn, seems to have persuaded citizens that it is risky for their local schools to depart too significantly from those in other cities, states, or even countries.

Second, other changes have tended to erode the social trust upon which local control of schools is based. In providing for local authority over education, the electorate expresses its confidence that such authority will be used reasonably. However, certain factors seem to have diminished that public confidence. The aging of the population has meant that a much smaller proportion of Americans are parents of school-age children. As a result, fewer local citizens have direct knowledge of the schools upon which to base their confidence in the value of what is taking place there. This phenomenon is not necessarily a simple conflict of interests between generations, in which the older generation has different priorities for the use of public funds than the support of public education. Such differing priorities might lead to less funding for education in general but not necessarily to a preference for state rather than local decision-making. But the recent willingness of the public to spend more for each student rather than less seems to rebut the presumption that an aging population demands less education for the young. By contrast, the lack of recent experience with local schools among a significant part of the population helps to explain why citizens as a whole are less willing to trust localities to make the fundamental decisions about education even as those citizens are more convinced about the importance of education.

The increased segregation of cities by economic status and as a result by ethnicity seems to have had a similar effect. On the one hand, the existence of distinct suburban and urban school districts may lead suburbanites to know little about urban schools and, thus, to seek to enforce on them the same model of education that exists in the suburbs, especially in light of the apparently poor performance of urban students. On the other hand, these same considerations may also lead urban communities to believe that they are being systematically deprived of resources and other advantages enjoyed by suburban schools. The continued low ranking of urban schools on state tests and other standardized measures truly exacerbates this mutual distrust, confirming to suburbanites that urban districts are chronically incapable of making good decisions about their schools and to urbanites that suburban districts indeed have more and better public resources. Both groups of citizens may be willing to surrender their local autonomy for the apparent advantages that a uniform state definition of schooling might bring—for urban schools, additional resources, and for suburban schools, the recognition and promulgation of their model of schooling.

These speculations about the sources of citizens' tolerance for increased state control of education, based in part on a demand for uniformity and in part on growing distrust among various social groups, might make this phenomenon understandable, but it does not necessarily make it justified. For the empirical claims upon which these explanations are based may be incorrect. That is, for instance, uniformity in education may very well not be the best way to make a nation's economy competitive. More to the point of this essay, the political values upon which these explanations are based may not, upon due consideration, prove to be justified. In what follows, I will consider what certain key American political values imply about the governance of schools and how those implications bear upon the changes in governance we have made and ought to make.

THE POLITICAL VALUES
OF SCHOOL GOVERNANCE

Abstract political ideals do not have direct and certain implications for concrete political institutions and practices. As will be clear, the major political values discussed in this section—liberty, equality of opportunity, and democracy—all imply that for some purposes and circumstances political authority should be centralized, and for others it should be decentralized. Nor do our most fundamental political ideals all necessarily agree in their implications for practice. Nevertheless, an analysis of these ideals can at the very least help us understand the ideological landscape upon which decisions about school governance are made, what values certain decisions may allow us to realize and what values we may be thereby sacrificing. And it can help clarify what empirical evidence we must gather in order to understand the implications of our decisions about school governance.

LIBERTY

Liberty can be understood as the freedom to decide matters that affect our lives. In the United States, we tend to treat liberty as a set of individual freedoms of self-determination, many of which are protected by the Constitution's Bill of Rights—freedoms of religious belief, association, and expression, for example. However, none of even these fundamental freedoms is absolute, largely because one person's exercise of a freedom may limit another's. If, for instance, my religious beliefs include a prescription about the religious beliefs of others, my having the full freedom of religious expression necessarily limits the freedom of religious expression that others may enjoy. Thus, individual liberty needs to be seen as a person's freedom to decide matters that is constrained so as to permit others a similar range of self-determination. Individual liberty is then one's control over a sphere of actions and decisions that affect oneself alone.

Of course, much of what we want to do has potential effects on others' lives. Here, liberty is not simply the freedom to make these decisions entirely on our own but rather to participate fairly in these decisions with others whom they affect. Thus, liberty encompasses not only individual rights but also political rights, that is, rights to be involved in making collective decisions that affect us.

LIBERTY AND LOCAL GOVERNANCE

Local governance is often thought to have a connection to both individual and political liberty. On the one hand, local governance permits individuals to shape institutions according to their personal beliefs about the good life; as such, it is a vehicle for personal expression. On the other hand, local governance permits collaboration in decisions that have an immediate effect on our own, our families', and our neighbors' lives; as such, it is a vehicle for participation in collective decisionmaking. As I have argued elsewhere, however, in the arena of public schooling, these connections between liberty and local governance are more apparent than real (Bull 1984). For, first, schooling decisions have clear effects on others' lives, at the very least on the lives of students. Therefore, they simply do not fall into the sphere of individual liberty; I simply do not have a right of unilateral decisionmaking about matters of such deep and lasting influence on the futures of other human beings. Second, schooling decisions, under contemporary circumstances, often (and perhaps usually) have effects that extend beyond the locality. Some argue that these effects are general to the entire society, influencing for instance the levels of economic productivity achieved in the society, which in turn influences the standard of living we all enjoy. Even if the effects of educational decisions are more limited than this, they are at the very least portable, so that schooling decisions affect other localities when the children who attend those schools move to other communities as adults. Thus, for example, one community's decision to neglect the education of their least able students in the belief that those students would not be able to afford to live in that community as adults could have potentially negative external effects on the communities in which those students eventually do reside.

For these reasons, then, neither individual nor political liberty provides an immediate justification for local control of schools. The members of a locality do not have a right based on their individual liberty to mold the lives of students as a means of expressing or achieving their own visions of the good life, for students are not simply a part of the environment to be used willy-nilly for the satisfaction of one's personal aspirations. Nor do members of one locality have a right based on their political liberty to make school decisions without taking into account the effects that those decisions may have on other communities, for schooling decisions at the very least impose externalities on the communities in which students reside as adults and perhaps on the nation as a whole.

LIBERTY AND CENTRAL GOVERNANCE

Seen in this light, larger units of government—states and nations—have two sorts of responsibilities in the governance of schooling. First, they must protect the individual rights of children to develop in ways that will enable them to become their own persons and thus to hold and pursue their own visions of the good life regardless of what aspirations their parents and current communities may have for them. Second, they must protect the rights of those affected by the long-term consequences of schooling decisions to participate in those decisions.

Apparently, then, considerations of liberty tend to justify control of schools by these larger units of government. However, not just any form of state and national control is justified by these considerations, for it must have the consequences of liberating children to live their own lives, on the one hand, and of enabling the larger society to benefit from children's education, on the other. And, upon careful inspection, the most prevalent contemporary strategy for state and national school governance— systemic or standards-driven reform—meets neither of these liberty-based criteria.

In a nutshell, systemic reform proposes to control schooling in two ways. First, states or nations are to prescribe three sets of interconnected standards for the conduct of schools—outcome standards to define the student achievements at which schools are to aim, curriculum standards to define the subject matter and instruction to which students are to be exposed in order to attain those outcomes, and opportunity-to-learn standards to define the resources to which students are to have access in order to learn the specified curriculum and to attain the prescribed outcomes. Second, states or nations are to align their various school policies to these standards—notably, student testing, student promotion and graduation, teacher certification, professional development, professional compensation, school accreditation, and school funding policies (Smith and O'Day 1991).

LIBERTY AND THE JUSTIFICATION OF THE STANDARDS-BASED MODEL OF CENTRAL GOVERNANCE

Most obviously, this approach to school governance fails to protect children's rights to develop into their own persons. If anything, defining student achievement in detailed and specific ways, prescribing their curriculum and educational resources, and enforcing these standards through restrictive testing, promotion, and graduation policies explicitly denies students the right to participate in shaping the ends and means of their own education.

Now, it might be argued that schooling has such systematic and extensive consequences for society in general and for others with whom children interact in particular that individual children's rights to self-determination in education are entirely overshadowed by the interests that others have in their education. Of course, such a claim needs to be substantiated by clear evidence about the empirical effects of an education in which children are enabled to become their own persons, but let us suppose for the sake of argument that such evidence would show that an education in which children have a significant say does impose demonstrably negative externalities on others in the society. Even if this were the case, it is doubtful that systemic reform would have salutary consequences for the legitimate interests that others have in children's education.

Proponents of systemic reform argue that it will in particular enhance the economic growth and social vitality of the nation and thereby benefit us all (Smith, Fuhrman, and O'Day 1994). Systemic reformers believe that high and uniform standards coupled with policy alignment to those standards are the surest way to achieve higher levels of student performance and therefore the economic and social benefits that are thought to come in the wake of improved student performance.

Unfortunately, this prescription for social and economic growth is highly implausible (Bull 1996). To generate such growth, systemic reformers assume that the knowledge upon which improvements in our social and economic systems depend would expand under the imposition of uniform educational standards. However, the growth of knowledge is an inherently unpredictable affair, for predictions about the growth of knowledge must be based on what we already know, and by definition the growth of knowledge is beyond what we know. Under such conditions of uncertainty, it is unwise for a nation that wishes to promote the expansion of knowledge to restrict itself to a single, favored version of where progressive improvements of knowledge might originate and how they might develop. However, this is just what the development and enforcement of uniform curriculum standards would do. In developing these standards, we would inevitably need to make choices about matters that are hotly contested in the various disciplines, especially if the standards are to reflect disciplines on the leading edge of knowledge. And the enforcement of such standards throughout the schools would inevitably promote a single authoritative, if controversial, version of the disciplines. In turn, this would narrow how the disciplines are understood in the society, constrict the development of the disciplines, and ultimately reduce the capacity of the disciplines to generate and expand knowledge. In short, uniform and governmentally enforced curriculum standards, no matter how sophisticated they might be, would actually undermine the schools' capacity to contribute to the expansion of knowledge and therefore to economic and social growth.

Thus, the currently favored approach to state and national governance of schooling, standards-driven reform, fails to meet either criterion for such governance suggested by a consideration of liberty: It is unlikely to enable students to become their own persons or to serve the interests of others who are affected by students' education.

THE DIVISION OF CONTROL BETWEEN CENTRAL AND LOCAL AUTHORITIES AS PROMOTING LIBERTY

Interestingly, however, local control of schooling, properly constrained by state and national governments, might be more successful in meeting these criteria. Now, some localities may have a tendency to ignore children's rights to become their own persons either for selected groups of children (based, say, on their race or social status) or for all children. If so, they may wish to determine at least some children's personhood completely, based perhaps on particular religious beliefs or beliefs about what particular categories of children are good for. Clearly, then, larger units of government must prevent these beliefs from becoming the basis upon which these children's education is conducted. But they need not adopt systemic reform for this purpose. Instead, they can, first, establish and enforce children's civil rights to an education that is free from sectarian religious or discriminatory doctrines. Second, they can establish general expectations about the breadth and depth of the education that all children are to receive, expectations that need not take the form of detailed outcome and curricular standards. Third, they can provide adequate funding to be used by local schools to provide an education of sufficient breadth and depth. Within this limited framework of state and national governance, localities can then be encouraged to develop their own robust conceptions of and plans for schooling. The variety in education to which this local planning would lead is a far firmer foundation for disciplinary, social, and economic development than the uniformity imposed by systemic reform.

EQUALITY OF OPPORTUNITY

In a sense, considerations about the contribution of education to individual and political liberty speak to the amount and quality of educational opportunity available within a society. Educational opportunity seen from this perspective must be sufficient in quantity and of the right kind to enable citizens to lead lives that they find fulfilling and to contribute to the fulfillment of others' lives. And, therefore, those whose lives are affected by decisions about the educational opportunities made available in a society must ultimately be empowered to make those decisions.

Beyond this, however, we also care about how these opportunities are distributed among citizens. If, for example, citizens decide that making a certain kind of educational opportunity available would be beneficial to them collectively, the chance to take advantage of that opportunity should be made fairly available to all. In part, a fair chance to take advantage of an opportunity means that citizens should be allowed to qualify for that opportunity based upon their demonstrated abilities. But it also means that citizens should also be given a fair chance to acquire the abilities that would allow them to qualify.

These two elements of fair equality of opportunity in education—a chance to acquire abilities and a chance to qualify for opportunities based on ability—are the basis for a conceptual distinction within a society's educational institutions. To some extent, these institutions are to be universal, giving all citizens a chance to develop their abilities, and to some extent they are competitive, giving all a chance to use their developed abilities to qualify for further education (Gutmann 1987).

EQUAL OPPORTUNITY AND UNIVERSAL EDUCATION

On this analysis, unless all are given an opportunity to gain the qualifications for various further opportunities, the competition for further education (or for subsequent positions of employment) would be unfair. From this premise, it is sometimes concluded that the universal element in a society's educational institutions must provide a chance for all to acquire precisely the same abilities. This conclusion is erroneous, however, for at least two reasons. In the first place, preparing oneself for a further opportunity, whether in education or employment, necessarily means that one has to concentrate one's efforts in the realization of some but not all of one's potentials, namely those potentials that are relevant to the particular opportunity one seeks. For example, it is highly unlikely that the potentials one needs to develop in order to qualify to become a ballet dancer would be the same as those needed to become an electrical engineer. In other words, trying to take advantage of one opportunity necessarily means that one has to foreclose other opportunities. Second, unfairness results, not when one opportunity is foreclosed in favor of another (as must inevitably happen), but only when one has no say in the opportunities that can be pursued. Thus, it is unfair to prevent girls from trying to become electrical engineers, but as long as that opportunity is genuinely open to them, any particular girl's decision to prepare for a career in dancing rather than engineering is perfectly fair. In other words, equality of educational opportunity even in the universal element of a society's educational institutions does not necessarily imply that students have to develop the same abilities. All that is required here is that the choices about such differential development not be made, either in fact or in effect, by anyone other than those whose development is at stake.

What a society must do to maintain fairness in the distribution of educational opportunities is to protect the rights of those who are educated to decide upon the paths of their own development and to provide a reasonable level of educational resources to permit them to embark upon those paths. To be sure, there may need to be some common elements in all children's education. For instance, having a fair chance to determine one's path of future development probably requires that all children have a reasonable understanding of the various opportunities that might be available to them in their society, and some skills may be of such general application that they will be needed no matter what path of development is chosen. However, the universal education that a society makes available cannot be fairly limited to these common learnings. Otherwise, the chance to prepare for further opportunities would depend entirely upon the resources available in one's family, something that the doctrine of equal opportunity is supposed to correct. In other words, equality of educational opportunity implies that all children in a society should have a reasonable chance to be different in ways that advantage them in the competition for further educational and employment opportunities.

EQUAL OPPORTUNITY AND THE JUSTIFICATION OF STANDARDS-DRIVEN REFORM

Apparently, then, the doctrine of equal educational opportunity provides a clear role for units of government beyond the locality, for the rights to decide the course of one's own development must be protected across the entire society. It would be unfair for some localities to decide to restrict the developmental pathways available to the members of a particular race or gender. Thus, it falls to state and national governments to protect these rights. Once again, however, the current approach to state and national governance—namely standards-driven reform—proves to be an ineffective, indeed entirely inappropriate, mechanism for protecting these rights even though systemic reformers have claimed that this approach is justified in large part as a strategy to equalize opportunity.

O'Day and Smith (1993) argue, first, that previous reforms have exhausted their capacity to equalize the school performance of advantaged and disadvantaged students. An earlier focus on minimum competency standards, they say, did have a modest effect of encouraging schools to improve the performance of students from poor families and from racial minorities. However, widening social and economic disparities and the increasing need for achievement above these minimum levels render those reforms insufficient to reduce the achievement gap any farther. Second, holding all schools to higher-order student performance and curriculum standards and enforcing opportunity-to-learn standards to ensure that all schools have the resources to meet those expectations are asserted to guarantee that the most disadvantaged students have the chance to learn challenging content and complex skills. State and national adoption and enforcement of these standards are necessary, according to O'Day and Smith, to make certain that the chance for sophisticated learning is not restricted solely to those schools and school systems that serve primarily advantaged children. Thus, systemic reform is essential to widen the distribution of the most beneficial forms of school improvement and, therefore, to provide equal opportunities to disadvantaged children.

As might be obvious, this argument for systemic reform assumes that equal educational opportunity implies that all students should have the opportunity to learn the same things. And as we have seen, such equality of learning simply does not capture the basic meaning of this political value. After all, the opportunity to be equalized is the chance to gain an advantage in the competition for scarce positions in the educational and employment systems. It is difficult to understand how identical schooling, no matter how sophisticated it may be, provided to those already disadvantaged by their and their family's social status could provide them with such an advantage. In fact, by dictating what is sure to be the vast majority of disadvantaged students' instructional time and resources, systemic reform makes it less and less likely that their public schools will be able to provide the distinctive educational advantages that their families cannot. Oddly enough, then, systemic reform may actually amplify the educational advantages that better-off students receive as a result of their families' social position (Bull, in press).

Equally disconcerting, systemic reform also seems systematically to deprive students, especially disadvantaged students, of the right to decide upon the paths of their own development, one of the key elements of equal opportunity. As noted, these rights may imply some common learnings necessary to enable children to understand what opportunities are available in the society, how to make good decisions about them, and how to prepare for them once a decision is reached. Oddly enough, systemic reformers do not seem to be concerned about these matters. Instead, they assume that there is a fully specifiable and common pathway to success in a society and wish to set all children upon it, whatever their individual talents and proclivities may be. Unfortunately, under systemic reform socially advantaged children are likely to be able to exercise their rights to decide the course of their lives more fully than disadvantaged children because their families are more likely to provide more robust decisionmaking skills and information, because they may need to spend less of their school time to meet the outcome standards (and thus have more time to explore alternative pathways of development in school), and because their families have more private resources to introduce them to alternatives to the officially prescribed developmental path (Bull 1996).

THE DIVISION OF CONTROL BETWEEN CENTRAL AND LOCAL AUTHORITIES AS PROMOTING EQUAL OPPORTUNITY

The real challenge of equal educational opportunity is, then, to provide to disadvantaged children the right and the resources to determine their own development intelligently in light of the full range of social opportunities available in their society. And indirectly local control of schooling may have an important role in meeting this challenge. Now, no one would hold that local schools should have the prerogative of providing an incompetent education to disadvantaged children, and state and national governments have an important role in preventing that from happening. But it is not necessary or even desirable to adopt systemic reform for that purpose. Instead, these larger units of government could provide at least roughly comparable and probably superior funding for the schools that serve disadvantaged children and require that schools use these funds efficiently to support some locally developed, coherent, and sophisticated educational plan, not the single uniform plan that the systemic reformers have in mind. Because of the variation that could develop among local plans, disadvantaged children would have a chance to gain the educational advantage at which equality of opportunity aims. Moreover, attention to local aspirations in developing these plans could enhance the likelihood that children would find their schooling to align with their own proclivities and talents.

DEMOCRACY

To this point in the argument, three conclusions seem justified. First, liberty and equality of opportunity imply clear responsibilities for governing education at the state and national levels. Second, systemic or standards-driven reform is not a plausible way of carrying out those responsibilities. And third, certain forms of constrained and supported local governance of schools seem more consistent with these responsibilities. However, systemic reform has been selected through apparently democratic political processes by the federal government and a wide variety of states as the preferred approach to school governance these days. If so, perhaps systemic reform should be considered to be justified—despite its arguably negative effect on liberty and equality of opportunity—just because it has been democratically chosen.

One might reject this conclusion on the basis of two arguments. On the one hand, one might claim that legitimate democracies must limit majority rule so as to protect liberty and equal opportunity. But this claim is hotly contested within democratic theory (Barber 1984). On the other hand, one might argue that the selection of systemic reform has not resulted from genuinely democratic processes because, say, our state and national governments are instruments of capitalistic domination rather than of the will of the people. Yet there is every indication that standards-driven reform is indeed publicly popular among a wide variety of American citizens. Rather than pursue these two lines of argument, I would like to consider the soundness of the conceptualization of democracy upon which systemic reform is apparently based. Democracy is, in general terms, the popular control of government, but this concept is broad enough to permit wide variation in how the purposes and instruments of government are conceptualized.

STANDARDS-DRIVEN REFORM AS BASED ON AN AUTHORITARIAN CONCEPTION OF DEMOCRACY

As I have argued elsewhere, systemic reform embraces a particular theory of democracy that I label democratic authoritarianism (Bull, in press). Systemic reform suggests that the key to education governance lies with the formulation of a coherent political will for a polity's future, that is, a popular agreement about what type of society we wish to become. Systemic reform's outcome, curriculum, and opportunity-to-learn standards for the public schools are then to be deduced from such a vision for our society's future so as to create the social capacity among citizens that will permit the realization of this vision. Once this vision has been agreed to and the educational standards have been inferred from it, a society's policies for operating and monitoring public institutions should be developed and implemented to achieve the ends that the democratic polity has articulated. Or, in the terms used by systemic reformers, policies should be aligned with the standards. This view of political organization is democratic because it allows for popular determination of the purposes of public institutions. It is authoritarian because once those purposes have been determined, all exercises of public authority must stem exclusively from that source.

This view of democracy is appealing for several different reasons. First, it embodies a common understanding of instrumental rationality, namely, that one is rational by choosing coherent ends and then determining one's actions in order to accomplish those ends. Second, it forbids the use of the instruments of public authority for any purpose except for those articulated by the public will, so that no one will be permitted to use the power of the government for his or her private ends. Finally, it provides a straightforward basis for determining educational policy, namely, by telling us to develop the intellectual and practical capacities of citizens in ways that will accomplish our collective purposes.

For all its superficial appeal, however, democratic authoritarianism is a deeply flawed conception of political organization. In part, these flaws stem from the empirical implausibility of its very account of the connection between political will and social capacity. This theory essentially tells us to imagine the preferred future state of our society and then to engineer our social capacities to achieve that state of affairs. However, this view does not recognize fully the extent to which our ability to imagine our future and what we may find worthwhile in the future are dependent upon our social capacities. To be sure, it does recognize that our existing social capacities can serve as a reality check on our imaginations by telling us either that some visions of our future might be unattainable because of seemingly intractable limitations in our capacities or that some visions might have to be delayed while we develop capacities that we do not currently possess. But it does not recognize two other important truths about the relationship between political will and social capacity: Initially, what we want or can imagine at any particular time depends upon what we can do. And, subsequently, what we will want in the future depends upon changes that have taken place in what we can do. Thus, the relationship between political will and social capacity is interactive and not simply hierarchical as democratic authoritarianism seems to assume. In other words, the supposition that we can come to a permanent collective agreement about our future and then simply change our capacities to achieve that vision is illusory because the changes we make in our capacities will, in turn, change our vision of the future.

But perhaps this problem can be overcome by simply accepting that our current aspirations are likely to change in the future. In other words, we might simply change our capacities today to achieve what we think we want tomorrow in the full recognition that what we think we want tomorrow may be different and may require us to change our capacities in yet other ways. But even this adjustment in democratic authoritarianism is inadequate; indeed, it reveals an even more fundamental flaw in that conception of democracy. For this revised version of democratic authoritarianism is essentially a recipe for an unplanned, deeply irrational future. From a larger perspective, we can see such a society as profoundly schizophrenic, both believing that it should pursue a particular vision of its future and knowing that attaining that vision will inevitably prove unsatisfactory in entirely unpredictable ways.

A PROGRESSIVE CONCEPTION OF DEMOCRACY

John Dewey suggested a more intelligent solution to this problem of the interactive relationship between political will and social capacity, and on that basis he developed a progressive theory of democracy (Dewey 1927). Like democratic authoritarians, he viewed today's social problems as reflecting a discrepancy between our aspirations and our capacities. Unlike them, however, Dewey recognized that tomorrow's social problems will be almost certainly different from today's and recommended that we view our current social capacities and our current social aspirations as equally important starting places for the continual construction and reconstruction of our democratic polity.

From Dewey's perspective, the tasks of a democracy are twofold—to pursue the solution of today's social problems by changing our social capacities and to follow the imminent opportunities for developing today's social capacities so as to change our social aspirations. But to avoid either the stasis or the ultimately directionless evolution of democratically authoritarian societies, these two tasks must be undertaken interactively. To accomplish this, we must avoid premature and rigid judgments about just what our social problems are by permitting multiple and diverse definitions of those problems and fostering diverse strategies to overcome them. Just as important, we must also cultivate free and open communication among those who are working at these various definitions and strategies, for in this way the various elements of a society can become resources for one another, offering a storehouse of alternative social aspirations and capacities from among which a continuously evolving but progressive future for the society as a whole might be fashioned.

In this light, local communities and especially local schools have an important role in Dewey's vision of progressive democracy. They can act as the sites at which varying hypotheses about our society's problems are formulated and at which varying strategies for developing social capacity to meet those problems are tried out. However, communities and schools cannot serve in this role if they are excessively constrained by central authorities, no matter how popularly constituted. To be sure, there are important roles for central authorities in a progressive democracy—in prescribing participatory mechanisms for problem identification and solution at the local level, in preventing local communities from following hypotheses about the society's future that are known to be anti-progressive, and in allowing open communication among communities to flourish.

These roles bear little resemblance to those prescribed by systemic reformers. And, thus, the theoretical basis upon which the current shift from local to state and national control of schools rests is not justified as an expression of a legitimate democratic polity. In such a polity, the task of central and local authorities is not simply for the central authorities to determine what ends should be accomplished and for the local authorities to work out the means by which to achieve those ends. Rather, both are to have a significant role in the progressive evolution of our ends and means, that is, our social aspirations and capacities.

CONCLUSIONS ABOUT THE BALANCE OF LOCAL AND CENTRAL CONTROL OF SCHOOLS

The political values of liberty, equal opportunity, and democracy prescribe several general criteria for a society's public school system. First, the society's educational opportunities should be sufficient in quantity and quality to enable children to become their own persons and to benefit others whose lives they affect. Second, the society's educational opportunities should be distributed in a way that allows children a reasonable degree of control over the potentials that they will realize and that gives them a chance to become successful in the pursuit of positions of further educational, social, and economic advantage. Finally, the school system should enhance the likelihood that the society's aspirations and capabilities will change in progressive ways.

All of these criteria encompass obvious tensions—between individual autonomy and social benefit, between self-direction and social advantage, and between political will and social capacity. Thus, it is not necessarily the case that what a child needs to become his or her own person is what will benefit others in the society most fully, that the choices children may make about their own development will prove socially advantageous to them, or that the direction a society sets for itself will provide for the most fruitful development of its collective knowledge and ability. Nor is it necessarily the case that what most enhances freedom will also promote equality and progressive change. Because of these tensions within and among our various political values, the precise form that our political institutions should take, including the arrangements we make for their governance, is inevitably a matter of sustained and continuing thought, investigation, and deliberation. Nevertheless, the detailed consideration of these values in the previous sections does generate certain hypotheses about the school governance arrangements that are and are not likely to allow us to realize and harmonize these political priorities.

Most clearly, the discussion thus far throws considerable doubt upon the currently favored strategy for the governance of the public school system. Standards-driven reform shifts control over the substance and conduct of public education in ways that make the achievement of individual and political liberty, genuine equality of opportunity, and democratic polity problematic. To be sure, none of these values implies that our schools have a right to provide an incompetent education to our children as a group or to any significant segment of them. Thus, it is understandable that the public's concern over the adequacy of our educational system might lead them to suppose that an increasingly centralized and highly prescriptive strategy of control over that system is the only remedy that is likely to be effective. Nevertheless, our analysis suggests that this treatment may be worse than the disease. For, on the one hand, it threatens to limit the capacity of our school system to enable children, especially socially disadvantaged children, to control their own lives and futures and even to gain a meaningful chance to distinguish themselves in our society. But, ironically, it also undermines the likelihood that our society will grow in productive and progressive ways, instead promoting the very outcome that is, I suspect, the real worry at the basis of our collective concern about the competence of the school system. Making our school system even more uniform and restrictive is simply not a good strategy for advancing the vitality of our civilization.

THE LEGITIMATE ROLES OF CENTRAL AUTHORITIES

Thus, the real challenge before us is to determine a strategy of school governance that will produce the diversity upon which a free and promising future for our society can be constructed. As the discussion to this point suggests, the way to meet that challenge includes responsibilities for both central and local school authorities. In particular, central authorities must play a number of critical and related roles:

1. Ensuring children's basic civil right to an education that is not restricted to a narrow conception of their possibilities, particularly a conception based upon a single sectarian vision of the good life or a conception known to interfere with the progressive development of society as a whole;

2. Ensuring children's basic civil right to an education that does not prescribe particular social roles based on, for example, children's race, religion, ethnicity, gender, or familial economic status;

3. Defining and prescribing any genuinely common learnings necessary for all children to have an informed choice about the visions of the good life and

the related educational opportunities they will pursue;

4. Defining and prescribing general guidelines about the breadth and depth of study that any adequate education must meet for all children to have an informed choice about their visions of the good life and to have a genuine opportunity to succeed;

5. Ensuring that local processes for determining the content and procedures of education are genuinely participatory;

6. Providing for free and robust communication among localities as they shape and reshape their decisions about educational content and procedures; and

7. Guaranteeing that localities will have access to sufficient resources to provide an education that meets the foregoing requirements.

THE LEGITIMATE ROLES OF LOCAL AUTHORITIES

Within this broad, centrally maintained framework, localities also have critical responsibilities for governing the public schools that fall within their jurisdictions. Most obviously, they are to maintain a lively, ongoing, and participatory debate about the content and procedures of their students' education. This debate is to be mindful of children's individual liberties in education—essentially their right to become their own persons without undue constraint by the idiosyncrasies of their communities or of their status within them. Equally important, however, this debate is also to be concerned about the success of individual students and the community as a whole. Thus, the range of choices permitted to students may be defined by the community's honest and reflective judgments about where future opportunities for its own constructive development seem most likely to lie and about how their children can best flourish as the community tries to take up those opportunities. In other words, each community has an obligation to define its own understanding of and its standards for its children's education with an eye, on the one hand, on the free development of those children and, on the other hand, on the progress of the community as a whole.

DIVIDED GOVERNANCE AND SCHOOL FUNDING

This recommended division of labor between central and local educational authorities provides a far different view of educational governance than that of the systemic reformers, who seem to believe that any creative thinking about the purposes of education is to take place at the central levels of government, relegating localities to the task of compliance with those purposes. By enforcing an exclusively compliant role upon local citizens, administrators, and teachers, systemic reformers effectively forfeit the contributions that local experience, intelligence, and energy may make to the formulation of educational purposes. Ironically, the compliance mentality is also likely to undermine teachers' and communities' creative contributions to the reform of instructional procedures, where the systemic reformers hope that these educators will find constructive and context-sensitive ways of achieving the centrally prescribed purposes of education. For, as Dewey taught us, the ends and means of action are inextricably linked so that restrictions on our authority to consider our purposes concomitantly impose restrictions on our ability to think about the means by which those purposes can be accomplished (Dewey 1939). As Dewey would have predicted, state and national adoption of detailed and precise educational standards is now creating a demand from teachers for equally precise prescriptions of the instructional procedures whereby those standards can be met rather than fostering teachers' creative instructional energies.

The alternative view of educational governance outlined in this chapter provides a role for central and local authorities in developing and revising both the ends and means of education. And crucially this role is one of investigation and experimentation, not simply of prescription. On the one hand, localities must be involved in the thoughtful consideration of their own problems and how to overcome them in and through the education of their children. Importantly, this task requires deliberation about what education is for as well as how it is to be conducted. On the other hand, central authorities, too, must be thoughtfully engaged with a variety of important issues—what rights and liberties are most justified in education, what common learnings (if any) are actually connected to the realization of those rights and liberties, what breadth and depth of content are needed for children to succeed, how local participation can be best achieved, how open communication among communities can be made to flourish, and so on.

A crucial lesson about school funding is implied by this view of educational governance. One central premise of government finance is that those who benefit from a decision have an obligation to pay its cost. This premise has been taken to imply that the authority to make educational decisions and the obligation to pay for them must always rest at the same governmental level. That is, it is said, if localities are allowed to make decisions about their schools, they must also be required to raise the revenue to support those decisions. However, this conclusion is profoundly, even perniciously, fallacious. For, as I have argued in this chapter, local control of schools if properly defined and executed can make a crucial contribution to the productive development of the entire society because localities can be a source of the diversity, intelligence, and experimentation that progressive change in the society requires. Under these conditions, the premise that requires those who benefit to pay actually implies that the society as a whole has an obligation to pay for the maintenance of system of schooling in which localities have a significant degree of control over their own schools.

REFERENCES

Barber, B. (1984). *Strong democracy: Participatory politics for a new age*. Berkeley, CA: University of California Press.

Bull, B. (1984). Liberty and the new localism: Toward an evaluation of the tradeoff between educational equity and local control of schools. *Educational Theory, 34*(1), 75–94.

Bull, B. (1996). Is systemic reform in education morally justified? *Studies in Philosophy and Education, 15*(1), 13–23.

Bull, B. (in press). National standards in local context: A philosophical and policy analysis. In Bruce Jones (Ed.), *Educational leadership: Policy dimensions in the 21st century*. Stamford, CT: Ablex.

Dewey, J. (1927). *The public and its problems*. New York: H. Holt and Company.

Dewey, J. (1939). *Theory of valuation*. Chicago: University of Chicago Press.

Gutmann, A. (1987). *Democratic education*. Princeton, NJ: Princeton University Press.

O'Day, J. A., and Smith, M. S. (1993). Systemic reform and educational opportunity. In S. Fuhrman (Ed.), *Designing coherent education policy: Improving the system* (pp. 250–312). San Francisco: Jossey-Bass.

Smith, M. S., Fuhrman, S. H., and O'Day, J. (1994). National curriculum standards: Are they desirable and feasible? In R. F. Elmore and S. H. Fuhrman (Eds.), *The governance of curriculum* (pp. 12–29). Alexandria, VA: Association for Supervision and Curriculum Development.

Smith, M. S., and O'Day, J. (1991). Systemic school reform. In S. Fuhrman and B. Malen (Eds.), *The politics of curriculum and testing* (pp. 233–267). London: Taylor & Francis.

3

THE LIMITS OF STANDARDIZATION AND THE IMPORTANCE OF CONSTITUENCIES: HISTORICAL TENSIONS IN THE RELATIONSHIP BETWEEN STATE AUTHORITY AND LOCAL CONTROL

Nancy Beadie[1]
University of Washington

1 I would like to thank Marge Plecki, Thomas Mauhs-Pugh, Jeff Bardzell, and Neil Theobald for expert help and valuable suggestions at various points in the development of this essay.

The tension between local control and central authority is an endemic and perhaps dynamic characteristic of schooling in the United States. Historically, it's clear, the scope of central government authority in all areas of American life has increased tremendously over the last two centuries of the nation's existence. Schools were part of this expansion. Indeed, in many ways the increased involvement of central government in individual and community welfare originated with schooling.[2]

And yet it would be erroneous to characterize the historical relationship between local control and state authority in schooling as simply linear or reciprocal in development, with state control progressively increasing and local control steadily declining. Rather, a close look at the history of school funding and governance reveals a seesaw between assertions of central authority and assertions of local control on a range of issues. Increased local prerogatives and contributions to schooling have often been followed by increases in state prerogatives and contributions, and vice versa. It is perhaps more accurate to portray the relationship between local control and state authority as a perpetual balancing act in which the loads being balanced are constantly increasing.

There are a number of ways to look at this seesaw relationship between local control and state authority historically. One way is to analyze the shifting balances in this relationship in terms of party politics. Beginning in the 1830s and continuing through the nineteenth century the most aggressive efforts to systematize school funding and organization at the state and eventually at the national level were associated first with the Whig and then with the Republican parties. Correspondingly, local resistance to this assertion of state authority was commonly associated with the Democrats. Given these associations it is not surprising to find that a chronology of the rise and fall of various efforts to assert central authority in schooling follows closely the fortunes of the respective political parties within each state and at the federal level. Since the 1930s the party associations have somewhat reversed at the federal level, so that

---

2 For discussions of the relationship between schooling and state formation see A. Green (1990) and Beadie (1999b).

Democrats are commonly associated with assertions of central government reform in schooling, while a laissez-faire attitude toward school regulation and funding is associated with the Republican Party. Nonetheless party politics remain an important lens through which to consider shifts in the balance of local control and central authority in matters of schooling.

Another way to look at the seesaw relationship between local control and state authority historically is with respect to changes of economy. Not only the rise and fall of particular political parties, but growth and retrenchment in state political economies can be correlated with shifts in these relationships. In the nineteenth century the Panic of 1837 had a very specific negative effect on the state systems of schooling that early school reformers had just begun to establish. Not until the 1850s, with the next major surge of growth in state economies, were these plans significantly revived. Similarly, expansive plans for a federal system of schooling received significant setbacks in the Depression of 1873. As a result, Congress probably missed the one historical moment when the creation of a national system of schooling was politically feasible (McAfee 1998; Lee 1949; Warren 1974). During the Great Depression of the 1930s, by contrast, financial crisis led for the first time to a significant increase in the share of total school funding derived from state sources and in the leverage of state agencies with respect to school regulation. More recently, as Berne (1988) has shown, the state-level push for increased equity in school funding may have been significantly undercut by the simultaneous economic recession of the 1970s.

It would also be a mistake, however, to see the historical relationship between local control and state authority in schooling as a mere reflection of political and economic trends. Schooling itself has been a force of social, economic and political change in American society. Moreover, it has been strongly valued across both party and class lines to an extent perhaps unparalleled in other western nations. Thus, even when the authority of central governments over schooling was relatively weak, and plans for increased regulation, standardization and central funding of schooling were foiled, communities of all kinds continued to organize schools, and families of all classes and cultures continued to send their children to them. In many respects it was this demand for schooling and the voluntary organization of schools to meet that demand that established the norms, procedures and regulations that state school systems eventually adopted. Virtually every major innovation in state school law, it can be argued, followed, rather than preceded, its acceptance in common practice. Thus, as Kaestle (1983) has emphasized, common schools and common school attendance were already widely supported by localities before states required towns to establish them. Similarly, as T. F. Green (1980) and Tyack, James, and Benavot (1987) have suggested, school attendance was already nearing universality before states made such attendance compulsory at any given age. Comparable inquiries into issues of academic standards might well show that official certification requirements for teachers and achievement requirements for students have been effective only after the majority of teachers or students have already acquired that level of attainment on a non-compulsory basis.

Viewed from this perspective, the relationship between local control and state authority in schooling appears less conflicting and more complementary, with increases in local initiative and demands in schooling eventually bringing about increased support and authority for such innovations at the state level. Often this increase in state involvement has occurred in the name of making universal what had already become prevalent, and thus of equalizing access to a benefit already widely valued. Such efforts, however, have themselves often come into conflict with the values of self-determination or popular sovereignty that favored local initiative and innovations in the first place. In this way the relationship between local control and state authority can be seen as a value tension: the classic American tension between liberty and equality.[3]

What follows is an overview of key trends and historical turning points in the relationship between local control and state authority. This overview is divided into six standard his-

---

3 On some different ways of conceptualizing some of these tensions, see Labaree (1997), Benson and O'Halloran (1987), and Strike (1988).

torical periods: the colonial era (to 1780); the early national period (1780–1830); the antebellum period (1830–1860); the Civil War, Reconstruction and the post-Reconstruction era (1860–1890); the Progressive era (1890–1930); and the Great Depression, World War II and the postwar era (1930–1960). In developing this account I identify the 1850s and the 1940s as two historical turning points when state authority over local schooling increased significantly. Also as part of the discussion, however, I highlight two enduring tensions in the relationship over time: the limits of standardization and the importance of political constituencies.

THE COLONIAL PERIOD: PARENTAL RESPONSIBILITY AND LOCAL INITIATIVE

In the colonial and early national period the responsibility for educating children belonged squarely with parents, masters and other legal guardians. As a result of such parental responsibility, common schooling and basic literacy were already widespread through many parts of the colonies by the 1740s and 1750s, one hundred years before publicly supported state systems of schooling were in place. These schools were almost wholly a product of local initiative and demand. They included both (a) entrepreneurial or independent pay schools, in which individual master teachers and mistresses taught basic reading, writing and arithmetic and some higher subjects on a fee per subject basis, usually in their homes; and (b) subscription or rate schools, in which parents effectively pooled their resources to hire someone to teach the common subjects to their children and wards in a school, church or other community setting.

The two main exceptions to parental responsibility for education in the colonial era lay at the ends of the spectrum of social class, where parental responsibility was insufficient to support educational services regarded as having public value. For the urban poor, who could not afford the school fees or rate bills necessary to carry out their educational responsibilities as parents, "charity schools" provided basic education for large groups of students at the same time. Generally funded by churches or missionary societies, these schools also sometimes received municipal subsidies and/or state funds. At the other end of the spectrum, for the small proportion of male youth who sought to enter politics and the professions, grammar schools provided education in Latin and Greek and other subjects of the classical curriculum. Because grammar schools were more expensive to staff than common schools, and because the full cost of such schooling was regarded as too great to be borne entirely by the parents availing themselves of such services, grammar schools were often supported by central funds. These included town and municipal taxes, but also some colonial land grants and/or proceeds from excise taxes and licensing fees.

Considerable regional variation existed in the extent to which colonial governments reinforced parental responsibility and local initiative in schooling. New England colonies were exceptional in that they required towns of a certain size to maintain schools as early as the 1640s and 1650s. To support such schools New England colonies also allowed (though they did not require) towns to levy local taxes. Connecticut law specified taxation as one of several possibilities, including a direct charge to parents or any other method of raising funds on which the town could agree. Most towns used some combination of methods, including general taxes, but also rate bills for parents and in-kind contributions. Grounded in the tradition of established churches, the tithing of local inhabitants in support of religious instruction was not a new idea. It is likely that the impetus for such laws lay in the attempt to redress a perceived lapse in accepted practice rather than in an attempt to innovate (Urban and Waggoner 1996).

Moreover, New England school laws were often resisted by localities. As Sklar (1993) has shown with respect to late eighteenth and early nineteenth century Massachusetts, for example, some towns violated colonial law by directing all their public funds into Latin grammar schools for boys, thereby providing no common English education for girls or for boys who were not destined for the professional class. Other towns, by contrast, violated colonial law by making no provision for Latin grammar schools, thereby concentrating all resources in the common schools. In both cases towns proved willing to pay a fine rather than change local practice to conform to Massachusetts law.

Everywhere but New England, school laws were permissive rather than regulatory. In the southern colonies, where the established church was Anglican, and hierarchical, the dispersal of the population and the lack of a strong institutional infrastructure in the colonial context seems to have resulted in weak provisions for the kind of formal schooling that might commonly be associated with parish organization in the British context. In the Middle colonies, where religious and cultural diversity was greatest, school organization depended on local community and church responsibility, and also on more secular entrepreneurial initiative on the part of schoolmasters.

To summarize, then, two main rationales existed for intervention by a central government in the educational responsibilities of parents or in the school initiatives of localities during the colonial era. The first was the failure or inability of parents to provide for the basic education of their children through schooling, apprenticeship or household instruction. The second was the insufficiency of local funding procedures and parental school fees to cover the high cost of classical schooling for boys seeking to enter the professions. New England colonies took by far the most activist approach to promoting school organization, with Connecticut and Massachusetts both requiring that towns of a certain size maintain schools by some means. There is little evidence of serious enforcement of these New England provisions, however. Well into the nineteenth century towns seem to have violated school laws as often as they honored them.

In this way the organization of schooling in the colonial era clearly depended on parental demand and local initiative. This lack of central responsibility and control of school provisions was not necessarily to be regretted. The practice of relying on parental duty and local initiative resulted in the highest rates of literacy and the widest distribution and accessibility of schooling that existed anywhere in the western world at the time.[4]

---

4 Although literacy rates in colonial British America apparently exceeded those elsewhere in the world before the Enlightenment, the

THE EARLY NATIONAL PERIOD:
CREATION OF PERMANENT SCHOOL FUNDS

Central government involvement in schooling increased in the early national period as a direct result of the territorial expansion that occurred after the Revolutionary War. Initially, this increased state involvement derived less from any recognized state authority in matters of schooling than from acknowledged state authority over public lands and other sources of common wealth. Beginning in the 1780s and 1790s with lands ceded by the British and appropriated from Native Americans after the Revolutionary War, and continuing throughout the nineteenth century with further federal appropriations and land grants, states dedicated certain portions of their public lands and of other sources of state income to the support of schools. Much of the first state legislation regarding schools thus revolved around the terms upon which these school lands would be sold and their proceeds invested and distributed.

This early legislation most often reinforced and rewarded local initiative and control of schooling by leaving the management and use of lands and funds up to the localities. Increasingly in the 1820s and 1830s, however, states consolidated control of such school funds and specified the terms upon which localities could qualify for shares of the proceeds. Again, many of these early provisions effectively reinforced and institutionalized existing practices of local initiative and control. At the same time, however, states often established the groundwork upon which later, more coercive and elaborate state regulatory powers were erected. In this way the creation of permanent school funds became an entering wedge for increased state involvement in schooling later in the nineteenth century.

Lands appropriated from Native Americans formed the foundation of a number of these funds. Due to the terms of the Treaty of Paris, but even more to the questionable U.S. interpretation of the treaty as implying the defeat of Britain's Indian al-

---

first universal, state-sponsored school systems was established not in America but in Prussia. For a summary of work on the history of literacy see Kaestle (1985). For a comparative international history of school system formation see A. Green (1990).

lies as well as of Britain itself, the United States and its member state governments asserted authority over vast new areas of land. In the land-based economy of colonial and early national society, this huge appropriation of land in turn represented a vast increase in the wealth of the nation and of each of its member states. Throughout the early republican period and well into the nineteenth century, the sale and/or lease of these new "public" lands, together with the processing and sale of the natural resources they contained (i.e., salt and timber), provided Congress and state legislatures with an essentially "free," non-tax-based source of capital for financing public improvement projects of all kinds. Among the chief beneficiaries of these resources were schools.

The appropriation of public lands for support of schools occurred in two main ways: through the authority of the federal government and through the authority of state governments. First, the original thirteen colonies settled boundary claims among themselves and asserted authority over lands within those boundaries that had not been previously allocated to titled property owners. Then the federal government assumed authority over territory not included in these state boundaries. Beginning in the 1780s with the organization of Ohio as a territory, Congress established a pattern of requiring that a certain number of lots within each section of the territory be dedicated to the support of schools. With some partial exceptions and variations, this policy continued to be followed throughout the nineteenth century (Swift 1911).

In addition to appropriating public lands for support of schools, some states (Rhode Island, Delaware and Virginia) established their first funds from sources such as license fees, fines, forfeitures, lotteries, and auctions. Bank stock, or the taxation of banks, also provided a major source of endowment for new funds (New Jersey, Vermont, Rhode Island, Virginia, and North Carolina) as well as an important means of increasing the income on endowments initially realized from other sources. As Muscalus (1945, p.7) concluded, the use of bank enterprises to finance public education became "rather general before the Civil War," and in some instances, "the money distributed to school districts by the State was derived entirely, or almost entirely from bank stock investment or taxation of banks."

Whether they did so through land appropriations, bank investments or the collection of license fees, virtually all states had some form of state school fund by the 1830s. These funds in turn became major beneficiaries of the surplus federal funds Congress returned to the states in 1836. For the first and, so far, the only time in history, the federal government earned a budget surplus that it then redistributed to the states. In accordance with the precedent established by federal land grants, Congress specified that some portion of the surplus funds be dedicated to the support of schools. In response most states added a portion of the federal surplus deposit funds to the principal of existing permanent school funds (Warren 1974).

Though the existence of permanent school funds was fairly universal by the 1830s, however, the ways in which the proceeds of such funds were distributed varied by region. At the beginning of the early national era, states generally followed the colonial tradition of directing central funds to schooling at the ends of the class spectrum—to charity schools for poor children, and to academies that provided classical education and other higher schooling to the professional classes. While this logic was common to states both north and south at the beginning of the early republican era, a change in the accepted logic of the political economy of schooling occurred in the North beginning in the nineteenth century, becoming fairly widespread by the late 1830s. Fueled in large part by the expansion of suffrage and the breakdown of aristocratic hierarchies in a commercial economy, northern legislatures in the Jacksonian era increasingly determined that the most politically astute use of common wealth was to benefit the common man through common schools.

With the rise of the common school reform movement in the 1820s and 1830s, legislatures began to tie the distribution of revenues from permanent school funds to state reform goals. Increasingly, states specified that state school funds be used to pay the salaries of "qualified" or "certified" teachers. Initially this meant that teachers had to be certified by local town or county commissioners. Eventually, however, states established more elaborate criteria for certification. Other major increases in state

authority derived from the terms upon which localities qualified for shares of state school fund revenues. These eventually
came to include requirements regarding the length of school
terms, and reporting requirements. In this way, the creation of
permanent school funds laid the groundwork for more coercive
state legislation later in the nineteenth century.

THE ANTEBELLUM PERIOD: ESTABLISHING THE PRINCIPLE OF "FREE" COMMON SCHOOLING

In the mid-nineteenth century, state governments substantially increased their involvement and authority in schooling,
eventually establishing the principle that states had a compelling interest in guaranteeing and even requiring a common education for all children. This construction of state educational authority occurred in several stages and did not occur without resistance. Indeed, one could go a long way in reading the whole
of nineteenth century school legislation as a continual seesaw
between a localist (and largely Democratic) politics of decentralized power and a cosmopolitan (and largely Whig and Republican) politics of centralized power.

The first stage of this construction of state authority occurred in the 1820s and 1830s as states sought to consolidate
control over central funds and to specify the terms upon which
such funds were distributed. These initial attempts at establishing central state authority were often short-lived, however, or
undercut by financial losses and government retrenchment in
the aftermath of the Panic of 1837. The Illinois legislature, for example, passed a law requiring that common schools open to all
white citizens be established in each county as early as 1825. A
small portion of the state treasury was to be devoted to the support of such schools, as was most of the income on a central state
school fund. Localities were to raise the rest of the necessary
funds, half from local taxes and half through tuition charged to
parents. In 1829, however, the legislature repealed these provisions. The next major state provision for support of schools did
not occur until 1855, when Illinois instituted a two-mill state tax
for their support, with additional funds to be raised by locality.

Meanwhile, in 1835, the state did establish a central state fund from which localities could qualify to receive a share of the proceeds. Much of that money, however, was "borrowed back" by the state government for other purposes following the panic of 1837 (Waltershausen 1994).

Similar scenarios played out in other states, both north and south. Michigan made state authority a provision of its first state constitution in 1835, establishing a precedent that other states followed later in the century. In the Panic of 1837, however, the state "borrowed" its common school fund to use for other purposes and dropped state provisions regarding the amount of county school taxes to be raised, the powers of the state superintendent, and the promotion of school construction (Tyack, James, and Benavot 1987). Many other states also experienced backlashes in the late 1830s and the 1840s. In Georgia an 1837 law allowing for the voluntary organization of common schools was repealed in 1840. In Massachusetts the state board of education established in 1838 came close to being abolished in 1840. In the same year (1840) the office of superintendent was abolished in Ohio and Connecticut (Kaestle 1983).

Generally speaking, until at least the 1850s, whatever state provisions existed for schooling were more permissive than regulatory. They allowed localities to organize common schools and/or to tax themselves for the purpose, or they required towns and counties to establish common schools but allowed the funds for such schools to be raised either by rate bills to parents or by taxation. Some states made central state funds for common schools available to localities who chose to apply for them and then attached some minimal requirements to districts or towns that did so. These systems of voluntary school organization met with varying responses. In Pennsylvania in 1847 more than three-fourths of existing districts took advantage of common school laws, voluntarily taxing themselves for school support. In North Carolina by 1846 a majority of districts had taken advantage of an 1839 common school law. Similarly, in Georgia slightly more than half the counties raised enough taxes to make them eligible for shares of state funds for charity schools. In Virginia, by contrast, only a few localities managed the two-thirds vote necessary to create a voluntary system of local taxation under legislation passed from 1846 to 1849 (Swift 1911).

The 1850s marked an important turning point in the construction of more coercive state power in the formation of common school systems. A number of states passed legislation in this decade that made the levying of local taxes for support of schools compulsory rather than voluntary. Although the practice of levying local school taxes had roots far back into the colonial era and was already widespread as a voluntary means of raising school funds, the legislatures of the 1850s fundamentally shifted the balance between local control and state government in the North by making this practice compulsory, and by combining local taxation with state taxes for support of schools. At the same time a number of new states admitted to the union during the 1840s and 1850s made such provisions part of their state constitutions.

This assertion of compulsory state authority occasioned tension and resistance. At issue were not only the collection of taxes at the state level, but the conditions upon which the state redistributed those funds to localities. Generally, states redistributed school funds on the basis of population, combining some allowance for the total size of a local population with the principle of distributing funds for the number of school-aged children served in the locality. Such funding formulas allowed for some redistribution of wealth to localities with low property valuations, but not without opposition.

Moreover, not all children were included in these funding formulas. Several northern states specifically limited their provisions for common schooling to white citizens. Beginning with their very first legislation in the 1820s and 1830s, for example, both Indiana and Illinois defined common schools as schools open to all white citizens. Illinois continued this tradition of defining common schools as "whites only" institutions when it instituted its first state tax for support of common schools in 1855. The legislation specified that the distribution of state funds collected through this tax be calculated according to the number of white children in each county (Waltershausen 1994). Similarly, Indiana defined public schools in racially exclusionary terms throughout the antebellum period (Reynolds 1998).

California, however, went further than either of these Mid-western states in using state funding and authority in schooling to enforce exclusion of non-white children from common schools. Beginning in 1852 with the state's first school laws, and its appointment of former southerner Andrew Moulder as State Superintendent of Public Instruction, California deliberately developed a "whites only" school system that not only discouraged but explicitly prohibited the attendance of Chinese, blacks or Indians in state supported schools. In 1858 Moulder recommended to the state legislature that they confer on him the authority to withhold state monies from any district that permitted the admission of "children of inferior races," whom he identified as "African, Mongolian and Indian." The California School Law of 1860 adopted this recommendation specifying that "Negroes, Mongolians and Indians shall not be admitted to the Public Schools" and granting the State Superintendent the power to withhold state funds from any district where such "prohibited parties" were found to be in attendance. This assertion of state authority went a step beyond allocating funds on a racially exclusionary basis by forcibly excluding non-white children from local schools receiving state support (Olson 1997, pp. 34–36).

The racially exclusionary school policies upon which states like California and Indiana distributed state funds were the object of considerable resistance on the part of minority communities and would become the subject of a number of court cases in the immediate postwar period. Probably the most widespread source of tension with respect to the view of school laws, however, was the issue of equity for taxpayers. Common school reformers such as Samuel Lewis and Horace Mann argued that it was "the duty of every government" to use its common wealth to even out the wide disparities in educational opportunities among different communities and ensure that the means of an adequate education "are provided for all" (Lewis 1838, pp. 1027–28; Mann 1846, p. 1098). When it came to effecting such policies, however, state school officials often experienced significant opposition. In Illinois, for example, the two-mill school tax first levied by the state in 1855 immediately produced a reaction from towns whose contributions to the state funds exceeded the

money they received in return. "The people are not against paying taxes," one county commissioner explained in 1856, "but
think that the money collected should not be taken out of the
county where raised." Similarly, another complained, "...justice
would seem to require" that the state school tax fund "should be
appropriated in the counties where the same is collected." Despite continued complaints of this kind, Illinois maintained its
two-mill tax and the same basic method of distribution for 18
years. At the same time, however, state officials established a
"state board of equalization" which adjusted property assessments on which the tax was based. As a result of these adjustments the per capita amount of school funds raised through
state tax declined significantly, as did the proportion of total
school funds that came from state sources. The share of total
funds derived from state sources declined from 64 percent in
1856 to 36 percent in 1862 (Waltershausen 1994, p. 63).

As in this example from Illinois, many state superintendents
found that in order to establish the principle of "free" tax-supported common schooling in the 1850s, they had to compromise
on some of their specific goals regarding the regulation of common schooling. In general, the legislation of the 1850s was less
aggressive than the earlier, short-lived legislation of the 1830s.
Pierce's 1837 plan for Michigan, for example, had included compulsory attendance and minimum teacher salary provisions.
Under his plan the share of school funds derived from local state
sources would be 50/50, thereby providing the state with the leverage necessary to enforce such requirements. This leverage
was lost, however, with the loss of state funds in the Panic of
1837, and would not again be in reach for another hundred
years. Although at the time of the Civil War a number of states
had established the principle of tax-supported common schooling, most of the regulation of school practice still lay far in the
future.

CIVIL WAR, RECONSTRUCTION, AND THE POST-RECONSTRUCTION ERA, 1860–1890: EFFORTS AT STANDARDIZATION

Before the 1850s, the essential dynamic of state involvement in schooling was to encourage local initiative by empowering localities to organize and tax themselves for support of schools, and by providing what amounted to "start-up funds" and financial incentives for localities to facilitate such organization. After the 1850s, by contrast, the central dynamic of state involvement in schooling became increasingly regulatory. Beginning in the late 1850s and continuing through the post-Reconstruction era of the 1870s and 1880s, state governments undertook a number of efforts at school standardization. These efforts included strategies for standardizing textbooks and curricula, teacher certification, student achievement, high school accreditation and graduation, and teacher salaries.

A survey of these efforts at standardization reveals the considerable limits of state authority in the face of traditions of local control, the dynamics of party politics, and the forces of supply and demand. Even with the establishment of compulsory state systems of common school funding and the organization of state departments of education, compliance with state standards often remained voluntary in important respects. The result of these efforts at standardization, then, was often the elaboration of a two-tiered system of school operation in which some students, teachers and schools met *state* standards of accreditation and certification, while most met merely *local* educational standards.

Looking closely at school laws in an individual state provides examples of how these double standards developed. In New York, most of the specific powers of the state superintendent derived from the authority to apportion state funds, including those now raised by compulsory state tax. In order for districts to be eligible for their share of the funds to which they had already been forced to contribute by law, they had to operate common schools for a minimum term, employ qualified teachers to teach in those schools for the whole of that term, and submit annual reports regarding pupil attendance, teacher employment, and funding of those schools.

Through these provisions the state superintendent gained a kind of bureaucratic power over the operation of the system as a whole. According to the consolidated school laws of 1864, these powers included the right to inspect any common school in the state, the power to appoint school inspectors, the authority to certify teachers and other school personnel, and the power to remove school officers or commissioners who willfully neglected or violated their duties as specified by law or as determined by order of the state superintendent. With these powers the state superintendent also indirectly acquired authority over the fixing of district boundaries, the examination of schools and teachers, the maintenance and safety of school buildings, and the moral fitness, learning, and ability of existing teachers at the local level (New York 1864).

As this summary of state law suggests, the state superintendent technically enjoyed several sources of authority and influence over the conduct of local schools. In practice, however, the superintendent's actual powers were in reality quite limited. These limitations derived in part from traditions of local control. Although the superintendent technically had the power to issue his own teaching certificates, for example, in practice almost all teacher examinations and certificates were awarded by local school commissioners. As these commissioners were elected by local voters and operated under their own set of legal mandates and guidelines, the state superintendent's powers in this respect were more a matter of arbitration than of directive.

Perhaps even more effective in limiting the authority of the state, however, were forces of supply and demand. The numbers of teachers trained in the state normal schools or certified directly by the state superintendent were a tiny fraction of the total numbers of teachers employed each year. Even the hundreds of independent academies and city high schools not under direct state control did not come close to educating the numbers of teachers necessary to operate the schools in the state. Producing an adequate supply of minimally qualified teachers was thus a far more pressing problem than one of determining how high the standards of qualification should be. On the demand side the relative rarity of a normal school certificate made it quixotic to set hiring standards as high as the state superintendent might like.

As a result of these limitations on state authority, some schools hired teachers whose credentials had state standing while others hired teachers whose credentials carried only local authority. This language of "local" versus "state" certificates became explicit in the 1860s and 1870s in New York and other states. Local teaching certificates were granted on a short-term basis by local school commissioners or school boards. Good for a year or two at a time, or perhaps only for three or six months, these certificates qualified a teacher to teach within the locality, but did not transfer to other jurisdictions. State certificates, by contrast, usually conferred by formal and more rigorous examination, were good for extended periods, perhaps for life, and applied to any district in the state.

Throughout the nineteenth century the numbers involved in these state and local distinctions were extremely skewed. In New York in 1886, 93 percent of the teachers employed by common schools held "local" certificates, 4 percent held normal school certificates, and 2.5 percent held certificates granted by the state superintendent. In effect, then, a two-tiered system of certification developed within the public schools, one which included the vast majority of teachers and was subject to local authority and control, and another constituting a tiny translocal elite of teachers of state standing (Pugh 1994, pp. 212–14).

Additional limitations on the state's capacity to effect standardization existed with respect to other aspects of school operations. Generally, when it came to issues of curriculum, the leverage of state superintendents was much weaker than it was for the qualification of teachers. Although the basic subjects of a common education were not in dispute, the question of how those subjects were to be taught (i.e., with which textbooks) was contentious. In Virginia, for example, under the new constitution of 1870, the State Board of Education acquired the legal authority to dictate the selection of textbooks. This authority proved more technical than practical, however. To hold onto his position in the face of the resurgent power of conservative southern Democrats in the 1870s, state superintendent Ruffner had to back down on these and other provisions for central authority over the schools. In 1875 Ruffner considerably loosened the state's textbook adoption procedures, allowing the exercise of local choice (Link 1986, pp. 16–20).

California's authority over textbook selection also proved susceptible to political backlash. Perhaps in part because he failed to adopt the more conciliatory approach of Ruffner, but also because of his strong Republican party affiliations, state superintendent Swett did not survive the first serious challenge to his authority over textbook selection in 1867. Beyond his tenure, the textbook issue continued to be contested. Eventually, in 1879, the state lost its central authority over a number of such educational matters. Under a new state constitution, textbook selection, teacher certification, racial exclusion and other special school provisions moved from state jurisdiction to that of city and county school boards (Tyack, James, and Benavot 1987, p. 103).

Efforts to establish standards of academic achievement at the state level also proved subject to significant limitations. One of the most ambitious attempts to establish such standards was the New York State Regents' exams, developed in the 1860s and 1870s. Instead of promoting standardization through direct regulation of schools, New York asserted standards of academic achievement through the testing of individual students. Depending on their performance on these exams, students could earn certificates or diplomas. Presumably the competitive demand of students for these state credentials would in turn exert a regulating influence on the schools. To further encourage such beneficial influence, the state attached small amounts of supplemental funding to schools for each student who successfully completed each level of the examination system (Beadie 1999b).

Even this more diffuse assertion of centralized education authority suffered setbacks, however. Although virtually all schools participated in the system, very few ever required successful completion of the exams for admission or graduation, as the regents initially imagined. Most academies and high schools continued to award their own certificates and diplomas according to their own criteria even as they also awarded Regents certificates and diplomas. As with the certification of teachers, the number of students who received "local" certificates and diplomas greatly exceeded those who received Regents credentials.[5]

Although New York's system was distinctive in its use of examinations, other states tried to standardize the meaning of a high school diploma by other means. In 1871, for example, Michigan instituted a "diploma system" of accreditation for high schools that met University of Michigan standards of admission (Angus and Mirel 1999, p. 8). Similarly, Indiana designated certain high schools as "commissioned" high schools beginning in the 1880s. Graduates of these schools could automatically gain access to state colleges without further examination. To achieve this designation a high school had to meet minimal criteria regarding curricula, length of school terms and qualifications of teachers. By commissioning some high schools as credentialing institutions, however, and others not, the state effectively created a two-tiered system of higher study within the public schools. In effect the educational authority of some schools was "merely" local while the authority of others was legitimated by the state and thereby carried an exchange value within state borders (Stahly 1998, pp. 67–68).

These distinctions between "local" and "state" standards also often reinforced distinctions between rural and urban schools and populations. Standards of accreditation and certification were often defined by urban principals and superintendents and modeled on urban schools. Rural school principals and constituencies thus sometimes complained that such standards gave urban students and schools an unfair advantage over rural students. In addition, some state systems of standardization reinforced racial hierarchies and discrimination. Mississippi, for example, established a statewide teacher salary scale in 1886 that effectively legitimated unequal pay for black and white teachers, even when teachers of different races achieved the same level of certification on the same statewide certifica-

---

5 In 1890, the regents found that students earned a total of 2,978 different school-based diplomas, as compared with 1,633 Regents diplomas (Beadie 1999b).

tion exam (Bond 1934, p. 94).[6] In some respects, the Mississippi effort represented a stronger assertion of state authority than northern states exercised at the time. Although state systems of teacher certification were being developed across the country, few states claimed to administer them through a single, uniform teacher exam. Eventually, discriminatory systems such as these occasioned renewed assertions of local initiative and control on the part of black communities.

PROGRESSIVE ERA, 1890–1930: DEFINING THE ISSUE OF LOCAL CONTROL

During the Progressive Era, a national network of educators and administrators actively sought to increase the power of states to enforce standardization. One way they did so was by framing the issue of standardization as a problem of school finance. Reformers like Ellwood P. Cubberley recommended changes in school laws that would substantially increase the share of total school funds derived from state sources and tie state funds to specific school improvements. These laws often provoked considerable resistance on the part of rural districts, and in some instances rural constituencies organized politically against them. In this way it could be said that the issue of local control was a creation of the Progressive Era. Although the tension between state authority and local prerogatives had existed from the beginnings of the common school movement in the 1820s and 1830s, it was not until the first decades of the twentieth century that the principle of local control gained clear articulation as a rallying point for organized political action.[7]

---

6   The system established a state salary scale, but did so using salary ranges that legitimized wide variations in what a local district actually chose to pay an individual teacher. The salary range stated for the highest grade certificate was the widest, permitting someone paid at the top of the range to earn over twice as much per year as someone paid at the bottom of the range, even though they performed equally well on the licensing exam.

7   As Kaestle (1983) has emphasized, resistance to the centralizing tendency of common schools reform was widespread in the antebellum era, but unorganized.

The issue of local control was defined in the Progressive Era in response to a direct assault on the practice of local school governance by an increasingly powerful national network of progressive reformers. As Tyack (1974) and others have shown, an "interlocking directorate" of university professors and presidents, city and state superintendents effectively used the National Education Association to develop a consensus among school leaders.[8] One of the strategies adopted by this network was to promote standardization through the school finance system.

In his 1906 study, *School Funds and Their Apportionment*, E. P. Cubberley specifically analyzed the systems of school funding employed in various states with an eye toward illustrating significant disparities between rural and urban districts and of presenting a financial strategy for addressing those disparities. From his perspective, the failure of rural districts to meet state (and urban) standards derived mainly from inequalities in taxable wealth. To address this disjunction between mostly urban and mostly rural districts Cubberley recommended that states substantially increase the share of total school funds derived from state sources, and that they apportion school funds on the basis of need and effort rather than on the basis of wealth and population. These recommendations in turn implied a substan-

---

8 The existence of such a network of educators and policymakers was not new. During the common school reform movement, state superintendents and self-appointed schoolmen had similarly drafted school legislation and developed models of school finance policy with reference to each other. They had also assisted each other in the lobbying efforts necessary to put their plans into law. As early as the 1830s and 1840s these educators came together in national organizations and conventions to share information and strategies. These associations generated a number of proposals for promoting common school principles and practices across state lines. In 1857 some of the participants of this nationalizing effort formed the National Teachers Association, a progenitor of the National Education Association (Mattingly 1975). This organization in turn assumed an instrumental role in securing establishment of the first U.S. Department of Education in 1867, and in lobbying for some of the numerous bills aimed at establishing a national system of education introduced in Congress in the 1870s and 1880s (Warren 1974; Lee 1949).

tial increase in central state authority, both to generate increased funds and to determine effort and need.

Cubberley did not end his analysis here, however. He went on to recommend an extensive supplemental funding system in which additional state funds would be tied to specific educational programs and school improvements. These included funds dedicated specifically to secondary schooling and to various "special advantages" such as kindergartens, manual training, physical training, evening schools, special education, parental schools, and vacation schools. Framing his proposal as an issue of equalization, Cubberley pointed out that as long as secondary schooling and special programs were a matter of local prerogative and permissive taxation, only the wealthier urban districts would be likely to provide the full range of educational advantages. With the provision of supplemental state funds, however, smaller communities could provide such programs.

Cubberley's method of presenting his recommendations implied that he was not promoting any particular set of school reforms. What Cubberley apparently sought was a new *method* of promoting school improvement, rather than any specific set of provisions. And yet this very lack of apparent concern about the content of such measures itself was a kind of programmatic intent. Rather than write legislation that specifically designated which special programs would receive additional grants or special funding, Cubberley suggested, officials should write apportionment legislation in general terms so as to allow extra funds to be granted to *any special program* adopted by a central state office of education. Such a general set of provisions would "at once" make it possible to recognize "any or all of these newer efforts," thereby eliminating the need of amending the apportionment law. "Most of the recent educational efforts" Cubberley went so far as to suggest in the concluding paragraph of this chapter "are so valuable that some provision ought to be made for them which will lead to their more general adoption by the smaller communities of the state" (Cubberley 1906, p. 249).

In effect, then, Cubberley proposed a school finance system calculated to provide state-level educators with a general license to determine which program ought to be part of the state system of education. Although Cubberley's plan did not necessarily become an exact blueprint for legislative changes in specific states, it was highly influential. Efforts to refine the use of school finance systems to promote school reform became widespread in this era. As with earlier standardization efforts, these strategies were neither politically nor racially neutral, though promoters like Cubberley presented them in as neutral a way as possible. With respect to rural districts, for example, Cubberley presented his analysis as specifically aimed at relieving the problems of small schools and rural districts. Under the guise of promoting funding equity, however, Cubberley actually proposed to make mandatory a number of educational programs and provisions that rural communities had long resisted. For example, Cubberley suggested that special state subsidies be apportioned for "concentration of rural schools," meaning rural school consolidation.

Rural school consolidation was a direct assault on the principle of local control as understood by rural districts of the time. Much has been written about the urban version of consolidation (i.e., Tyack 1974; Reese 1986; Mirel 1990), which involved the elimination of ward-based systems of political representation and the establishment of small, citywide school boards elected on an at-large basis. By the end of the nineteenth century most cities had adopted such a system, which decreased the influence of (often ethnic) neighborhoods over local schools. Beginning in the late 1890s national education leaders promoted similar changes for rural areas. An 1897 report on rural schools issued by the National Education Association pronounced the individual school district as "the most undesirable unit possible." It went on to advocate the large-scale elimination of local school districts and an aggressive consolidation of rural schools (Pugh 1994, p. 247).

In the 1910s and 1920s a number of states passed school consolidation laws. These laws eliminated the taxation and spending powers of individual districts and replaced them with small boards representing larger territories on an at-large basis. In effect these changes decreased the influence of smaller communities by diluting their voting power in that of larger population areas. At the same time, such school laws often lowered the requirements for forcing a vote on school consolidation and increased the authority of state-appointed commissioners to propose and approve such changes. With school board officials elected at-large and the more commercial populous districts enjoying greater voter strength than smaller districts, a school consolidation could more readily be pushed through against the wishes and united resistance of the district inhabitants whose schools stood to be eliminated. In addition, many states established financial incentives for school consolidation. Often this two-pronged strategy developed in separate steps, with the changes in governance effectively increasing the pressure to take advantage of incentives.

These coercive aspects of school consolidation predictably occasioned considerable resistance on the part of affected districts. As Tyack, James, and Benavot (1987) have shown, litigation over district boundaries, district creation, and school consolidation all increased significantly in the period after 1917, and continued at a high level through the 1940s and into the 1950s. In some states resistance went beyond such efforts at legal redress and became the object of organized political action. New York State provides a particularly dramatic example of this process of politicization. Belatedly awakened to the consequences of changes in school governance effected by a 1917 "Township Law," rural New Yorkers organized a successful campaign to repeal it.

As part of this campaign rural leaders articulated a principle of local control in school governance as a positive social good. At issue from their perspective was both the educational value for students of schooling conducted in a close community environment, and the democratic value for students, parents, and citizens alike of direct involvement in decisions regarding education. This progressive-sounding vision of education echoed the language of Dewey, and rural leaders recognized this fact. In the wake of their successful repeal of the 1917 Township Law, organizers of this rural school constituency went on to develop and promote a vision of rural school improvement that would be rooted in local initiative and community rejuvenation. Taking a case study from the work of Evelyn Dewey as an explicit model, editors of the *Rural New Yorker* declared that if school improvement was to "be in any way permanent it must be developed and carried on by the people of the district" (Pugh 1994, p. 378).

This example illustrates how the aggressive centralization policies of progressive reformers helped define the issue of local control. Other examples of central school policies that galvanized local initiative are provided by the racially oppressive policies of southern states. During the Progressive Era, southern state governments established increasingly elaborate methods of diverting public school funds from black to white schools.[9] As a result of these policies the gap between school provisions for white and black children continually widened in southern states over the period from 1880 to 1920. Anderson (1988, p. 154) found "the disparity in per capita expenditures between blacks and whites in the public schools was greater in 1910 than in 1900 and greater in 1900 than earlier, in every southern state." Bond (1934, p. 104) details gaps in per capita expenditures for white and black children as high as 30 to 1 in some counties of Mississippi in 1908–09. In response to these worsening school conditions, many black communities in the South funded and constructed their own schools through voluntary fundraising and "double taxation." Having raised the funds and taken the initiative to organize these schools, southern black communities managed to hold onto a considerable degree of control, even though they usually handed over title to the buildings and submitted to state and county supervision in order to get what they

---

9 These strategies depended on developing a gap between the terms upon which the state allocated central funds to local districts and those upon which local districts allocated funds to individual schools. Although local districts received the same per pupil funding from the state for each of their black as well as white students, county school officials organized fewer schools, hired fewer teachers and paid lower salaries for black children than they did for the same numbers of white children. What was not allocated for the education of black children then became eligible for the education of whites. Moreover, given the per child basis of allocating state funds, the possibilities for high levels of funding for white schools increased as the proportion of blacks in the population increased. In other words, the greater the proportion of black children in the local population, the greater the resources subject to diversion to white schools (Bond 1934; Anderson 1988; Benson and O'Halloran 1987).

could of public funds. In an indirect and unintended way, then, systematic state policies of depriving black schools of funds and diverting them to white schools stimulated a surge of local initiative and control in black schools (Anderson 1988; Walker 1996, 1998).

This surge of local initiative in response to systematic state policies of discrimination considerably complicates the history of relationships between state authority and local control. Instead of a simple story of tension between state and local authorities, the southern case reveals conflicts between different local constituencies (black and white) in which one constituency enjoyed considerably more access and influence in state-level politics and policy than the other. To assert local control, black communities thus had to resist both the oppression of local authorities and that of state laws that facilitated that oppression.

Complexities such as these were not simply the product of a peculiar southern politics, however. A close look at the dynamics of progressive era policies in cities reveals a similarly complex relationship between state authority and local control. These complexities are illustrated by a little-known essay by John Dewey published in the *New Republic* in 1915. In the essay, Dewey criticized the work of the New York State education department as "largely in the hand of routineers." State officials, according to Dewey, were more interested in "improving mechanical uniformity" and in "that kind of administrative efficiency denoted by reports and examinations" than in real educational leadership (Dewey 1915, p.179). Dewey made these remarks in the context of a very specific battle in the school wars of New York City. This battle, like many others before and since, was ultimately over the degree to which the city schools should be under the control of city government. Dewey, like other New York reformers at this time, favored increased city control as a plan more conducive to the exercise of strong leadership in the direction of reform. Indeed, the main point of Dewey's essay was to make the somewhat shocking proposal that the New York City School Board should be eliminated entirely. The thrust of the proposal, however, was not to suggest that state authority should be increased, but rather to suggest that the operation of the schools should be absorbed into city government. In making this proposal, Dewey seems to have imagined that urban education would be administered in much the same way as other urban services such as transportation, water, recreation and police. That is to say, schools would no longer be subject to the decisions of a lay, elected board, but would be administered by a department of public servants and professionals.

For those familiar with the particular history of progressive schools reform in New York City, this position put Dewey squarely with the coalition of university and business leaders associated with the ultimately disastrous imposition of the Gary Plan on New York City Schools (Ravitch 1974). In addition to providing a rare glimpse into Dewey's perspective on the *realpolitik* of urban schooling, however, his comments are illustrative of the problems of defining issues of local control for urban districts in the twentieth century. On the one hand a proposal for absorbing school administration into city government would seem to be a case for increasing local control of schools, and to some degree it was presented as such by Dewey himself. On the other hand, to present this example as an assertion of local control would be misleading. For starters, this change in school governance was to be accomplished through a special act of the state legislature. Indeed, it could be said that the reformers in this case sought to exploit their greater influence in politics at the state level to effect changes they could never win support for in local politics. The state in this regard was less an authority over city school administration than a tool for increasing the power and resources of certain urban coalitions in their struggles with each other.

This strategy of seeking special legislation at the state level in order to change the balance of power at the local level is a recurrent pattern in the history of schooling generally, but particularly in the history of urban schooling in the twentieth century. As cities grew in size and significance during the Great Depression and World War II, so did the political and financial leverage of leading urban constituencies.

THE GREAT DEPRESSION, WORLD WAR II, AND THE POSTWAR ERA: THE CONSOLIDATION OF STATE AUTHORITY

Despite the groundwork laid by progressive era reformers, the consolidation of schools and of state regulatory authority was largely a post-1920, and even a post-World War II, phenomenon. Depression-era conditions facilitated this consolidation. During the first half of the 1930s, school districts experienced drastic cuts in school funding from both state and local sources, even as enrollments increased steadily, especially in urban schools. By the mid-1930s this combination of increasing demand and declining resources led coalitions of teachers, school leaders, citizen groups, and some businessmen to lobby state governments for special legislation to provide new sources of funding for schools.

At the same time as legislatures established new sources of school funding, they also sought to achieve greater efficiencies in schooling. In response to demands for solutions to the school crisis, a number of states commissioned special state-level investigations focused specifically on the financial efficiency of existing school systems. A common recommendation of such reports was the need for more aggressive policies of school consolidation. Together, these depression-era measures initiated significant increases in the shares of total school funds derived from state sources and in the regulatory powers of state departments of education.

In addition to these measures, a number of political factors contributed to the consolidation of state authority in the 1930s and 1940s. One of these factors was the increasing influence of urban constituencies in state politics. A second factor was the increased political organization and effectiveness of teacher unions. In a number of cities teacher unions cooperated with local school officials, citizen groups, and even business leaders to win new state funding and appropriation provisions that would benefit local schools. Later, these same unions sometimes went on to secure legislation that would protect teachers' interests statewide. In other cities, however, opposing business interests successfully prevented teacher unions from securing relief at the state level. In these ways the relationship between state and local control varied according to the power and interests of different constituencies.

Precipitating all this political and financial activity was the severe decline in tax revenues experienced by school districts during the Great Depression. By 1932 most teachers' salaries had been cut and many teachers had been let go. As the depression continued, school boards imposed hiring freezes, eliminated most special programs, and forced remaining teachers to accept unpaid furloughs, delayed paychecks, and partial payment of salaries in scrip. In rural areas some districts returned to the practice of boarding teachers in local homes in lieu of salary, while others closed their schools entirely. In Alabama, for example, 85 percent of all counties closed their schools in 1933. Everywhere school construction programs were suspended, school years were shortened, vacations were extended, and new school openings were postponed or reversed (Tyack, Lowe, and Hansot 1982; Moreo 1996, p. 43).

Compounding the effects of these staff and budget cuts were simultaneous increases in the enrollment and persistence of children in school. These increases occurred primarily at the high school level, where the virtual elimination of employment opportunities for youth led to a fundamental historical change in youth's school attendance patterns. For the first time in the 1930s, the majority of 14- to 17-year-olds attended school instead of dropping out to seek employment or to work in the family. By the end of the decade this change had translated into higher graduation rates as well. In 1939 for the first time nearly half the relevant age cohort earned high school diplomas (Angus and Mirel 1999; Green 1980).

These shifts in attendance patterns were most profoundly felt in urban areas because youth employment and school-leaving rates had been higher there before the depression. In San Francisco, for example, the graduation rates of children entering the system as first graders went from 29 percent in 1930 to 86 percent in 1940. Needless to say, such changes in attendance patterns deepened the already considerable financial crisis of depression-era schools. In Detroit, for example, high schools experienced a 43 percent increase in student enrollments over the same five-year period that the school district cut its budget by one-third (Angus and Mirel 1999, pp. 60–61).

The effects of the Great Depression were not only economic, however, but also political. As a result of the depression-era collision between increased demand for schooling and declining school resources, a number of constituencies organized politically over school issues. These included not only teachers whose livelihoods were affected directly by budget cuts, and administrators who were responsible for maintaining the system, but businessmen who were the creditors of heavily-borrowing school systems, women's groups who were concerned with child welfare and school reform, and parents and students who were on the receiving end of reduced school services.

One common response to the cuts imposed by local school boards was public protest. In Chicago in 1933 over 25,000 people showed up at a protest meeting just nine days after the school board announced drastic budget cuts (Wrigley 1982, p. 228). Nationwide, student strikes and parent picket lines were common throughout the 1930s. Perhaps the most regular and persistent of these occurred in New York City, where a tradition of parent and student protest was already well-established. Issues such as building maintenance, overcrowding, free speech, and student transfers occasioned boycotts there in this period. Student and parent protests were not confined to the largest cities, however. In smaller places such as Hazleton, Pennsylvania, Youngstown, Ohio, and Lenoir City, Tennessee, students and parents staged demonstrations to protest teacher dismissals and other spending decisions (Moreo 1996, pp. 95–105).

Such activism on the part of students and parents was generally aimed at local school decisionmaking, however. It did not address the larger problems of declining revenues. Moreover, these larger conditions could not generally be addressed under existing tax practices. To significantly change the crisis conditions of schools required new sources of school revenue and new appropriation policies. In pursuit of such resources many school officials, educators and civic leaders sought relief from higher levels of government. At the federal level, state officials and national educational organizations, including the NEA, lobbied for a relief program aimed specifically at replacing lost tax revenues in existing school budgets. The Roosevelt administration preferred channeling funds into new programs, however, and this lobbying effort was clearly failing by 1935 (Tyack, Lowe, and Hansot 1982, pp. 92–112). In the meantime, at the state level, local school officials, city politicians, civic groups, and teachers' associations lobbied for new laws that would make schools less dependent on property taxes for funding, and that would guarantee schools minimum levels of school appropriations.

A number of states passed new school funding laws by the mid-1930s. A common provision of such laws was to institute sales taxes and license fees that were earmarked specifically for school support. In Michigan, for example, a state aid package passed in 1935 dedicated a fixed portion of sales and liquor taxes to support of schools (Mirel 1993, p. 127). In California in 1933 a constitutional amendment dedicated revenue from sales taxes and other sources to the support of schools, and guaranteed a minimum annual per pupil appropriation from the state (Peterson 1985, p. 173). Similarly, North Carolina established a 3 percent sales tax for support of schools in 1933 (Moreo 1996, p. 44).

These new sources of revenue contributed to a substantial shift in the proportion of school funding derived from state sources. During the last decades of the nineteenth century and the first decades of the twentieth, northern states such as New York, Michigan, and Illinois contributed a very small share of school expenditures, ranging between 10 percent and 20 percent from decade to decade (Pugh 1994; Mirel 1993; Waltershausen 1994). Western and southern states tended to contribute larger shares, but some states, such as Iowa, raised virtually all school funds from local taxes. As a result of depression-era changes in school funding policies, state shares of school expenditures increased. In Michigan, for example, the state share of school expenditures went from 20 percent in 1930 to 45 percent in 1939 (Mirel 1993, p. 129). Nationwide, the percentage of school funds derived from state sources increased from 17 percent to 30 percent between 1930 and 1940 and continued to climb through the following decade (Berne 1988).

As the state share of total school support increased, so did the leverage states enjoyed for enforcing regulations and policies. At the same time as they instituted new tax and appropriation measures, a number of states launched state-level investigations into the costs and efficiency of existing school systems. The resulting reports often promoted aggressive policies of rural school consolidation. In Illinois a series of such reports in the 1930s (1934, 1935, and 1939) eventually led to the formation of a State Advisory Commission on School Organization. The work of this commission in turn reduced the number of school districts in the state by more than half in just six years—from 11,955 in 1944 to 4,540 in 1950–51 (Waltershausen 1994, p. 108). Similarly, New York commissioned "An Inquiry into the Cost and Character of Public Education in the State of New York" in 1934. The resulting 12-volume report in turn led to the creation of a state "Master Plan" that reduced the number of school districts in the state 62 percent by 1958 (Pugh 1994, pp. 447–450).

Overall, it can be said that a significant increase in state education authority occurred in the late 1940s with the victory of the school consolidation movement. This change had begun to take shape at the turn of the twentieth century with the rhetorical campaign initiated by the NEA. It then matured in the 1910s and 1920s as a number of states passed laws promoting consolidation through local governance changes and financial incentives. Not until the late 1940s, however, did it come to fruition. As Pugh (1994, p. 434) explains with respect to New York State, the first wave of consolidation, from 1925 to 1945, succeeded in eliminating school districts, but not necessarily in eliminating schools. In this early period the main thrust of consolidation was to facilitate the organization of central high schools, often leaving one-room schools to continue to operate at the elementary level. In the postwar period, by contrast, state departments of education became much more aggressive in their goal of eliminating schools as well as districts. In addition to providing financial incentives for the construction of central schools and the transportation of students, states developed increasingly refined methods of forcing the closure of existing schools. Often these methods involved regulations requiring that all schools provide certain physical facilities and meet certain standards of construction and sanitation. Similar regulations regarding curriculum might require that all schools provide instruction in subjects such as personal hygiene by teachers certified in that subject. In order to command the resources necessary to meet these requirements schools would then find themselves forced to consolidate. If they failed to do either, they would face the prospect of having their facilities condemned and/or their state funds withheld.

This carrot-and-stick approach to forcing consolidation followed closely the model suggested by Cubberley in 1906. It had taken nearly five decades, however, for the model to be realized. From this perspective, the surge in state regulation of the most minute aspects of school building, hiring, curriculum, and organization is of comparatively recent origin. Although complaints about the overregulation of schools by state authorities date at least from the turn of the century, and though visions of close state and even federal control of such matters took form in the heads of school reformers as early as the 1830s, it was not until the 1940s and 1950s, after two world wars and the Great Depression, that state governments gained the kind of resources and leverage necessary to realize such visions.

One way to look at this shift in power is as a result of changes in social demography. The victory of the school consolidation movement in particular represented a decline in the relative importance of rural constituencies in state politics. As Mirel (1993) has shown for Michigan, the battles over state funding sources and levels in the late 1930s and the 1940s were closely associated with battles over apportionment of seats in the legislature among urban and rural districts in the state. Nationally, the proportions of the population living in rural and urban areas had substantially reversed themselves in the one hundred years since common school reform, from 84 percent rural in 1850 to 36 percent rural in 1950 (U.S. Bureau of the Census 1960). The stimulus to manufacturing initiated by the two world wars in particular promoted migration from rural areas to cities. In many respects it can be said that the centralization of authority effected by state departments of education in the 1940s represented the victory of an urban over a rural model of schooling.

Whether this centralization of authority meant a loss of local control for urban districts is much less clear than it is for rural districts, however. After all, many of the depression-era funding provisions were passed in response to the demands of urban districts. At the state level urban constituencies from the same city often cooperated with each other to win state provisions that would benefit local schools. In Atlanta, for example, the schools had traditionally derived a high proportion of their operating funds from annual city appropriations. When the size and predictability of these appropriations declined during the depression, a coalition of local teachers, school officials, civic groups and city leaders successfully lobbied for special legislation that guaranteed a certain proportion of city revenues to support of schools (Peterson 1985). Similarly, in Detroit, a coalition of local educators, city officials, and civic groups played a significant role in winning the state aid package that provided relief for schools in 1935. Moreover, this cooperation continued at least through the 1940s. In 1949, for example, a similar coalition successfully lobbied for legislation that freed Detroit schools entirely from city appropriations and authorized the raising of school funds through special levies (Mirel 1993). In these cases it could be argued that some new state funding provisions represented an assertion of increased local autonomy on the part of urban districts.

Teacher unions were an important part of the success of such efforts, and in the postwar period the political power of teacher unions continued to increase. Having used the power of their numbers and the strength of their association with organized labor to win relief for schools during the Great Depression, teacher unions often went on to win other legislative victories such as minimum teacher salaries, state tenure policies, and the elimination of married-teacher laws (Murphy 1990). These new provisions circumscribed the authority of local districts in important respects, but they did not arise as an effort by state officials to increase their authority over schools. Rather, they represented the increased political organization of educators themselves.

In some cases the political organization of educators developed in direct response to that of other constituencies. Chicago is the cardinal example of a district in which the political organization of teachers developed as a counterpoint to the power of other interest groups. Beginning shortly after the turn of the century, Chicago teachers organized against the failure of major local corporations to pay their taxes and thus to make good on promised increases in teacher salaries. This episode in turn became just one in a long line of conflicts between educators and businessmen in that city. As a result of this history of conflict, the coalitions of teachers and civic groups that helped win state aid for schools in other states during the Great Depression did not prove effective in Chicago. Instead, teacher and civic groups seeking relief for schools ran into direct opposition from a powerful and effective business elite. Drawing on the organizational power of the Commercial Club of Chicago and on the financial leverage of Chicago bankers, these leading businessmen formed an extra-legal commission on public expenditures that forced drastic cuts in school programs and teaching staff and salaries while derailing the efforts of civic groups, teachers, and school officials to win relief for schools at the state level (Wrigley 1982; Shipps 1995, 1997).

Although Chicago is an extreme example of organized opposition between teachers and business interests, other organized attacks on teachers' bargaining power did occur. Beginning in the late 1940s, when teachers in many locations violated no-strike policies to win their first significant pay raises in nearly twenty years, a number of individual teachers and teacher associations began finding themselves the subject of public investigations into un-American activities at both the state and federal levels. These attacks continued into the height of the McCarthy era in the 1950s and formed the backdrop of teachers' subsequent efforts to win academic freedom and collective bargaining agreements (Murphy 1990).

Viewed from the perspective of these cases, the important question to emerge in the post–World War II era was not state versus local authority, but which constituencies enjoyed the greatest access to influence in higher-level politics and policy making. From this perspective state authority was a tool to which multiple constituencies sought recourse in conflicts with each other. Just as there was no procedural way to ensure that the tool would always be in the "right" hands or used in the "right" way, so there was no reason to believe that if the tool were somehow taken away, the conflicts that gave rise to its use would disappear.

CONCLUDING DISCUSSION

In the 1960s and 1970s not only teacher unions but civil rights groups became important participants in efforts to secure state and federal legislation that would regulate the operation of local schools. Again school finance provided a means of enforcing these new state and federal policies. Local districts failing to comply with new state and federal mandates stood to lose their shares of state and federal funding. Many localities resisted these assertions of central authority over the operation of local schools. In virtually every state and locality the principle of "local control" became a rallying cry for maintaining school segregation. At times, however, not only white communities but black constituencies advocated community control over neighborhood schools.

The historical consequences of these more recent battles over state authority and local control are still being debated. In many respects, however, state and federal mandates seem to have failed to achieve their intended results. Despite various equal opportunity programs, for example, the most needy children continue to be concentrated in the same schools without a corresponding concentration of the resources necessary to meet those children's needs (Benson and O'Halloran 1987; Kozol 1991; Kantor 1998). Similarly, with respect to teacher salaries, the compromise necessary to effect state salary controls and guarantees has arguably kept the salaries of many teachers, especially those in the most challenging urban areas, artificially low (Theobald and Picus 1991; Theobald and Hanna 1991; Picus 1991).

In response to such conditions, many policy experts and school officials are currently advocating more decentralized approaches to school funding and regulation that would allow greater flexibility for individual schools to allocate staff resources and meet the needs of children (Odden and Clune 1998; Odden 1994). These proposals range from modest calls for deregulating teacher salaries, to thorough efforts to decouple school funding and regulation, and finally to full-scale charter school and/or voucher plans. At the same time, however, other reform proposals seem to point in the direction of greater central control of schooling, particularly with respect to such matters as setting academic standards, developing systems of school accountability, and ensuring that all schools are funded at a level of educational adequacy (Angus and Mirel 1999; Clune 1994). Without attempting to evaluate any of these proposals as they pertain to current contexts, it is worth considering what the foregoing historical discussion might suggest about these simultaneous impulses toward centralizing and decentralizing school authority.

For starters, it should be noted that these impulses generally focus on different aspects of school decisionmaking. While the tendency toward centralization focuses on academic standards, the tendency toward decentralization focuses on spending decisions. In this respect current reforms refer to at least two different precedents in the history of school funding and regulation. This first of these precedents is the standardization efforts of the Reconstruction era, which focused on raising curriculum and performance standards. The second precedent is the consolidation efforts of the Progressive, Great Depression, and World War II eras, when states capitalized on increased state funding levels to increase state leverage over program and spending decisions at the local level. Each of these precedents raises its own set of questions about future relationships between local control and state authority.

In the case of Reconstruction-era efforts at standardization, the past reminds us of the limits to assertions of state authority in matters of curriculum and teacher qualifications. These limits include not only traditions of local control, but also the dynamics of party politics and matters of supply and demand. More specifically, the historical case reminds us that there are political limits to how high standards can be set, or at least enforced, at the state level.[10] These limits are shaped in large part by existing

---

10 For a fuller discussion of how the limits to standardization have worked historically, see Beadie (1999b).

supply. To put the matter broadly, history suggests that if the criteria for awarding educational credentials are set higher than the vast majority of candidates already attain, two eventualities are likely. One possibility is that state standardization efforts will suffer a political backlash sufficient to lead to the withdrawal of state authority to administer such standards. A second possibility is that local resistance will force a compromise along the lines of the two-tiered credentialing systems common in the Reconstruction Era. Such systems effectively recognized differences between state and local standards (or between minimum standards and achievement incentives), by awarding credentials of differing significance.

With respect to the consolidation efforts of the Progressive, Great Depression, and World War II eras, the past reminds us of the importance of organized constituencies for securing and maintaining high levels of school funding from the state, and for legitimizing state authority over program and staffing issues. Although Cubberley and others advocated the use of state finance systems to achieve specific programmatic and organizational goals in the Progressive Era, it was not until constituencies organized to demand increased state funding of schools during the Great Depression that states acquired the financial leverage they used to effect such policies in the postwar era. The question raised by the historical case is what effect the decentralization of school spending decisions would have on the formation and maintenance of such constituencies at the state level. If spending decisions become more school- or district-based, will constituencies become more school-based as well?

To some extent this eventuality is exactly what reformers have in mind when they imagine breaking the hold of teacher unions on school policy or increasing the accountability of schools to local communities. It is worth asking in that case, however, which constituencies will have the organizational power necessary to influence state-level decisions about funding levels for schools. While it may make theoretical sense to decouple decisions about school spending from those about fundraising and apportionment, it is also true that in the United States public fundraising at any level requires strong and effective constituencies, particularly in times of government retrenchment. In the twentieth century these constituencies have included urban coalitions of citizen groups, business leaders, and city officials, but also statewide organizations of educators themselves. Arguably, however, much of the capacity for such cross-group coalition building in urban contexts was lost in the 1970s and 1980s. What are the possibilities for renewed coalition building in the first decade of the new century? How would decentralization affect that capacity? It is important that a focus on the procedural relationship between state and local authority not obscure political issues that in the long run have a lot to do with the degree of educational equity and adequacy it is possible to achieve.

REFERENCES

Anderson, J. (1988). *The education of Blacks in the south*. Chapel Hill: University of North Carolina Press.

Angus, D., and Mirel, J. (1999). *The failed promise of the American high school, 1890–1995*. New York: Teachers College, Columbia University.

Beadie, N. (1999a). Female students and denominational affiliation: Sources of success among nineteenth-century academies. *American Journal of Education, 107*(2), 75–115.

Beadie, N. (1999b). From student markets to credential markets: The creation of the regents examination system in New York, 1864–1890. *History of Education Quarterly, 39*(1), 1–30.

Beadie, N. (1999c). Market-based policies of school funding: Lessons from the history of the New York academy system. *Educational Policy, 13*(2), 296–317.

Benson, C. S., and Halloran, K. (1987). The economic history of school finance in the United States. *Journal of Education Finance, 12*(4), 495–515.

Berne, R. (1988). Equity issues in school finance. *Journal of Education Finance, 14*(2), 159–80.

Bond, H. M. (1934). *The education of the Negro in the American social order*. New York: Prentice Hall.

Clune, W. H. (1994). The shift from equity to adequacy in school finance. *Educational Policy, 8*(4): 376–94.

Cubberley, E. P. (1906). *School funds and their apportionment*. New York: Teachers College, Columbia University.

Dewey, J. (1915). State or city control of schools? *New Republic, 2*(20), 178–180.

Green, A. (1990). *Education and state formation: The rise of education systems in England, France and the USA*. New York: St. Martin's Press.

Green, T. F. (1980). *Predicting the behavior of the educational system*. Syracuse: Syracuse University Press.

Kaestle, C. F. (1983). *Pillars of the republic: Common schools and American society, 1780–1860*. New York: Hill and Wang.

Kaestle, C. F. (1985). The history of literacy and the history of readers. In E. D. Gordon (Ed.) *Review of Research in Education 12* (pp. 11–15). Washington, DC: American Educational Research Association.

Kantor, H. (1998). Dismantling the educational state?: Observations on Title I of ESEA and federal education policy, 1965–1900. Paper presented at the annual meeting of the History of Education Society, Chicago.

Katz, M. (1968). *The irony of early school reform: Educational innovation in mid-nineteenth century Massachusetts*. Cambridge, MA: Harvard University Press.

Kozol, J. (1991). *Savage inequalities*. New York: Harper Collins.

Labaree, D. (1997). Public goods, private goods: The American struggle over educational goals. *American Educational Research Journal, 34*(1), 39–81.

Lee, G. C. (1949). *The struggle for federal aid: A history of the attempts to obtain federal aid for the common schools, 1870–1890*. New York: Teachers College, Columbia University.

Lewis, S. (1838). First annual report of the superintendent of common schools 1838. Reprinted in part in S. Cohen (Ed.) (1974), *Education in the United States: A documentary history* (pp. 1027–1029). New York: Random House.

Link, W. A. (1986). *A hard country and a lonely place: Schooling society and reform in rural Virginia*. Chapel Hill: University of North Carolina Press.

McAfee, W. M. (1998). *Religion, race and reconstruction: The public school in the politics of the 1870s.* Albany: State University of New York.

Mann, H. (1846). Tenth annual report of the secretary of the board. Reprinted in part in S. Cohen (Ed.) (1974), *Education in the United States: A documentary history* (pp. 1095–1099). New York: Random House.

Mattingly, P. H. (1975). *The classless profession: American schoolmen in the nineteenth century.* New York: New York University Press.

Ment, D. (1975). *Racial segregation in the schools of New England and New York.* Ph.D. dissertation, Columbia University.

Miller, G. F. (1922). *The academy system of the State of New York.* Albany, J. Lyon.

Mirel, J. E. (1990). Progressive school reform in comparative perspective. In D. Plank and R. Ginsberg (Eds.), *Southern cities, southern schools: Public education in the urban south* (pp. 151–174). Westport, CT: Greenwood Press.

Mirel, J. E. (1993). *The rise and fall of an urban school system: Detroit, 1907–81.* Ann Arbor, MI: The University of Michigan Press.

Moreo, D. W. (1996). *Schools in the Great Depression.* New York: Garland.

Mucalus, J. A. (1945). *The use of banking enterprises in the financing of public education, 1796–1866.* Philadelphia, University of Pennsylvania.

Murphy, M. (1990). *Blackboard unions: The AFT and the NEA, 1900–1980.* Ithaca, NY: Cornell University Press.

New York State (1864). An act to revise and consolidate the general acts relating to public instruction. *Laws of New York.* Albany: Van Bethuysen, 1211–1290.

Odden, A. (1994). Decentralized management and school finance. *Theory into Practice, 33*(2), 104–111.

Odden, A., and Clune, W. H. (1998). School finance systems: Aging structures in need of renovation. *Educational Evaluation and Policy Analysis, 20*(3), pp. 157–177.

Olson, S. (1996). *The legalization of Chinese segregation in the San Francisco Public Schools, 1850–1902.* M. A. thesis, University of Washington.

Peterson, P. E. (1985). *The politics of school reform, 1870–1940.* Chicago: University of Chicago.

Picus, L. O. (1991). Cadillacs or Chevrolets?: The evolution of state control over school finance in California. *Journal of Education Finance, 17*(1), 33–59.

Pugh, T. (1994). *Rural school consolidation in New York State, 1795–1993: A struggle for control.* Ph.D. dissertation, Syracuse University.

Ravitch, D. (1974). *The great school wars: New York City, 1805–1973: A history of the public schools as battlefield of social change.* New York: Basic Books.

Reed, H. S. (1942). *The period of the academy in Connecticut, 1780–1850.* Unpublished Ph.D. dissertation, Yale University.

Reese, W. J. (1995). *The origins of the American high school.* New Haven: Yale University Press.

Reynolds, M. A. (1998). The challenge of racial equality. In W. B. Reese (Ed.) *Hoosier schools: Past and present* (pp. 173–193). Bloomington, IN: Indiana University Press.

Shipps, D. (1995). *Big business and school reform: The case of Chicago, 1988.* Unpublished Ph.D. dissertation, Stanford University.

Shipps, D. (1997). The invisible hand: Big business and Chicago school reform. *Teachers College Record, 90*(1), 73–116.

Sklar, K. (1993). The schooling of girls and changing community values in Massachusetts towns, 1750–1820. *History of Education Quarterly, 33*(4), 511–542.

Stahly, T. (1998). Curricular reform in an industrial age. In W. B. Reese (Ed.) *Hoosier schools: Past and present* (pp. 53–77). Bloomington, IN: Indiana University Press.

Strike, K. (1988). The ethics of resource allocation in education: Questions of democracy and justice. *Microlevel school finance: Issues and implications for policy* (pp. 143–180). Cambridge, MA: Ballinger Publishing Company.

Swift, F. H. (1911). *A history of public permanent common school funds in the United States, 1795–1905*. New York: Henry Holt and Co.

Swift, F. H. (1931). *Federal and state policies in public school finance in the United States*. New York: Ginn and Company.

Theobald, N. D., and Hanna, F. (1991). Ample provisions for whom?: The evolution of state control over school finance in Washington. *Journal of Education Finance, 17*(1), 7–32.

Theobald, N. D., and Picus, L. O. (1991). Living with equal amounts of less: Experiences of states with primarily state-funded school systems. *Journal of Education Finance, 17*(1), 1–6.

Tyack, D. (1974). *The one best system: A history of American urban education*. Cambridge: Harvard University Press.

Tyack, D., and Hansot, E. (1982). *Managers of virtue: Public school leadership in America, 1820–1980*. New York: Basic Books.

Tyack, D., James, T., and Benavot, A. (1987). *Law and the shaping of public education, 1785–1954*. Madison, WI: The University of Wisconsin Press.

Tyack, D., Lowe, R., and Hansot, E. (1982). *Public schools in hard times: The Great Depression and recent years*. Cambridge, MA: Harvard University Press.

Urban, W., and Waggoner, J. (1996). *American education: A history*. New York: McGraw Hill.

Vinovskis, M. (1985). *The origins of public high schools: A reexamination of the Beverly High School controversy*. Madison, WI: The University of Wisconsin Press.

Walker, V. S. (1996). *Their highest potential: An African American school community in the segregated south*. Chapel Hill: University of North Carolina.

Walker, V. S. (1998). The professional Black educator in legally segregated schools in the South. Unpublished paper presented at the annual meeting of the History of Education Society, Chicago, Illinois.

Walter, S. (1998). "Awakening the public mind": The dissemination of the common school idea in Indiana. In W. B. Reese

(Ed.) *Hoosier schools: Past and present* (pp. 1–28). Bloomington, IN: Indiana University Press.

Waltershausen, C. B. (1994). *A study of equity in the Illinois general state aid formula, 1818 to 1993.* Unpublished Ph.D. dissertation, University of Illinois at Urbana-Champaign.

Warren, D. (1974). *To enforce education: A history of the founding years of the U.S. Office of Education.* Detroit: Wayne State University Press.

Wrigley, J. (1982). *Class politics and public schools: Chicago, 1900–1950.* New Brunswick, NJ: Rutgers University Press.

4

RECENT LITIGATION AND ITS IMPACT ON THE STATE-LOCAL POWER BALANCE: LIBERTY AND EQUITY IN GOVERNANCE, LITIGATION, AND THE SCHOOL FINANCE POLICY DEBATE

John Dayton
The University of Georgia

In the introduction to this year's American Education Finance Association Yearbook, Theobald and Bardzell (2000) recognize the important roles of liberty, equity, and efficiency in the school finance policy debate. Though recognizing the significance of efficiency concerns for public policy makers, this chapter focuses on the roles of liberty and equity in governance, litigation, and the school finance policy debate. A commitment to the often competing values of liberty and equity is deeply rooted in American political and legal history, from the U.S. Declaration of Independence (1776) to the most recent public school funding equity cases. American public policy concerning public school funding cannot be fully comprehended without an understanding of the essential American principles of liberty and equity.

This chapter reviews the integral roles of liberty and equity in the American system of governance. A review of the significance of liberty in American constitutional history, political philosophy, law, and in limiting and balancing powers among the federal, state, and local governments is provided. And to illustrate the delicate balance between liberty and equity concerns in American public policy debate, a brief review of funding equity litigation since *Serrano v. Priest* (1971) is also provided. This chapter concludes with a discussion of significant recent funding litigation, the future of funding litigation, and the roles of liberty and equity in this process.

LIBERTY, GOVERNANCE, AND THE DELICATE BALANCE OF POWER

Over two centuries after cries for liberty and objections to taxation resulted in the birth of a new American nation, U.S. citizens' passions for liberty continue to play a central role in public policy debates. From taxpayer revolts to demands for local control, comprehending the deep historical roots of liberty in American culture is essential to understanding the perennial role that liberty plays in debates concerning governmental policy in the United States. Liberty remains the centerpiece of American political thought.

LIBERTY AND CONSTITUTIONAL GOVERNANCE

Since the American Revolution, Americans have recognized that the preservation of liberty requires eternal vigilance, and a constitutional system of governance capable of maintaining the delicate balance of power and adapting to changing circumstances. The U.S. Constitution (1787) is the foundation for this system of governance, incorporating broad democratic principles intended to serve as "a distant beacon: clear enough to provide manifest direction and guidance, but distant enough to allow for debate regarding the best route to our common goal" (Dayton and Glickman 1994, p. 68). As Daniel Webster stated: "We may be tossed upon an ocean where we can see no land— nor, perhaps, the sun or stars. But there is a chart and a compass for us to study, to consult, and to obey. The chart is the Constitution" (Public Papers 1981, p. 802).

As the U.S. Supreme Court has recognized, the Constitution is a living document embodying broad principles that provide guidance in the struggles with the pressing issues of the day, while vigilantly protecting the people's liberties (*Missouri* 1920, p. 443). These principles require interpretation of their meaning in light of changing circumstances. Clearly, the Constitution's founders did not intend that their words would be interpreted in a narrow and final way. Instead, American constitutional democracy is a dynamic process entailing an eternal dialogue, forever debating and balancing competing ideals and interests, while maintaining fidelity to the Constitution's original fundamental principles. It is in this fragile balance of competing interests, dialogue and debate, that liberty thrives.

To promote and protect liberty, Jefferson drafted a Declaration of Independence (1776) that advanced a very different theory of governance authority than its historical predecessors. Jefferson rejected the "divine rights of kings" theory (LaMorte 1999, p. 7). For example, the Magna Carta (1215) had ordained King John "by the grace of God king of England" asserting a system of governance power that flowed from God to the king, God's appointed governor, and through a descending hierarchy of nobles and other royal appointees in governance over the people. In contrast, Jefferson's proclamation in the Declaration of Independence (1776) inverted the earthly part of this governance equation by declaring:

> We hold these truths to be self-evident: that all men
> are created equal; that they are endowed, by their

Creator, with certain unalienable rights; that among these rights are life, liberty, and the pursuit of happiness. That to secure these rights, governments are instituted among men, deriving their just powers from the consent of the governed; that whenever any form of government becomes destructive of these ends, it is the right of the people to alter or abolish it, and to institute new government, laying its foundation on such principles, and organizing its powers in such form, as to them shall seem most likely to effect their safety and happiness.

The Declaration of Independence recognized a system of governance in which government authority flows from the Creator to individuals equally endowed by the Creator with liberty and fundamental equality, and all legitimate government power is derived from the consent of the people. Government is not recognized as a divinely appointed ruler over the people, but as a servant to the people, necessary to protect the rights of life, liberty, and property. All individuals are endowed by the Creator with certain unalienable rights. But without a common government to protect the rights of life, liberty, and property, individuals' rights would be lost in anarchy.

Accordingly, government's legitimate role is to impartially protect the rights of all individuals, so that civil society, commerce, agriculture, and other beneficial activities may flourish, when the rights and liberties of all persons are secured. Under the diligent watch of the people, government is lent only those powers necessary to achieve these ends, and when government fails in its social compact with the people the Declaration of Independence proclaims that "thereby the legislative powers, incapable of annihilation, have returned to the people at large for their exercise."

LIBERTY AND A SYSTEM OF CHECKS AND BALANCES

Within the U.S. Constitution, the architects of American democracy established systems of governance in which the powers of governance were separated and distributed to limit excesses and protect liberty. But under the U.S. Constitution, not only are powers divided among the federal and the state governments, but also the ultimate scope of government is limited. The documents that founded the nation reflect the Lockean theory of equality, natural rights, social contract, and limited governmental power (Locke 1690). According to this theory, when autonomous individuals left the state of nature and agreed to submit to collective governance for their common protection, individuals retained certain basic rights and it was the duty of a just government acting under the consent of the governed to protect those rights. While governments may legitimately regulate those elements that are properly within the sphere of public control, all persons retained certain fundamental rights that remain within the private sphere and are not proper subjects for public control absent a compelling governmental interest.

Further, even compelling governmental actions that impinge on fundamental rights must be narrowly tailored to achieving the compelling interest. Accordingly, government officials should be judicious in rule making, being careful not to over-regulate or exceed their authority. Unnecessary and repugnant laws infringe on liberty and diminish respect for government. In government as in physics, for every force there is a counter force in equal and opposite proportion. Extreme governmental actions are likely to produce extreme forces in opposition.

To avoid the abuse of power, the U.S. Constitution created a federal government of limited powers, all other powers being reserved to the states or to the people under the Tenth Amendment. Further, federal powers were divided between three coequal branches of government: the legislative branch, the administrative branch, and the judicial branch. State constitutions also create these three coequal branches at the state level. This diffusion of power, and the system of checks and balances among the multiple branches of the federal and state governments, deters an accumulation of power, which, as Lord Acton (1877) recognized, would inevitably lead to abuse. Lord Acton is most frequently quoted as stating: "Power tends to corrupt, and absolute power corrupts absolutely" (Hyman 1989, p. 9), indicating the necessity to limit the accumulation of governmental power. Further, state governments generally delegate many governance powers to local government agents for the daily administration of government in recognition that local government officials are most likely to understand unique local concerns and exercise greater sensitivity to the concerns of people they have regular contact with. It is within these majestic ideals of liberty and the recognition of the necessity for limited government to protect those liberties that U.S. public school policy is established.

LIBERTY AND THE GOVERNANCE OF PUBLIC SCHOOLS

Concerning the governance of public education, as the U.S. Constitution's Tenth Amendment (1791) states: "Those powers not delegated to the United States by the Constitution, nor prohibited by it to the States, are reserved to the States respectively, or to the people." Accordingly, the federal government may only exercise those powers that are granted to the federal government by the Constitution. The U.S. Constitution contains no provisions concerning education. Therefore, the domain of education is reserved to the states or to the people.

Although the federal government has entered the realm of public education, primarily through civil rights legislation, the offering of conditional federal funds, and remedial desegregation efforts, all 50 states recognize in their constitutions that public education is the responsibility of the state government. But the states have historically allowed broad local control of education, not only delegating significant governance powers, but also delegating local responsibilities for the funding of public education. Although state constitutions create a state-level duty to support public education, allowing local funding of public schools has resulted in significant funding disparities among many states' public schools. Persons disadvantaged by these funding disparities have challenged state funding systems based on local wealth, resulting in significant litigation. To limit unconstitutional inequities among their state's schools, many courts have attempted to balance efforts to foster local liberty in the governance of local public schools with concerns for equity in public school funding.

EQUITY AND SCHOOL FUNDING
LITIGATION SINCE *SERRANO V. PRIEST*

Although state constitutions recognize state-level duties to provide for public education, liberty may be promoted through local control. Through local control, citizens may play a more active role in governing local schools and enjoy greater liberty in establishing educational policy for their children and communities, including decisions concerning taxation and funding. But systems of public school funding based on local wealth have produced inequities and inadequacies in educational resources affecting the quality of children's lives and the economic and social futures of economically disadvantaged communities. Property-tax-based systems of funding are in many instances harmful to the most vulnerable and disadvantaged children. Funding policies that rely on local property wealth to support education make many already disadvantaged children the recipients of an inadequately funded education that compounds their other disadvantages.

EQUITY LITIGATION

Advocates for these children have sought redress of their disadvantaged educational circumstances. Failing to achieve reform through the legislative process, public school funding reformers turned to federal and state constitutions and the assistance of courts to obtain relief. Efforts to obtain relief under the federal Constitution were unsuccessful. In *San Antonio v. Rodriguez* (1973), the U.S. Supreme Court upheld the Texas system of public school funding despite substantial funding disparities. Nonetheless, school funding reform advocates have achieved some success in litigation based on state constitutional provisions.

Although school funding litigation has a long history, most scholars recognize the Supreme Court of California's decision in *Serrano v. Priest* (1971) as the beginning of the modern era in school funding litigation (LaMorte 1999, p. 352; Sparkman 1990, p. 197). The court's decision in *Serrano v. Priest* resulted in a victory for funding equity plaintiffs, and established a model for similar litigation in other states. The *Serrano* case was the first successful challenge to a state aid system of public school finance. In addition, *Serrano* was the first case to establish a judicially manageable standard for courts in addressing inequities in school funding. This standard has been described as the *Serrano* principle. The *Serrano* principle commands that the quality of a child's education cannot be a function of the wealth of the local community, but instead must be a function of the wealth of the state as a whole.

In *Serrano* the court held that education was a fundamental right, requiring strict scrutiny in reviewing governmental actions that impinged on this fundamental right. To survive strict judicial scrutiny, a government action must be premised on a compelling governmental interest, and narrowly tailored to achieving that interest, a very rigorous judicial standard that challenged government actions rarely survive. The court applied strict scrutiny to the California system of public school funding, determining that California's system, which caused substantial disparities in per pupil revenue among school districts, discriminated against students in poorer districts and violated the equal protection clause of the Fourteenth Amendment. The court rejected the defendant's argument that promoting local control constituted a compelling state interest, noting that the state's system rather than being necessary to promote local fiscal choice, "actually deprives the less wealthy districts of that option" (*Serrano* 1971, p. 1260).

The plaintiffs in *Serrano* were Los Angeles County children and their parents. They represented all public school children in the state of California and the parents of those children who pay real property taxes, except those in the most privileged district. *Serrano* framed the issues that would become prominent in subsequent school funding cases based on equal protection claims: (1) whether education is a fundamental right; (2) whether the court would apply strict scrutiny in reviewing the challenged funding system; and (3) whether the state's goal of promoting local control constituted a sufficient state interest to justify funding disparities under the court's standard of review.

The *Serrano* court noted the wide fiscal disparities created by the California system of public school funding. Assessed valuation per average daily attendance "ranged from a low of $103 to a peak of $952,156—a ratio of nearly 1 to 10,000" (p. 1246). The court further found that within Los Angeles County, per pupil expenditures ranged from $577.49 to $1,231.72 (p. 1248). The court also addressed the issue of taxpayer equity, noting "as a practical matter districts with small tax bases simply cannot levy taxes at a rate sufficient to produce the revenue that more affluent districts reap with minimal tax efforts" (p. 1250). In the words of the court, "affluent districts can have their cake and eat it too: they can provide a high quality education for their children while paying lower taxes. Poor districts, by contrast, have no cake at all" (p. 1251).

The court bolstered its ruling that education was a fundamental right by citing *Brown v. Board of Education* (1954) and the U.S. Supreme Court's recognition that "education is perhaps the most important function of state and local governments" (p. 493). The court also weighed the importance of education in comparison with the right to vote and the rights of defendants in criminal cases, two fundamental interests which the U.S. Supreme Court had already protected against discrimination based upon wealth. The California Supreme Court concluded: "We are convinced that the distinctive and priceless function of education in our society warrants, indeed compels, our treating it as a fundamental interest" (p. 1258).

In *Serrano*, the defendants argued that if the court were to find that wealth discrimination in public education violated the equal protection clause, the court must then be deemed to "direct the same command to all governmental entities in respect to all tax-supported public services" and that "such a principle would spell the destruction of local government" (p. 1262). The court rejected the defendant's argument, stating that "although we intimate no views on other governmental services, we are satisfied that, as we have explained, its uniqueness among public activities clearly demonstrates that education must respond to the command of the equal protection clause" (p. 1262). The court then remanded the case to the trial court with directions to proceed consistent with the court's opinion.

Since *Serrano*, 35 states' highest courts have ruled on the merits of constitutional challenges to their states' funding systems, with 18 states' highest courts upholding states' systems of public school funding and 17 states' highest courts declaring school funding systems unconstitutional (see Table 4.1). Those disadvantaged by public school funding systems continue to turn to state courts seeking a judicial declaration that the existing funding system is unconstitutional, and requesting a judicial mandate for funding equity reform. Funding reform advocates hope a favorable judicial decision will serve as a catalyst for legislative reform.

TABLE 4.1. STATE SUPREME COURT
OPINIONS SINCE *SERRANO V. PRIEST*

Declaring Funding Systems Unconstitutional

Arizona: *Roosevelt v. Bishop* (1994)

Arkansas: *Dupree v. Alma School District* (1983)

California: *Serrano v. Priest* (1971)

Connecticut: *Horton v. Meskill* (1977)

Kentucky: *Rose v. Council for Better Education* (1989)

Massachusetts: *McDuffy v. Secretary* (1993)

Montana: *Helena v. State* (1989)

North Dakota: *Bismarck Public School District v. State* (1994)[1]

New Hampshire: *Claremont School District v. Governor* (1997)

New Jersey: *Abbott v. Burke* (1990)

Ohio: *DeRolph v. State* (1997)

Tennessee: *Tennessee Small School Systems v. McWherter* (1993)

Texas: *Edgewood v. Kirby* (1989)

Vermont: *Brigham v. State* (1997)

Washington: *Seattle School District v. State* (1978)

West Virginia: *Pauley v. Kelly* (1979)

Wyoming: *Campbell County School District v. State* (1995)

Upholding Funding Systems Against
Constitutional Challenges

---

1 Affirming a district court judgment that "the overall impact of the entire statutory method for distributing funding for education in North Dakota is unconstitutional" but lacking the super-majority required by the North Dakota Constitution to declare statutes unconstitutional.

Alaska: *Matanuska-Susitna v. State* (1997)
Colorado: *Lujan v. Colorado State Board of Education* (1982)
Georgia: *McDaniel v. Thomas* (1981)
Idaho: *Idaho Schools v. Evans* (1993)
Illinois: *Committee v. Edgar* (1996)
Kansas: *Unified School District v. State* (1994)
Maine: *School Administrative District v. Commissioner* (1995)
Maryland: *Hornbeck v. Somerset* (1983)
Michigan: *Milliken v. Green* (1973)
Minnesota: *Skeen v. State* (1993)
New York: *Board of Education v. Nyquist* (1982)
Oklahoma: *Fair School Finance Council v. State* (1987)
Oregon: *Coalition v. State* (1991)
Pennsylvania: *Danson v. Casey* (1979)
Rhode Island: *City of Pawtucket v. Sundlun* (1995)
South Carolina: *Richland County v. Campbell* (1988)
Virginia: *Scott v. Commonwealth* (1994)
Wisconsin: *Kukor v. Grover* (1989)

But after many years of judicial intervention, substantial funding inequities continue. Even where legislative reforms have been enacted there has often been a tendency towards deterioration of equity gains (Camp and Thompson 1988, pp. 223–224). Through the disproportionate influence often afforded to those with economic and political power, wealthy districts may continue to dominate the legislative process, sometimes altering equity reform legislation to the degree that inequities may actually increase (Bevelock 1991, p. 489).

ALTRUISM VERSUS THE POLITICS OF SELF-INTERESTS

Advocates of funding reform have worked diligently to achieve greater funding equity. Despite their efforts, funding inequities and resulting inadequacies persist, making many children's educational opportunities largely a function of geographic accident and local economics. Significant human potential is wasted by failing to provide adequate educational opportunities for all children. Despite altruistic ideals in state constitutional provisions governing public education, state legislators continue to delegate much of their constitutional responsibility for funding public education to local authorities, resulting in considerable disparities in local abilities to fund education.

Historically, American schools were a local responsibility supported by local funds (*McDuffy* 1993, p. 529). But in recognition of the significance of public education, lawmakers in the early 1800s adopted state constitutional provisions addressing public education. Today, all 50 states have constitutional provisions describing the state's duty to support public education (Hubsch 1985, p. 134). Nonetheless, the perception that public school funding is a local obligation persists, as does substantial reliance on local property taxes for funding. Ideals of local control and liberty concerning local schools are so ingrained in American culture that many citizens would be surprised to learn that their state's constitution assigned ultimate responsibility for supporting public education to the state government and not the local district. Further, many citizens are unaware that all revenues collected for support of public education are in fact state funds rather than local funds (Valente 1985, p. 290).

It is in the conceptual gap between constitutional mandates and citizens' perceptions that the problem of school funding inequities unfolds. State constitutions establish a state-level duty to support public education, but citizens continue to insist on local liberty and assert ownership over local funds generated to support education. Within the ideological conflict between equity and liberty in funding is a tension between altruism and self-interest: the altruistic wish for educational opportunity for all children and an enhancement of the general welfare of the society versus the natural tendency to seek the best for one's own children and advance self-interests. Granting public education constitutional status was an altruistic gesture to set all children's educational interests above the political fray of self-interests. But egalitarian ideals are often frustrated by the realities of self-interests and limited resources. Proclamations that may have been attractive as constitutional ideals may become politically problematic when they result in additional taxation or the transfer of economic resources from one community to another.

Unconstitutional disparities in expenditures result from this conflict between altruistic ideals and the harsh political realities of self-interests. Although the state's constitution proclaims that the state owes a duty of educational support to all of the state's public school students, in order to appease local political concerns, ranging from lofty ideals of local liberty to more narrow self-interests, the state operates a system of public school funding that results in substantial disparities in educational support and tax burdens. Even though all children are under their state's constitution equally children of that state entitled to a state-supported free public education, some of the state's children are favored or disfavored based on geography and local wealth (Alexander 1991, p. 341).

Substantial variations in per pupil funding exist among school districts within many states. For example, in *Edgewood v. Kirby* (1989, p. 392), the Supreme Court of Texas recognized a per pupil spending disparity ratio of approximately 9 to 1. The wealthiest school district in Texas spent $19,333 per pupil, while the poorest district had only $2,112 per pupil for education. In *Helena v. State* (1989, p. 686), the Supreme Court of Montana recognized an 8-to-1 disparity in per pupil expenditures. Other states' systems of public school funding have also resulted in substantial disparities (Dayton 1992).

DOES MONEY MATTER?

In defending these inequities in funding, many states have asserted that it is not the amount of money expended that determines the level of educational opportunity offered by a school district, but instead, how that money is spent. Certainly spending more money on education does not by itself guarantee that students will receive a better education. Mismanagement and inefficiency could result in the waste of additional financial resources. But just as certainly, schools that cannot afford science labs and foreign language teachers are unlikely to produce students proficient in science and foreign language (Wise and Gendler 1989, p. 17). Common sense suggests that although money does not guarantee a better quality education, those with money can afford useful educational resources that those without money cannot. As the Supreme Court of New Jersey noted in *Abbott v. Burke* (1990, p. 406): "We therefore adhere to the conventional wisdom that money is one of the many factors that counts." Nonetheless, there has been extensive academic debate over this issue. And with expert witnesses testifying on both sides of this issue, it continues to be hotly debated in both academic and legal circles (Underwood 1989, pp. 414–15).

However, since *Serrano*, most courts have not shared the skepticism of some scholars regarding whether expenditures affect educational opportunity. The majority of courts instead reflect the common wisdom that although money alone does not guarantee educational opportunity, it is a significant factor (Dayton 1993). The existence of a positive correlation between expenditures and educational opportunity has been recognized by the highest courts in Arkansas, California, Connecticut, Georgia, Kentucky, Maryland, Massachusetts, Montana, New Jersey, New York, North Dakota, Tennessee, Texas, West Virginia, and Wyoming (Dayton 1998). No court has ruled that money makes no difference to educational opportunity. But the highest courts in Colorado, Idaho, Michigan, and Pennsylvania have found that the plaintiffs did not sufficiently carry their burden of proving this correlation (Dayton 1998).

For property-poor districts, inadequate educational resources and relatively high property taxes may create a cycle of poverty from which there is little hope of escape without greater equity in school funding and taxation (Dayton 1995). Because the local district must fund its schools by taxing a small tax base, the community will have relatively high property tax rates but a low financial yield leading to inadequate educational resources, inadequate education, and ultimately an unskilled local labor force. High property tax rates and an unskilled local labor force are then an additional disincentive for the economic development that is needed to improve the local tax base. Without state educational support and taxpayer equity it is unlikely that disadvantaged communities will be able to attract the quality business and residential investors that are needed to improve the community's tax base and public schools (Dayton 1995).

Continuing inequities in school funding are not merely an artifact of chance. It is well known among educational policy makers that reliance on local property wealth for funding public schools creates fiscal inequities (Ward 1992, p. 249). These disparities continue despite decades of pressure to equalize educational funding. There may be both ideological and practical explanations for the continuation of funding inequities. Ideologically, notions of liberty and equity are in conflict. Practically, these inequities continue in many states because those with economic and political power are advantaged by their continuation.

DISCUSSION

Conflicting ideals of liberty and equity are at the core of many disputes resulting in public school funding litigation. But while the battles may sometimes become unnecessarily bitter, the debate is essential in a democratic society. The goal in these debates must always be a workable and just balance of legitimate competing interests, not the predominance of one fundamental value over another. If either ideals of liberty or equity were pursued to their extremes, significant harm would result to individuals and the community. While the protection of liberty is essential in a democracy, it is not desirable to allow the powerful to overwhelm the weak in their pursuit of self-interests. And while equity is essential to justice, it is not desirable to reduce all individuals to the lowest common level. A just balance is essential, in which all persons are granted equity in educational opportunities, but retain the liberty to excel and make independent choices concerning their lives.

Americans would cease to be Americans without their love of liberty and their insistence that the common government respect their liberties. American liberty is the beacon that continues to draw new immigrants to American shores. In sharp contrast to many nations, the American creed of liberty holds that all persons are created equal, and that all persons have certain unalienable rights, including life, liberty, and the pursuit of happiness. To protect liberties from those that would intrude on the life, liberty, or property of individuals, Americans recognize that a just, common government is necessary to secure these rights.

To achieve this end, individual citizens lend some of their powers to a common government, so that this common government may act on their behalf in protecting their rights. Through a pooling of resources, a common government can then fund police and fire protection, roads, water projects, schools, and so forth, that individuals could not fund by themselves, thereby promoting the common good while protecting the rights and liberties of all individuals.

But because all individuals lend some of their resources to the common government, the common government becomes an immense source of power, tempting to persons that might wish to exercise this power over others. To protect against this danger, government must be stringently limited in scope to only those powers necessary to the accomplishment of legitimate governmental purposes, and vigilantly scrutinized to assure that government officials are not intruding on private liberties or otherwise abusing governmental power. The means to achieve this include the separation of powers, constitutional limitations on the legitimate scope of governmental interests and powers, limitations on taxation, open meetings, open records, public accountability, and a strong preference for local control.

But Americans also have a firm commitment to equity. The Declaration of Independence declares that "all men are created equal" and the Fourteenth Amendment to the U.S. Constitution guarantees "the equal protection of the laws." State constitutions have similar provisions guaranteeing the equal protection of the laws (Dayton 1992). The American commitment to equity is also reflected in civil rights legislation, judicial efforts including *Brown v. Board of Education* (1954), and funding equity cases like *Serrano v. Priest* (1971) and its progeny.

Certainly, the American pursuit of equity has been a difficult, slow, and painful journey, with many tragic errors. For example, the U.S. Supreme Court held in *Scott v. Sandford* (1857) that African-Americans as slaves were not citizens of any state or of the United States and could therefore be denied legal rights. Also, during World War II Japanese-Americans were imprisoned because of their ancestry (*Korematsu* 1944). And although many people fled to America to escape religious persecution, they subsequently persecuted other religious minorities in America. Individuals in America, as in the rest of the world, have been denied their fundamental rights because of irrational religious, race, gender, age, disability, and other prejudices.

But these failures in government actions are not due to the failures of democratic ideals. Instead, they are failures by government officials to fully comprehend, respect, and comply with these democratic ideals. Further, they are failures by the people at large, who failed either to fully comprehend these ideals, to live up to these ideals, or to require their elected representatives to respect these ideals. Nonetheless, although progress has been slow and imperfect, few would doubt that Americans have made significant progress in promoting equity based on religion, race, gender, age, and disability, in contrast to many other nations.

Ideals of liberty and equity are deeply rooted in American political thought, and are reflected in the ongoing debate concerning public school funding. Ideals of liberty are reflected in objections to taxation and in calls for local control, school choice, vouchers, home schooling, and so forth. Ideals of equity are reflected in desegregation and civil rights efforts, educational remediation programs, etc. Ideals of both liberty and equity are also reflected in the continued battle for greater equity in public school funding. Nearly three decades after *Serrano v. Priest* (1971), school funding litigation continues unabated.

In most of the post-*Serrano* litigation, the ideals of liberty and equity seemed to be in direct conflict. Following the U.S. Supreme Court's decision in *San Antonio v. Rodriguez* (1973), allowing states to justify disparate treatment in order to foster local control, many state courts upholding state systems of funding justified their unequal funding systems by citing the state's interest in advancing local control, thereby promoting local liberty in educational matters. In contrast, courts declaring state systems of funding unconstitutional focused on the state's failure to provide funding equity, as required by the state constitution's education or equal protection provisions. Although no court ordered exact expenditures in dollars per pupil, there was a clear focus on per pupil expenditures in litigation and in many judicial decisions.

But more recent judicial opinions appear to have found a possible middle ground between the competing ideals of liberty (defined as local control) and equity (defined as fiscal neutrality). Many of the more recent opinions focus on the provision of an adequate education, assuring equity in the provision of essential educational resources, regardless of per pupil expenditures, while still permitting local liberty to exceed the parameters of mere adequacy (*Abbeville* (1999); *R.E.F.I.T.* (1995); *Opinion of the Justices* (1993); *Tennessee* (1993); *Fair School* (1987)).

Courts in some more recent opinions have expressly outlined the parameters of what constitutes an adequate education under their state's constitution (*Abbeville* (1999); *R.E.F.I.T.* (1995); *Opinion of the Justices* (1993); *Tennessee* (1993); *Fair School* (1987)). By defining minimal constitutional requirements for an adequate education, courts are establishing substantive standards that could assure that every student receives the educational resources required by the state constitution, but still allow for local supplements that may exceed the parameters of minimal constitutional adequacy.

A similar approach has been endorsed by the Supreme Court of New Jersey in *Abbott v. Burke* (1998), and may finally end the nation's longest-running school funding equity dispute. Funding equity litigation began in New Jersey in 1970 when students from poorer urban schools sued to enforce the New Jersey Constitution's education guarantee. The Supreme Court of New Jersey declared the state's system of public school funding unconstitutional in *Robinson v. Cahill* (1973). Litigation has continued unabated through the court's decision in *Abbott v. Burke* (1998), in which the court predicted that "this decision should be the last major judicial involvement in the long and tortuous history of the State's extraordinary effort to bring a thorough and efficient education to the children in its poorest school districts" (p. 455).

In *Abbott v. Burke* (1997) the court approved a state plan establishing substantive educational standards as constitutionally adequate. The court stated: "With the promulgation and adoption of substantive standards that define a thorough and efficient education, New Jersey joins a trend in favor of a standards-based approach to the improvement of public education" (p. 427). The court noted: "At its core, a constitutionally adequate education has been defined as an education that will prepare public school children for a meaningful role in society, one that will enable them to compete effectively in the economy and to contribute and to participate as citizens and members of their communities" (p. 428).

The Supreme Court of South Carolina also recently endorsed statewide substantive standards for public education. In *Abbeville v. State* (1999) the court held that "the South Carolina Constitution's education clause requires the General Assembly to provide the opportunity for each child to receive a minimally adequate education" (p. *3). The court noted similar decisions by the highest courts of Alabama in *Opinion of the Justices* (1993), Kentucky in *Rose v. Council for Better Education* (1989), Massachusetts in *McDuffy v. Secretary* (1993), New York in *R.E.F.I.T. v. Cuomo* (1995), North Carolina in *Leandro v. State* (1997), Oklahoma in *Fair School Finance Council v. State* (1987), Tennessee in *Tennessee Small Schools v. McWherter* (1993), and West Virginia in *Randolph County v. Adams* (1995).

In defining what constituted an adequate education under the South Carolina Constitution, the Supreme Court of South Carolina stated in *Abbeville v. State* (1999):

> We define this minimally adequate education required by our Constitution to include providing students adequate and safe facilities in which they have the opportunity to acquire: 1) the ability to read, write, and speak the English language, and knowledge of mathematics and physical science; 2) a fundamental knowledge of economic, social, and political systems, and of history and governmental processes; and 3) academic and vocational skills (p. *4).

However, the court cautioned that: "We do not intend by this opinion to become super-legislatures or super-school boards" (p. *4).

But other courts have become more extensively involved in defining statewide educational programs. In *Pauley v. Bailey*

(1984) West Virginia courts were involved in reviewing and approving a "Master Plan for Public Education" that "defines the educational role of the various state and local agencies, sets forth specific elements of educational programs, enunciates considerations for educational facilities and proposes changes in the educational financing system" (p. 132).

Critics of these judicially approved statewide plans have suggested that courts are exceeding the boundaries of judicial restraint and competence in attempting to substantively define an adequate education, noting that the legislative branch is responsible for establishing laws governing public schools, and judges should not engage in the creation of laws through judicial activism. Critics note that judges are neither lawmakers nor experts on educational policy. As Justice Moore stated, dissenting in *Abbeville v. State* (1999): "The goal of ensuring all...children an adequate education is unquestionably a laudable one. Under our system of government, however, it is not one entrusted to the judicial branch" (p. *4).

But since the U.S. Supreme Court's decision in *Marbury v. Madison* (1803) it has been commonly recognized that courts have the power and duty of interpreting the law. Whether courts are engaged in improper judicial activism or constitutionally required judicial interpretation has been an issue of persistent debate in many school funding cases. However, likely anticipating charges of judicial activism, the Supreme Court of South Carolina noted:

> [T]he constitutional duty to ensure the provision of a minimally adequate education to each student in South Carolina rests on the legislative branch of government. We do not intend by this opinion to suggest to any party that we will usurp the authority of that branch to determine the way in which educational opportunities are delivered to the children of our state (p. *4).

But it should be noted that the court was not deferring to local authority in educational control, but to state legislative control of public education. Although the trend toward judicial emphasis on adequacy may limit the liberty-equity conflict over per pupil expenditures, the liberty-equity conflict over state-local control continues. Ideals of liberty would generally favor more local control, while the promotion of statewide equity indicates greater state involvement and control.

One consequence of judicial endorsements of statewide substantive standards is that these decisions may promote the growing domination of state authority over local control. Even casual observers of educational governance have most likely observed that state control is increasingly dominating public educational policy. From increased state curriculum mandates to state-legislated finance programs, states are increasingly asserting authority over local schools. As Theobald stated: "While we talk about local control, what we have is anything but local control. That is probably the biggest issue in school finance" (in Johnston and Sandham 1999, p. 19).

Statewide curriculum mandates are very visible exercises of state authority, but the primary decline in local control may be rooted in the shifting balance of funding. Johnston and Sandham (1999, p. 19) noted: "The state share of K–12 spending, on average, increased from 38.3 percent in 1971–72 to 47.5 percent in 1995–96, making state aid the single largest component of local school budgets." As Johnston and Sandham stated concerning the golden rule of funding: "He who has the gold, makes the rules" (p. 1). Accordingly, state influence has increased as state funding has increased.

However, it should be noted that state authorities generally do have the legal power to exercise plenary control over their state's public school systems. Most states' constitutions give their legislatures ultimate responsibility for supporting public schools, and broad legal authority in controlling these schools. The limitations on this state authority are primarily political in nature, rather than legal. If local citizens want to limit state authority over local schools, they must work for a change in state law, persuade their state representatives to change state policy, or replace their representatives with elected officials that favor more local control.

But despite concerns that state officials may be intruding on local control and liberty, there may be credible arguments for increased intervention in many states. While liberty creates the freedom to excel, it also allows the freedom to fail. Governor Gray Davis of California is quoted as saying that local control of schools has been an "abject failure...[w]hen you have an earthquake or natural disaster, people expect the state to intervene... we have a disaster in our schools" (in Johnston and Sandham 1999, p. 19). In addition to concerns over academic failure, state officials have also seized control of local schools, in some instances, to root out local waste and corruption. Given increased concerns regarding achievement, growing calls for accountability, and incidents of waste and corruption in local governance, state officials may be able to articulate a persuasive case for increased state control in many states.

Further, some state officials argue that the current focus on accountability may actually increase liberty for local schools, if local officials choose to exercise this liberty. Although 48 states now mandate statewide academic standards, 39 mandate statewide testing, 19 require exit exams, and 23 states have legislation allowing state takeovers of local schools (Johnston and Sandham 1999, p. 19): "Ironically, state leaders sell their reform proposals to the public with accompanying promises of decentralization through fewer regulations and more freedom to do what it takes to meet the new standards" (p. 20). State officials argue that while less liberty may now be available concerning what students are expected to learn, more liberty is available in determining how to accomplish the state-mandated mission. Colorado Commissioner of Education William J. Moloney is quoted as saying that local school officials fail to take advantage of freedoms available to them, stating: "Schools do a lot of the same stuff, and they look alike...When you ask why, the answer is not because of state or federal regulations, but because 'that's how we've always done it'" (in Johnston and Sandham 1999, p. 20).

The movement toward greater state control and accountability is certain to generate future political and legal conflict. But in addition, there are other issues that are likely to generate future political controversy and litigation. For example, there appears to be significant evidence of growing disparities in resources for rural and metropolitan area schools, and an escalating legal battle over financial resources between these districts

(Dayton 1998). Thompson recognized in 1990 that there were "indicators of growing legal discontent" and an "increasing factionalism along rural and urban battle lines" (p. 71). If the fiscal situation of rural schools continues to deteriorate, and if state lawmakers fail to provide adequate remedies, the only option for disadvantaged rural students may be litigation (Dayton 1998).

Increased reliance on sales taxes to fund public education is also likely to generate future political conflict and litigation. Clearly, legislators and local officials face a formidable task in adequately funding public schools. And in their search for new sources of revenue, government officials are increasingly turning to local sales taxes to supplement local schools. But funding systems using local sales taxes pose a growing threat to equitable funding for rural schools, as centers of commerce increasingly move from smaller communities to larger metropolitan areas. As the Supreme Court of Tennessee recognized in *Tennessee Small School Systems v. McWherter* (1993, p. 144), the use of local sales taxes to fund local schools significantly disadvantages rural school districts. The Supreme Court of Alabama also noted in *Opinion of the Justices* (1993) that "rural students are disadvantaged because they generally live in areas without large shopping centers and are thus unable to generate substantial sales tax revenues for support of their schools" (p. 124).

Nonetheless, because of the difficulty of acquiring additional funds for public schools in a political environment already aggravated by high taxes, funding schemes utilizing local sales taxes continue to attract supporters. Many property owners have been persuaded that local sales taxes provide a means of limiting property taxes by imposing part of the burden of funding local schools on out-of-district shoppers and persons who do not own property. But this use of sales taxes not only increases funding disparities between metropolitan and rural schools, but also imposes a regressive tax on poorer individuals. Further, it drains additional funds from poorer rural communities into metropolitan areas because rural residents must increasingly travel to metropolitan areas to shop for goods and services not available locally. It is unlikely that the political and fiscal dynamics that created and perpetuate these inequities will change in the near future. A legislative solution may be unlikely given the disadvantaged political status of many rural areas. Accordingly, litigation may be the only remaining option in achieving greater funding equity for some rural schools, and may be on the not-so-distant horizon in many states.

CONCLUSION

Liberty and equity are fundamental American democratic principles, and both principles have played central roles in the ongoing school funding debate. Debate over the proper balance between these often competing principles is necessary in a free and just society. In disputes over school funding, citizens have turned to constitutions and courts both to protect their liberty and property interests and to assert equity claims in funding and taxation. Although most would agree that change is needed in public school funding policy, disagreement continues regarding the direction of that change. As the Supreme Court of New Jersey recognized in *Abbott v. Burke* (1998, p. 527): "The crisis is obvious; the solutions are elusive." Further, disagreement exists regarding even the fundamental meanings of liberty and equity. Much of the post-*Serrano* litigation concerns disagreements between plaintiffs and defendants about what constitutes equity in funding. Concerning liberty, some would argue that the promotion of liberty requires greater local control. But, as the Supreme Court of California noted in *Serrano v. Priest* (*Serrano II*, 1976), allowing disparities in funding in the name of promoting local control may be a "cruel illusion" which far from being necessary to promote local control, "actually deprives the less wealthy districts of the option" (p. 948). Proponents of local control argue that recent accountability efforts by state officials limit local control. State officials counter that although they are attempting to promote efficiency and achievement through state-level accountability efforts, they are allowing greater liberty by allowing local districts greater discretion in how to meet-state imposed standards. As the founders envisioned, the debate continues, in an effort to achieve a just and workable balance among competing ideals.

REFERENCES

Abbeville County School District v. State, 1999 WL 244388 (S.C. 1999).

Abbott v. Burke, 575 A.2d 359 (N. J. 1990).

Abbott v. Burke, 693 A.2d 417 (N. J. 1997).

Abbott v. Burke, 710 A.2d 450 (N. J. 1998).

Acton, J. E. (1877). *The history of freedom* (James C. Holland ed., 1993). Ottawa: The Acton Institute.

Alexander, K. (1991). The common school ideal and the limits of legislative authority. *Harvard Journal on Legislation, 28*, 341–366.

Bevelock, T. (1991). Public school financing reform: Renewed interest in the courthouse, but will the statehouse follow suit? *St. John's Law Review, 65*, 467–493.

Brown v. Board of Education, 347 U.S. 483 (1954).

Camp, W. E. , and Thompson, D. C. (1988). School finance litigation: Legal issues and politics of reform. *Journal of Education Finance, 14*, 221–238.

Dayton, J. (1992). An anatomy of public school funding litigation. *Education Law Reporter, 77*, 627–648.

Dayton, J. (1993). Correlating expenditures and educational opportunity in school funding litigation: The judicial perspective. *Journal of Education Finance, 19*, 167–182.

Dayton, J. (1995). When all else has failed: Resolving the school funding problem. *Brigham Young University Education and Law Journal 1995*, 1–20.

Dayton, J. (1998). An examination of judicial treatment of rural schools in public school funding equity litigation. *Journal of Education Finance, 24*, 179–205.

Dayton, J., and Glickman C. (1994). American constitutional democracy. *Peabody Journal of Education, 69*, 62–80.

Edgewood v. Kirby, 777 S. W. 391 (Tex. 1989).

Fair School Finance Council v. State, 746 P.2d 1135 (Okla. 1987).

Harrison, M., and Gilbert, S. (Eds.) (1993). *Thomas Jefferson: In his own words*. New York: Barnes & Noble.

Helena v. State, 769 P.2d 684 (Mont. 1989).

Hubsch, A. W. (1989). Education and self-government: The right to education under state constitutional law. *Journal of Law and Education, 18*, 93–140.

Hyman, R. (Ed.) (1989). *The Pan dictionary of famous quotations.* London: Grange.

Johnston, R. C., and Sandham, J. L. (1999, April 14). States increasingly flexing their policy muscle. *Education Week,* pp. 1, 19–20.

Korematsu v. United States, 323 U.S. 214 (1944).

LaMorte, M. W. (1999). *School law: Cases and concepts* (6th ed.). Boston: Allyn & Bacon.

Leandro v. State, 488 S.E.2d 249 (N.C. 1997).

Locke, J. (1690). *Two Treatises of Government.* London: Macmillan.

Magna Carta (England, 1215).

Marbury v. Madison, 5 U.S. 137 (1803).

McDuffy v. Secretary, 615 N.E.2d 516 (Mass. 1993).

Missouri v. Holland, 252 U.S. 416 (1920).

Opinion of the Justices, 624 So.2d 107 (Ala. 1993).

Pauley v. Bailey, 324 S.E.2d 128 (W. Va. 1984).

Public Papers of the Presidents: Reagan (1981). Washington, DC: U.S. Government Printing Office.

Randolph County v. Adams, 467 S.E.2d 150 (W. Va. 1995).

R.E.F.I.T. v. Cuomo, 655 N.E.2d 647 (N.Y. 1995).

Robinson v. Cahill, 303 A.2d 273 (N. J. 1973).

Rose v. Council for Better Education, 790 S.W.2d 186 (Ky. 1989).

San Antonio v. Rodriguez, 411 U.S. 1 (1973).

Scott v. Sandford, 60 U.S. 393 (1857).

Serrano v. Priest, 487 P.2d 1241 (Cal. 1971).

Serrano v. Priest (Serrano II), 557 P.2d 929 (Cal. 1976).

Sparkman, W. E. (1990). School finance challenges in state courts. In J. K. Underwood (Ed.), *The impacts of litigation and legislation on public school finance* (pp. 193–224). New York: Harper & Row.

Tennessee Small Schools v. McWherter, 851 S.W.2d 139 (Tenn. 1993).

Theobald, N. D., and Bardzell, J. (2000). Introduction and overview: Balancing local control and state responsibility for K–12 education. In N. D. Theobald and B. Malen (Eds.), *Balancing local control and state responsibility for K–12 education*, Chap. 1. Larchmont, NY: Eye On Education.

Thompson, D. C. (1990). Financing rural and urban schools: A growing schism. *Planning and Changing, 21*, 67–77.

Underwood, J. (1989). Changing equal protection analyses in finance equity litigation. *Journal of Education Finance, 14*, 413–425.

U.S. Bill of Rights (1791).

U.S. Constitution (1787).

U.S. Declaration of Independence (1776).

Valente, W. D. (1985). *Education law: Public and private*. St. Paul: West.

Ward, J. G. (1992). Schools and the struggle for democracy: Themes for school finance policy. In J. G. Ward and P. Anthony (Eds.), *Who pays for student diversity?: Population changes and educational policy* (pp. 241–251). Newbury Park, CA: Sage.

Wise, A. E., and Gendler, T. (1989). Rich schools, poor schools: The persistence of unequal education. *College Board Review, 151*, 12–37.

PART III

STATE ACTIVISM IN THE LATE TWENTIETH CENTURY

5

CONVERGING FORCES: UNDERSTANDING THE GROWTH OF STATE AUTHORITY OVER EDUCATION

Frances C. Fowler
Miami University

Local control has long been one of American education's most sacred cows. Throughout most of the twentieth century, the invocation of its name in an argument has sufficed to throw worshipers of lesser deities into confusion. People who advocated such reasonable reforms as racial desegregation, more equitable school funding, or higher academic standards frequently found that their most carefully constructed rationales shattered when they encountered American devotion to local control. The simple observation, "But that would weaken local control" was often enough to end a debate. Nonetheless, as the new millennium begins, there are signs that local control is weakening as more and more power over educational resources and policymaking shifts to the state level. Yet, for the most part, this change has not resulted from new beliefs and values; most

Americans still worship at the shrine of local control. Rather, it results from a convergence of national and even international political and economic trends.

This chapter explores those trends, setting them in the broader context of the political and economic transformations of the last quarter of the twentieth century. Since understanding what has happened depends on a clear grasp of the true meaning of local control, the first section defines it from both a legal and structural perspective. The second section describes in detail the changes within the United States that have encouraged the shift of authority over education from the local to the state level. Next, these changes are set in the context of globalization. The chapter concludes with a brief discussion of the implications of these changes and some cautious predictions.

WHAT IS LOCAL CONTROL?

THE LEGAL FOUNDATIONS OF LOCAL CONTROL

WHY LOCAL GOVERNMENTS ARE NECESSARY

Even in ancient times, rulers recognized that it was impossible to make all governmental decisions in a single, centralized location. For example, under the Roman Empire—which was very far from being a free or democratic state—considerable authority was decentralized to the regional and local levels. Officials such as provincial governors, procurators, and the subservient monarchs of conquered kingdoms made the routine, day-to-day decisions about issues in their jurisdictions, maintaining public works, upholding civil order, and dispensing justice by trying and sentencing criminals. The central government in Rome laid down broad policies for the whole empire and made decisions only about extremely important matters. Today, too, national governments decentralize considerable power to lower levels of decisionmaking. However, there are two general approaches to decentralization: federalism and the unitary relationship.

THE FEDERAL RELATIONSHIP

The different levels of government within a nation enjoy a federal relationship when governments at more than one level have sovereign power. In the United States, for example, both the national government and the 50 state governments have sovereign powers. Washington has authority over such policy areas as defense, the regulation of trade with other countries, and the currency. The states have authority over many domestic policy areas such as property rights, marriage and divorce, and most aspects of criminal justice. Because the national government has no sovereign power over these domains, it can do little to affect them; they must be left to the states. The United States is not the only country that uses a federal system to divide power between two levels of government. Germany, Brazil, and Switzerland are among the other federal nations (Coulter 1984; Isaak 1987).

THE UNITARY RELATIONSHIP

The second contemporary approach to dividing power between different levels of government is the unitary relationship. In a country with a unitary government, multiple levels of government exist, but only the national level has sovereign powers. Lower levels of government operate within a policy framework laid down by the central government; and, although local officials may have considerable discretion, ultimately they are accountable to the national government. In fact, if the national government concludes that the officials at a lower level are not performing adequately it can oust them and, if they are locally elected, even call another election to replace them. Many democratic countries use this approach; the United Kingdom, France, and Japan are good examples (Coulter 1984; Isaak 1987).

THE RELATIONSHIP BETWEEN STATES AND SCHOOL DISTRICTS

Because the relationship between Washington and the states is a federal one, many Americans assume that the states have a federal relationship with their local governments, including school districts. For example, this author has heard school board members complain loudly about state mandates and exclaim in public meetings: "Who do those guys in the state legislature think they are? *We* were elected by the people to run this school system!" She has also heard educators express shock at the news that a state government has taken over a school district and wonder if such a drastic action can possibly be legal.

Both the school board members and the educators were mistaken about the legal status of school districts. The relationship between states and local governments is not federal, but unitary. States therefore have the legal authority both to create and abolish school districts. They also have the power to develop education policies at the state level and require local districts to adhere to them. Moreover, they have the legal right to take over local districts which they consider failures and operate them until they meet state standards—a step which they have recently taken in several states, including New Jersey and Ohio. Indeed, nothing obliges states to set up local school districts at all. Theoretically, they could include all the public schools within their borders in a single huge district administered from the state capital. Hawaii, in fact, does precisely that.

There is nothing new about the legal status of school districts as it has just been described; it has not changed. However, the states' approach to discharging their constitutional responsibility for providing public education has changed. Until 25 or 30 years ago, states were content to let public education remain "a state authority locally administered" (Goertz 1996, p. 179). Today, however, they are no longer content to abdicate their constitutional authority; instead, they are asserting the legal rights that they have always had.

THE STRUCTURAL LOCATION OF "LOCAL" CONTROL

It is also helpful to conceptualize local control of education in the United States from a structural perspective. In 1990 and 1991, the Organisation for Economic Cooperation and Development (OECD), an international organization based in Paris, conducted a study of "the patterns of the division of authority in educational decision-making" (OECD 1995, p. 3) in 14 member nations, including the United States. The OECD researchers identified four levels of government at which educational decisions could be made (central government, upper intermediate, lower intermediate, and school) and determined for each country the percentage of decisions made at each level. Table 5.1 summarizes the findings for the United States.

TABLE 5.1. THE STRUCTURE OF EDUCATION DECISIONMAKING IN THE UNITED STATES

Level of Government (OECD terms)	Level of Government (American Terms)	Percentage of Decisions Made There
Central government	Federal government	0%
Upper intermediate level	State government	3%
Lower intermediate level	School district	71%
School	Site or building	26%

Based on OECD (1995), p. 40.

Several interesting facts emerge. First, the OECD found that the federal level made no decisions at all; a finding consistent with the U.S. Constitution, which does not even mention education. Somewhat surprisingly, the OECD found that only 3 percent of decisions were made at the state level. Possibly if the study were carried out today, a higher percentage would be attributed to the upper intermediate level. The heavy concentration of decisionmaking authority at the lower intermediate, or district, level is particularly striking.

Finally, Americans do not always think of the school as a decisionmaking level of educational governance, but the OECD researchers did. It is somewhat ironic that, although one of the most common arguments for local control is that it permits educators to make decisions at a governance level close to the children, the OECD study found that only 26 percent of decisions in American education are actually made at the level closest to them—the school. In summary, the OECD study depicted an American decisionmaking structure in which authority is heavily concentrated at the lower intermediate level of government.

The American structure should also be seen in relationship to the findings for the other 13 countries, all in Western Europe. The United States was one of only 3 countries in which no decisions were made at the national level; the others were Belgium and Switzerland. Of the 14 nations, the United States concentrated by far the most power at the lower intermediate level; the next heaviest concentration occurred in Belgium, with 50 percent. Finally, 11 of the 14 countries gave more authority to the school site than did the United States. Even France—widely considered to have a highly centralized school system—gave its schools more decisionmaking power than the United States, with 31 percent of decisions made at that level. Thus, from an international perspective, the governance structure of American education is characterized by a very heavy concentration at a the lower intermediate level of government, no national authority at all, and considerably less authority at the school level than is typical elsewhere.

THE TRANSFORMATION
OF THE STATES

THE STATE-LEVEL
VACUUM OF THE PAST

Most readers have probably noticed the striking contrast between the legal power of state government as described above and the minimal exercise of that power suggested by the OECD (1995) study. Obviously, the real question is not simply, "Why are the states asserting power over education today?" but rather, "Why did the states abdicate their power over education for so long and then suddenly begin to assert it?" The answer to the first part of that question is that, throughout most of American history, a power vacuum existed at the state level. Although states had considerable legal and constitutional authority, they lacked the capacity to exercise it. Sometimes referred to as "that sick old man of the federal system" (Reichley 1974, p. 11), state government was at its best weak and at its worst hopelessly corrupt. Glaring defects were apparent in all three branches of state government.

Governors, for example, were hamstrung in many ways. They were not permitted to serve long enough to build power or carry out programs. As recently as the mid-1950s, 21 states limited governors to a single two-year term and in 17 others they were limited to a single four-year term. Moreover, they had little power to appoint other members of the executive branch of state government. "Long" ballots were common, with many top state officials popularly elected; in the 1950s the average state elected 12 top executive officials in addition to the governor. These other elected leaders were not necessarily members of the governor's party; and, even if they were, they had little reason to follow his lead in policy matters. Governors also tended to have small staffs, primarily because the financial resources for hiring a large one were not available. In 1956, the typical American governor had a staff of 11 people. Finally, governors usually lacked meaningful power over budget preparation and in many states could not veto legislation (Hedge 1998). Because of these weaknesses, most governors were older men who had long served as party "hacks." They saw the governorship as an appropriate reward for years of service rather than as an opportunity to affect state policy. Not surprisingly, most governors were held in low esteem, as suggested by the title of a 1983 book about reforms of the governorship, *Goodbye to Good-Time Charlie* (Sabato 1983).

State legislatures enjoyed even less respect than governors. An old saw had it that "no man's life, liberty or property are [*sic*] safe when the legislature is in session" (Rosenthal 1981, p. 1). Many factors contributed to this poor reputation. First of all, most state legislatures were very unrepresentative. Since districts were rarely redrawn, rural areas were greatly overrepresented while urban ones were correspondingly underrepresented. In general, an urban vote was worth half of a rural one. For example, in 1955 a mere 18 percent of Florida's voters could elect a majority in the statehouse; and Florida's situation was not unusual (Hedge 1998). Moreover, restrictions in many states discouraged African-Americans and members of other minority groups from voting. State legislatures were therefore typically dominated by white "small-town lawyers, bankers and businessmen" (Ehrenhart 1984, p. 1) who promoted the interests of their rural constituents and opposed needed modernization as too expensive.

State legislatures were also hampered in many of the ways that governors were. Under the state constitutions of the time, most legislatures met only every other year and their sessions were very short. Moreover, their procedures were antiquated and their staffs skeletal. This meant that almost all state senators and representatives were part-time legislators who struggled— usually unsuccessfully—to balance a full-time career with service in the legislature. Even those who wanted to make a difference usually could not. In the early 1970s, Jack Morris (1974) visited the Pennsylvania state legislature and wrote an article about what he found. His description was scathing; the floor sessions were disorderly and noisy, and—perhaps as a result— much official business was conducted in closed caucuses. The legislative staff was very small, and most of its members were unqualified party "hacks" who could not have provided effective support to the legislature even if they had wanted to. Morris pointed out that although 53 percent of the state budget went to public education, there was no way that the legislature could oversee the schools. Jannette Reibman, chair of the senate education committee, asked him: "How can I look at the program in any depth when I have only one part time staff member?" (Morris 1974, p. 82). Not surprisingly, then, Morris concluded that the Pennsylvania state legislature was incompetent, entitling his article, "A State Legislature Is Not Always a Model of Ideal Government." It is sobering to note that a national study of legislatures conducted about that time rated the Pennsylvania legislature "average."

State court systems were no better than the executive and legislative branches of state government. They were very fragmented, with a Byzantine structure consisting of many types and levels of courts, making the coordination of the justice system difficult. In addition, state judges were often unqualified politicians whose decisions were frequently based on the interests of their supporters rather than on the law. Therefore, it took a very long time to resolve an issue in a state court and the outcome was about as likely to relate to politics as to the law (Hedge 1998).

Given the shortcomings of state government up until the last quarter of the twentieth century, then, it is not surprising that "state governments were scorned by many as racist, incompetent, inflexible, and politically and economically anemic" (Van Horn 1996, p. 1). Nor is it surprising that the two other levels of government—the federal and the local—tended to expand into the power vacuum left by the states. In public education this meant that the superintendents and school boards of local school districts assumed responsibilities and leadership roles which they probably would not have taken on if state governments had been stronger.

During the last four decades of the twentieth century, though, state government was transformed. The next two sections describe six major converging influences that enhance state power: (a) changes in the electorate, (b) the impact of federal programs, (c) constitutional and legal reforms of state government, (d) the growth of the intergovernmental lobby, (e) the fiscal crisis of local government, and (f) globalization.

THE TRANSFORMATION OF STATE GOVERNMENT BY NATIONAL FORCES

While changes to state government resulted in part from new policies specifically designed to strengthen state government, to a considerable extent these changes were by-products of policies designed to achieve other ends. In this section, several of the national forces which converged to transform state government are discussed.

CHANGES IN THE ELECTORATE

During the 1960s, two important policy changes at the federal level combined to produce, over time, a new sort of electorate in state politics. Two U. S. Supreme Court decisions, *Baker v. Carr* (1962) and *Reynolds v. Sims* (1964), declared the states' method of establishing voting districts for their legislatures unconstitutional. State governments were thus forced to re-draw these districts in conformity with the "one person, one vote" principle. This reapportionment brought rural domination of state legislatures to an end. At about the same time, Congress passed legislation, such as the Voting Rights Act of 1965 (amended in 1970, 1975, and 1982), which made it more difficult for states to restrict the voting rights of African-Americans and citizens from other minority groups. In combination, these federal reforms dramatically changed the demographics of voters in state elections and gave city dwellers, African-Americans, Hispanics, women, and younger people improved chances of being elected to state office. As a result, state governments not only became more representative of the populations which they served but also became more attractive to young, well-educated people who were interested in political careers. Moreover, state governments gained a new legitimacy. Previously, they had been perceived as outmoded and racist; increasingly, they were seen as capable of playing an important role in American politics (Bowman and Kearney 1986; Ehrenhalt 1984; Hedge 1998; Nathan 1996; Van Horn 1996). By 1974, the Citizens' Conference on State Legislatures (CCSL) was able to write, "As arenas for the orderly resolution of conflict, [state] legislatures offer the only real hope of reversing the trend toward social disintegration in this country" (CCSL 1974, p. 85). Such a statement would have been unthinkable even 10 years earlier.

THE IMPACT OF FEDERAL PROGRAMS

The 1960s were not just the decade of changes in voting policy; they were also the decade of John Kennedy's War on Poverty and Lyndon Johnson's Great Society. Both Kennedy and Johnson were interested in spending federal funds on the education of poor children, but it was under Johnson that the Elementary and Secondary Education Act of 1965 was passed. This law channeled large sums of federal money to both public and parochial schools in the form of grants for compensatory education. Other federal education programs followed. Most of these laws gave states an important role to play in implementing the programs and overseeing the way that local districts spent federal money. However, soon the federal government realized that the weak, understaffed state departments of education (SDEs) of the period lacked the capacity to perform these tasks adequately. As a result, it developed programs to strengthen

SDEs, funding their expansion and thereby giving more power to the executive branch of state government. As these federally fortified SDEs administered the new federal programs, those who worked in them gained experience and visibility in their states. Gradually they felt competent to take on other forms of educational oversight as well (Goertz 1996).

CONSTITUTIONAL AND LEGAL REFORMS OF STATE GOVERNMENT

After World War II, states began to reform their constitutions and other laws in order to address the weaknesses identified above; indeed, as of 1996, forty states had either heavily amended their constitutions or adopted new ones (Van Horn 1996). These changes strengthened all three branches of state government: executive, legislative, and judicial.

EXECUTIVE BRANCH REFORMS

Reforms of the executive branch focused on the governorship, but were not limited to it. Contemporary governors are much more powerful than they were three decades ago. Forty-nine states now permit governors to serve two consecutive terms and forty-eight give them four-year terms. This means that almost all governors can anticipate serving for eight years, just as the president does. Longer terms make it possible for them to develop meaningful policy agendas for their states and to lead the process of adopting and implementing new policies. Another common constitutional reform reduced the number of popularly elected executive officials in a state; the average today is six. Since constitutional changes also often gave governors more power to appoint and remove officials, most governors can now select a cabinet that agrees with their political philosophy and is willing to work cooperatively with them. Governors' influence over the budget process has also increased. In all but a few states the executive branch now develops a budget proposal to send to its legislature. Gubernatorial veto power has grown as well, and many governors' staffs have dramatically increased in size; today the average American governor has a staff of fifty. In short, as political scientists like to say, the American governorship has been "presidentialized" (Hedge 1998; Van

Horn 1994). As a result, the people who are attracted to the position are quite different from the governors of 30 or 40 years ago. Today's governors are younger, better educated, and more diverse than those of the mid-twentieth century.

Legislative Reforms

State legislatures were also reformed. Indeed, the pressure on legislatures to change their ways was even more intense than the pressure on governors and court systems. During the 1960s and 1970s, the CCSL, funded by the Ford Foundation, studied all 50 legislatures and rated them in terms of how representative, accountable, functional, informed, and independent they were. The CCSL used its findings to make numerous recommendations for legislative reform; and, as the states amended their constitutions or wrote new ones, they drew on the CCSL's work (Hedge 1998).

Some of the most important reforms were procedural. Legislative sessions were lengthened considerably and became, for the most part, annual rather than biennial. For example, immediately after World War II, only four state legislatures met every year; today forty-three do. (The exceptions are Arkansas, Kentucky, Montana, Nevada, North Dakota, Oregon, and Texas.) Moreover, the process for handling bills was streamlined and committee systems were reorganized. These changes greatly enhanced the ability of legislatures to produce legislation.

A second area of reform related to ethics. Conflict of interest laws were strengthened and restrictions were placed on the type of gifts which legislators could accept. Perhaps even more important was the passage of laws which increased the public's right to know what the legislature was doing. By the late 1970s all states had open meeting laws and 47 had open records laws, making it necessary for legislatures to conduct their business in plain view of the public and the media. The practice of making most decisions in closed caucuses, which Morris (1974) had observed in Pennsylvania in 1970, became largely a thing of the past (Hedge 1998; Van Horn 1996).

Finally, legislatures were provided with much larger staffs than they formerly had. The number of people working for state legislatures tripled between 1965 and 1995. Legislative staffs also became more professional, including more people with degrees in political science, public administration, law, and related fields. Today's state legislators have both a clerical support staff and a staff of professionals, making it easier for them to research proposed legislation and serve their constituents more efficiently (Hedge 1998; Van Horn 1996).

All these changes have made serving in a state legislature much more appealing than it used to be. Many aspiring young politicians start their careers in a state legislature; indeed, increasingly legislators make a full-time career out of their work in the state capital. Just as the governorship has been "presidentialized," state legislatures have been "congressionalized."

REFORMS OF THE COURT SYSTEM

Those who sought to reform state government did not ignore the courts. In fact, the transformation of state court systems began in the 1940s, with the passage in many states of laws requiring judges to have legal experience. In addition, most states now either appoint judges or use low-visibility, nonpartisan elections to select them. State court systems have been consolidated and streamlined; today the most popular organizational model is a three-tiered one, with a trial court at the county level, regional appellate courts, and a state supreme court. Finally, a professional court administrator who is able to provide considerable coordination of judicial activity now manages most state court systems. As a result of these changes, the capacity of state courts has increased dramatically. With this increased capacity has come a greater willingness to tackle controversial political issues. In fact, some state courts are as activist as the U.S. Supreme Court was when Earl Warren was Chief Justice in the 1950s. The inequity of school finance systems has been an especially popular area for judicial activism at the state level. School finance systems have been challenged in the courts of more than half the states (Hedge 1998).

THE GROWTH OF THE INTERGOVERNMENTAL LOBBY

Another factor in the increasing power of state governments is the intergovernmental lobby and related organizations.

Throughout most of American history, state governments operated in relative isolation from each other. The "Good-time Charlie" governors and part-time legislators of the past lacked the
time and resources—and perhaps the inclination—to cooperate
with each other to push for specific policy agendas in many
states at the same time. Recent decades, however, have seen the
growth of "intergovernmental" lobbying groups that permit
state governments to work together to influence state and national policy. Three especially influential groups of this type are
the National Governors' Association (NGA), the National Conference of State Legislatures, and the Council of State Governments. These organizations facilitate the exchange of information among state leaders and provide a vehicle both for coordi-
nating state policy change and lobbying in Washington
(Bowman and Kearney 1986). The activities of the NGA illustrate how the intergovernmental lobby works. The NGA's headquarters are in Washington, D. C. where it had ninety staff members in 1996. These professionals were divided into three
branches: state service, research, and lobbying. Every year the
NGA holds a conference for governors where up-to-date information on new state policy initiatives is exchanged and governors can talk and plan. The NGA has been especially interested
in education policy; in fact, its first study of a key state policy
area, conducted in 1986, focused on education (Beyle 1996;
Fowler 2000).

The work of the intergovernmental lobby in education policy is greatly enhanced by the Education Commission of the
States (ECS). This organization is a policy network that the National Governors' Conference set up in 1966. Its headquarters
are in Denver, and both the federal government and foundations finance it. Every year it convenes a national meeting on education policy which state school superintendents, governors,
state legislators, and other top leaders attend. There they are
briefed on the latest ideas in education policy and hear reports
about the success or failure of policies in various states. The ECS
also has an ambitious research agenda and publishes reports on
the status of various education policies in the 50 states (Fowler,
in press).

Since effective organization is a major source of power, the development of the intergovernmental lobby has further enhanced the power of state governments. Working collaboratively through these organizations, the states have been able to advance a multifaceted policy agenda, including education reform, with considerable success.

THE FISCAL CRISIS OF LOCAL GOVERNMENT

Important as changes in the electorate, the impact of federal programs, constitutional reforms, and the growth of the intergovernmental lobby were in transforming state governments, they do not fully explain the altered relationship between state and local governments. A piece of the puzzle is missing. That piece is the fact that while states' power was growing because of the changes just discussed, the power of local governments was simultaneously declining because of the fiscal crisis of the 1970s and 1980s. This crisis was caused by what some political scientists call "the three Rs." These "three Rs" are not, of course, "Reading, 'Riting, and 'Rithmetic," but "tax revolts, recessions, and reductions in federal aid" (Hedge 1998, p. 5).

Local governments have long depended on the local property tax as a major source of revenue. Yet, in the 1970s this tax came under heavy attack from taxpayer groups across the country. The reason is easy to understand. The 1970s were a decade of high inflation rates; in some years inflation exceeded 10 percent. This meant that real estate increased in value more rapidly than most people's salaries. As property values soared, homeowners began to experience their property taxes as a crushing burden and sought relief. As a result of popular referenda sponsored by tax revolt groups and of pressure on state legislatures, many states passed tax and expenditure limitations, or TELs. Since TELs usually limit the amount of money which can be raised through property taxes, local governments—including school districts—were much harder hit than were state governments. Over time they found it increasingly difficult to keep up with inflation (Bowman and Kearney 1986).

Recessions were another factor in the fiscal crisis of local government. The U.S. economy—and, indeed, the world economy—expanded very rapidly until about 1970, largely as a result of the enormous economic stimulus provided by the rebuilding of Europe and Japan after World War II. Starting in the 1970s, however, problems became apparent. Inflation and unemployment rates climbed simultaneously, although according to economic theory, this was not supposed to happen. Wages stagnated, and the gap between the rich and poor began to grow. In addition to the general economic malaise of the 1970s, 1980s, and early 1990s, several recessions occurred which were longer and more severe than the recessions of the recent past. Local governments, which have a relatively inelastic tax structure, felt the impact more than states. The fiscal crisis of the big cities was especially severe, but school districts were hard hit, too (Fowler, in press).

Finally, the federal government reduced its aid to local governments. As the funds available to local governments through federal revenue sharing and other programs declined during the 1980s, state governments had to step in to try to bridge the gap. In fact, between 1980 and 1986 alone, state spending on local government increased by 57 percent. In many cases, in order to be able to assist local governments, states reformed their revenue systems, improving their tax structure by adopting income taxes and, in 22 states, lotteries. They also developed more profitable approaches to investing public funds. But, of course, as they provided more resources to local governments, state governments also wished to oversee local programs more closely than they had in the past (Bowman and Kearney 1986; Hedge 1998; Van Horn 1996). The result has been "increased centralization of fiscal and programmatic authority in the states" (Bowman and Kearney 1986, p. 22)—a development that has affected most local governments, including school districts.

THE TRANSFORMATION OF STATE GOVERNMENT BY INTERNATIONAL FORCES

GLOBALIZATION

As the previous section explained, five national forces have converged over the last 40 years to transform state governments, increasing both their capacity and their power. The combination of changes in the electorate, the impact of federal programs, constitutional and legal reforms of state government, the growth of the intergovernmental lobby, and the fiscal crisis of local government altered the relationship between state and local governments. During the same period, state governments felt the growing impact of globalization, an international trend which has also contributed to their transformation. Globalization is "the increasing interdependence and interconnectedness of national economies" (Lazar 1996, p. 274). It is the result of several worldwide developments, but particularly of the revolution in communication which has been brought about by the introduction of such new technologies as the computer, the FAX machine, the Internet, e-mail, and cable television. Because of the rapid communication possible today, capital and ideas anywhere in the world can be exchanged almost instantaneously. Moreover, many services—such as electronic data entry—can be performed at a distance. Modern transportation has also made it possible to move goods and people very rapidly. As a result, governments and the relationships between governments are changing.

JIHAD VS. MCWORLD

Benjamin Barber (1995) has succinctly summarized the social and political forces unleashed by globalization as "Jihad vs. McWorld." On the one hand, the growth of global trade and multinational corporations is encouraging the development of "McWorld," a homogeneous world culture symbolized by the presence of McDonald's hamburger restaurants in every city of any size, from Moscow to Buenos Aires. Although McDonald's is American, "McWorld" does not operate in a single direction. Americans are often troubled when they learn that large portions of supposedly "domestic" automobiles were assembled in Korea or Mexico; and most Americans probably do not even realize that such common goods in their stores as Dannon and Yoplait yogurt and Bic pens and razors originated in Europe. Cultural influence is multidirectional, and McWorld reflects not one, but many countries.

On the other hand, globalization is fragmenting nation-states. The main reason is that multinational corporations are becoming increasingly large and powerful, with several exceeding most nations in wealth and power. For example, Toshiba's 1992 profits were $25 billion—just slightly under Argentina's total budget; and in 1991 the earnings of Domino's Pizzas were greater than the total expenditures of Senegal, Uganda, Bolivia, and Ireland together (Barber 1995). The enormous growth of the multinationals means that today few, if any, nations can control their national economies; as a result, they have lost status in the eyes of their citizens. As Susan Strange (1996) notes: "Popular contempt for [high-ranking officials] and for the head of state has grown in most of the capitalist countries—Italy, Britain, France and the United States are notable examples" (p. 3). As the power of national governments declines, fragmentation along subnational lines accelerates. In some countries this takes the form of the resurgence of deeply rooted ethnic groups: the growing demands of the Basques in Spain and France, the splitting of Czechoslovakia into two countries along ethnic lines, and the conflict in Yugoslavia come readily to mind. In others, secession movements have gained prominence: Northern Italy and Quebec provide good examples. In still others, the fragmentation takes the form of the increased autonomy of subnational governments. In Asia the city-states of Hong Kong, Taiwan, and Singapore illustrate this form of fragmentation; in North America, the growing assertiveness of the American states is another instance of this development. Since this fragmentation often involves intense hatred or fierce competitiveness, Barber (1995) dubs it Jihad, after the "holy war" of Islam, and argues, "Jihad and McWorld operate with equal strength in both directions, the one driven by parochial hatreds, the other by universalizing markets, the one re-creating ancient subnational and ethnic borders from within, the other making national borders porous from without" (p. 6).

THE "NEW FEDERALISM" FROM A GLOBAL PERSPECTIVE

In the global economy, the new multinational corporations and the old nation-states—which have been the dominant actors on the world's political stage for several centuries—are rivals. National governments are a hindrance to the growing power of multinationals because they still seek to regulate corporations and impose taxes on them just as they did when most corporations operated within the boundaries of a single country. As a result, these gigantic corporations pressure national governments both to relax the environmental and labor laws that they believe interfere with their freedom of action and to reduce corporate taxes. Usually, they argue that such changes are necessary if they are to be truly competitive in world markets. In addition, they seek to influence politics in order to weaken national governments generally. Daniel Drache (1996) observes: "A radically downsized nation-state structure is the hope of business everywhere" (p. 43). He also asserts that "business has…a vested interest in weakening national governments. Multinational business has long understood that the nation-state is the only counterweight to its global reach"(p. 55).

In the United States, this weakening of the national government has been apparent in a succession of policies which are loosely referred to as the "New Federalism." President Richard Nixon's administration was the first to move in this direction. In 1972 it initiated general revenue sharing with the State and Local Assistance Act; this shift of power toward the states accelerated with the introduction of block grants in the Comprehensive Employment and Training Act (1973) and the Housing and Community Development Act (1974). These laws gave state governments more power to decide what to do with federal funds than they had previously enjoyed. Not surprisingly, this trend continued under Republican President Gerald Ford; less predictably, Democratic President Jimmy Carter—who had been one of the "new" governors before he entered the White House—also put programs in place which further strengthened the states at the expense of Washington (Bowman and Kearney 1986).

President Ronald Reagan came to office with the support of a wide array of conservative interests, including business, so he not only continued this power shift, but also intensified it. In his 1982 State of the Union address, he sketched out how he planned to "curb the size and influence of the federal government" (Bowman and Kearney 1986, p. 7). Over the next few years, his administration enhanced state power by combining federal programs into block grants, giving states more discretion about how they used grant monies, moving federal oversight of grant implementation to the state level, and giving states more regulatory power. It should be noted, however, that although Reagan shifted power to the states, he also significantly reduced their federal funding, "forcing them to assume a greater burden of financial responsibility for health, welfare, education, and other programs" (Bowman and Kearney 1986, p. 7). As might be expected, state and local officials often opposed these changes, even though they enhanced their power.

Reagan's departure from office did not stop the trend. Bill Clinton's "Reinventing Government" has continued it, and the Republican-dominated 104th Congress which was elected in 1994 set about weakening the federal government with a vengeance. During its first hundred days, it created numerous block grants for entitlement programs. As Richard Nathan (1996) observes, "These devolutionary policies of the new majority in Congress do not stand alone. They are part and parcel of the strong movement in the country towards conservatism and limiting government" (p. 22).

COMPETITIVE FEDERALISM
AND LOCAL CONTROL

Because of the political and economic environment created by the New Federalism, state governments realized that in the new global economy, little help would be forthcoming from Washington. As a result, they increasingly developed policies in areas that previously had been left to the federal government. For example, in 1970 only four American states had trade offices in other countries; today, most do, and all fifty have an official relationship with the World Trade Organization (Pierce 1997). This dramatic change is well illustrated by the North Dakota Consensus Council's (NDCC) Web site (NDCC 1998). In a two-page piece entitled "Responding to the Changing National and International Environment," the NDCC refers to the "global squeeze on North Dakota" (p. 1) and asserts "Never before have North Dakotans faced the level of competition they will encounter in the coming years" (p. 1). They go on to argue that members of the North Dakota Legislative Assembly will have to understand and study "the changing international environment" (p. 1). Only by doing so will they be able to "capitalize on these new trends" (p. 1). Significantly, the NDCC's reference to the federal government is a brief allusion to "congressional members and committees" (p. 1) as one of several groups with which they will need to collaborate.

In this new competitive environment which stimulated the NDCC's efforts, 49 of North Dakota's competitors are other American states. In the fragmentation caused by the "Jihad" aspect of globalization, the states compete against each other to lure businesses (and, therefore, new jobs and taxes) to locate within their borders. They use several tactics in their competition. One is to loosen environmental regulations and to weaken labor laws to create an attractive business environment. A second is to offer tax breaks, which may include local property tax abatements. Another is to provide a local workforce with the necessary skills and appropriately docile attitudes. In some cases, they may also wish to use some academically superior public schools and school districts as bait to attract top executives to settle in their state. In other words, education policy is an important aspect of this new competitive federalism. As a result, states can no longer afford to leave the schools under largely local control. Increasingly, they are placing demands, setting standards, and enforcing accountability programs. They want to be "prepared to compete with producers of goods and services worldwide" (NDCC 1998, p. 1) and they have no intention of letting local control—no matter how sacred a cow it is—stand in their way.

WHITHER LOCAL CONTROL

As the previous discussion suggests, the gradual shift of control over education from the district to the state level has been overdetermined. Even if one or two of the forces that have converged during the last 35 years to strengthen state authority had been absent, this shift would probably have occurred anyway. With all six active at once, the change has been virtually inevitable. And, since all six forces will shape the foreseeable future, it is likely that the trend will continue. However, because local control has "sacred" status in many American minds, authority will probably shift slowly and the process will be a gradual "hollowing out" of local control until only its empty shell remains, rather than a sudden revolution. This author's cautious prediction, then, is that over the next generation, the actual decisionmaking structure of American education will become much more similar to the legally defined structure than it has been in the past.

Does this mean that American educators must sit quietly by while more and more power is centralized at the state level and taken away from those who know our nation's children the best? Not necessarily. Seen from an international perspective, the traditional structure of decisionmaking in American education has been unbalanced, with excessive authority centralized at the lower intermediate level of government. In fact, one could legitimately ask: "Just how local is the lower intermediate level?" Even in countries noted for great centralization at the national level, school sites have more authority than they have traditionally had in the United States (OECD 1995). Every valid argument that can be made for maintaining decisionmaking at the district level can be made even more forcefully for increasing the decisionmaking authority of schools. If American educators fight for the authority now concentrated at the district level to be redistributed both upward and downward, they may be successful, especially since they can support such a position with multiple international examples. If they can achieve such a redistribution of power, control over education in the future may well be more truly local than it is today—but the meaning of local will have changed.

REFERENCES

Barber, B. R. (1995). *Jihad vs. McWorld*. New York: Times Books.

Beyle, T. (1996). Governors: The middle men and women in our political system. In V. Gray and H. Jacob, *Politics in the American states*, 6th ed. (pp. 207–252). Washington, DC: CQ Press.

Bowman, A. O'M., and Kearney, R. C. (1986). *The resurgence of the states*. Englewood Cliffs, NJ: Prentice-Hall.

Citizens' Conference on State Legislatures (1974). Report on an evaluation of the 50 state legislatures. In W. P. Collins (Ed.), *Perspectives on state and local politics* (pp. 85–88). Englewood Cliffs, NJ: Prentice-Hall.

Coulter, E. M. (1984). *Principles of politics and government*, 2nd ed. Boston: Allyn and Bacon.

Drache, D. (1996). From Keynes to K-Mart: Competitiveness in a corporate age. In R. Boyer and D. Drache (Eds.), *States against markets* (pp. 31–61). London: Routledge.

Ehrenhart, A. (1984). Introduction: Power shifts in state capitals as new breed takes over leadership. In *Power in the states: The changing face of politics across America*, pp. 1–3. Washington, DC: Congressional Quarterly.

Fowler, F. C. (2000). *Policy studies for educational leaders: An introduction*. Upper Saddle River, NJ: Prentice-Hall.

Goertz, M. E. (1996). State education policy in the 1990s. In C. E. Van Horn (Ed.), *The state of the states* (pp. 179–208). Washington, DC: CQ Press.

Hedge, D. M. (1998). *Governance and the changing American states*. Boulder, CO: Westview Press.

House, E. R. (1998). *Schools for sale*. New York: Teachers College Press.

Isaak, A. (1987). *Politics*. Glenview, IL: Scott, Foresman and Company.

Lazar, F. (1996). Corporate strategies. In R. Boyer and D. Drache (Eds.), *States against markets* (pp. 270–296). London: Routledge.

Morris, J. H. (1974). A state legislature is not always a model of ideal government. In W. P. Collins (Ed.), *Perspectives on state and local politics* (pp. 77–84). Englewood Cliffs, NJ: Prentice-Hall.

Nathan, R. P. (1996). The role of states in American federalism. In C. E. Van Horn (Ed.), *The state of the states* (pp. 13–32). Washington, DC: CQ Press.

North Dakota Consensus Council, Inc. (1998). *Theme 16: Responding to the changing national and international environment.*

Downloaded December 5, 1998. Available at: www.bisman. com/ndcc/future16.html

Organisation for Economic Cooperation and Development (1995). *Decision-making in 14 OECD education systems*. Paris: OECD Publications.

Pierce, N. R. (1997). Nation state: Is its time up? *Neil Pierce Column*, April 16, 1997. Downloaded December 5, 1998. Available at www.chss.montclair.edu/hadisb/batkay.htm.

Reichley, A. J. (1974). The states hold the keys to the cities. In W. P. Collins (Ed.), *Perspectives on state and local politics* (pp. 11–26). Englewood Cliffs, NJ: Prentice-Hall.

Rosenthal, A. (1981). *Legislative life*. New York: Harper & Row.

Sabato, L. (1983). *Goodbye to Good-time Charlie: The American governor transformed*. Lexington, MA: Lexington Books.

Strange, S. (1996). *The retreat of the state*. Cambridge, UK: Cambridge University Press.

Van Horn, C. E. (1996). The quiet revolution. In C. E. Van Horn (Ed.), *The state of the states* (pp. 1–12). Washington, DC: CQ Press.

6

STATE POLITICS AND SCHOOL REFORM: THE FIRST DECADE OF THE "EDUCATION EXCELLENCE" MOVEMENT[1]

Tim L. Mazzoni
University of Minnesota

During the ten years from 1983 to 1993, the American states engaged in a massive use of policy in seeking to reform their public schools. Whether or not these nationwide efforts had a momentous impact on education, they might well have had such an impact on governance. Certainly the states, more than

---

1 This chapter was originally presented as a paper to an AERA symposium in New Orleans on April 7, 1994. In a reduced version it later was published as "State Policymaking and School Reform: Influences and Influentials" in the 1994 Politics of Education Association Yearbook. It is appearing here with the permission of Taylor & Francis Ltd.

ever, became the *de facto* as well as *de jure* policymakers for the schools. And within state policy arenas, political leaders and their business allies were depicted as giving direction to the reform thrust (Kirst 1994).

This chapter focuses on state education policy systems and how they appear to have changed. More specifically, the chapter examines from a state perspective—and a political-influence perspective—the causes, processes, and consequences of the first decade of the "education excellence" movement. It does so by placing events in historical context, by drawing upon research findings, and by applying an open-systems perspective, one concerned as much with contextual influences *upon* systems as with actor influence *within* systems.

Before beginning, two limitations need to be acknowledged —the first having to do with the systems, the second with research. State education policy systems are complex, shaped by external forces, and unlike one another in countless ways. The emphasis here will be on change over time more than on variability across space. Yet the presence and pervasiveness of interstate variability always must be kept in mind. As Fuhrman (1989, p. 64) aptly expresses it: "While pattern exists, variation in policy and process persists."

The second limitation has to do with the scholarly literature (for general reviews see James 1991; Lehne 1983; McGivney 1984; Mitchell 1988). Despite advancements, the research on which to portray state education politics remains spotty. And there still is considerable truth in Burlingame's and Geske's 1979 conclusion that analysts have "spent a good deal of time in some states, some time in a few states, and no time whatsoever in a great many states" (p. 60). As with variability across states, shortcomings in research limit prospects for generalization.

EXPANDED STATE ACTIVISM

The years from 1983 to 1993 witnessed an extraordinary eruption of state school policy. Though some states were vastly more aggressive than others in enacting detailed programs and broad-scale packages, the education excellence movement left no region untouched as it spread swiftly across the country.

Mandating rigorous standards for students and teachers was the dominant theme of the "first wave" of school reform (Firestone, Fuhrman, and Kirst 1991). In 1986, a "second wave" commenced, with attention shifting from bureaucratic intensification through state prescription to school restructuring through decentralized authority. By the end of the decade, some analysts and advocates were proclaiming the beginnings of a "third wave," one which called for the systemic redesign of K–12 education (Murphy 1990).

BACKGROUND FORCES

The "why" of the 1980s policy eruption has been cast by some scholars in broad interpretive frames. Social historians (e.g., Cuban 1990; Tyack 1993) look upon these events as yet another cycle in the recurring cycles of education reform that are rooted deep in America's past. Comparative analysts (e.g., Plank and Adams 1989; Ginsberg 1991), on the other hand, identify international trends, with many countries described as seeking to utilize their school systems to cope with underlying social, political, and economic problems. Other scholars (e.g., Clark 1993; Kirst 1984; Guthrie and Koppich 1988), concentrating more narrowly in time and space, point to a confluence of forces in the United States as setting the stage for reform, including: (1) America's slow—sometimes stagnant—economic growth, punctuated from 1978 to 1983 by soaring double-digit inflation followed by a severe national recession; (2) escalating global competition, with the loss by the United States of market share to other nations; (3) public unease and unhappiness about the ascent of economic rivals, notably the Japanese; (4) two decades of well-publicized reports decrying the softening in American schools of academic standards and the slide of student achievement test scores; and (5) elite and, to a lesser degree, popular dissatisfaction with the perceived productivity of America's public schools and inability—or unwillingness—of local school officials and educators to improve them.

FEDERAL IMPETUS FOR REFORM

In the context of these background forces, a political interpretation also has gained credence. The interpretation credits the federal government during the Reagan administration with creating the opportunity, stimulus, and agenda for state involvement on school reform issues. From this viewpoint, opportunity grew out of President Reagan's ideological commitment to the devolution of education policy and his political push to move program and funding responsibility from the federal to state and local levels. According to Clark and Astuto (1987), the consequence of Reagan's devolution quest, coupled with the failure of opponents to reassert a vigorous federal role, was to "leave the territory open to the states and they are claiming the territory" (p. 71).

If devolution offered a new opportunity for state activism, it was the Reagan administration's exuberant use of what Jung and Kirst (1986) call the "bully pulpit strategy" that stimulated and shaped that activism. Symbolic politics replaced substantive policy as federal commissions and officials relied on evangelizing and exhortation, rather than on expenditures and enforcement, to inspire a school "excellence" crusade (Boyd 1988). The first and most telling pulpit was afforded the National Commission on Excellence in Education, appointed by Secretary of Education Terrell Bell. The Commission adopted the strategy with the publication in 1983 of *A Nation at Risk*, a report crafted and released with a keen eye toward both arousing—and bounding—public debate on improving education in the United States (Wimpelberg and Ginsberg 1989).

However simplistic as policy analysis and crimped as social vision, *A Nation at Risk* was galvanizing as political manifesto. The imagery was one of a country in grave peril, its economy floundering and prey to foreign competitors, because a "rising tide of mediocrity" had been allowed to erode the quality of its educational foundations. Not only was the message dramatic, it was disseminated. Within a year millions of citizens had heard though print and electronic media about the dismal condition of American schools and what was necessary to fix them. That the indictment of schooling was unbalanced (Bracey 1991)—and the connection between economic competitiveness and education's deterioration unexamined (Cuban 1992)—hardly detracted from the report's appeal. Popular myth is the grist of mass politics. In the competition for public attention and agenda status, "simple, dramatic problem formulations," Hilgartner and Bosk (1988) observe, "are more likely to survive competition. Stock explanations that draw on widely shared, stylized 'political myths' are likely to triumph over sophisticated, subtle analyses" (p. 62).

If *A Nation at Risk* became, in Ravitch's words (1990, p. 48), the "paradigmatic educational statement of the 80s," it was far from alone in its message. Most of the national commission reports published during the decade, and there were dozens of them, promulgated similar diagnoses and prescriptions. The influence of these reports was magnified by constant reiteration and reinforcement—amplified by extraordinary media coverage as big-circulation newspapers, national magazines, and television networks discovered the schools (Kaplan 1992). Impact was further magnified by President Reagan's fervent—if belated—embrace of the bully pulpit strategy. And when, in Reagan's second term, William Bennett became Secretary of Education the reform thrust had a true "pit bull in the bully pulpit," a federal official whose zeal, rhetoric, and combativeness sparked one controversy—and media account—after another (Ravitch 1990, p. 48).

Some scholarly observers writing at the time attributed great—even controlling—impact to the education policy strategy of the Reagan administration. "The education reforms of the 1980s may best be viewed as a single national education reform with state variations," concluded Lutz (1986b, p. 1). And, he added: "Education reform of the 1980s has been a torrent of state reforms driven by the 'bully pulpit' of national rhetoric" (p. 2). In a similar vein, Astuto and Clark (1986) contended that as of the mid-1980s state education policy was simply "mirroring federal policy and consequently reinforcing the federal preferences in state policy options" (p. 30). Writing a few years later, Cooper (1988) observed that "since the Reagan years began, we have seen the New Right platform appearing in state after state. President Reagan and his second Secretary of Education, William Bennett, may have few new national programs to show. But they appear to have won the hearts and minds of the nation" (p. 286).

There surely is evidence to support interpretations that point to *A Nation at Risk*, other commission reports, and the Reagan administration's bully pulpit strategy as explaining the onset, pace, and content of state policy activism on school reform issues. In the wake of these influences, state-level task forces, commissions, and committees did spring up across the country. Every state had at least one; many had several meeting at the same time. National influences also contributed to mounting elite and popular pressures on state policymakers to "do something" about education. The invocation of crisis, a repeated theme in commission reports and pulpit pronouncements, infused urgency into the cause. Not only did these pressures—and the popularity to be gained by responding to them—create political incentives for state officials to risk the hazards of policy leadership, they were accompanied by education reform "solutions" that could be readily adopted by lawmakers. The national commission reports, write McDonnell and Fuhrman (1986, p. 56), "gave the impression that easily understood, simple solutions (albeit some expensive ones) were available. By providing, seemingly, straightforward policy solutions, these reports made it easier for state officials to propose and enact legislation quickly."

STATE SOURCES OF ACTIVISM

National commission reports and bully pulpit exhortations, along with high-profile advocates, undoubtedly influenced education reform initiatives in many states. Still, interpretations that narrowly single out these political forces give too little recognition to state activities that preceded *A Nation at Risk* and too much recognition to similarities—rather than to differences—in how state education policy systems sought in the 1980s to improve their public schools. To begin, the states had long been active on education issues. They did not need the federal government to cede them that terrain; they already occupied most of it (on state activism in the 1960s and 1970s see particularly Campbell and Mazzoni 1976; Fuhrman 1979; Iannaccone 1967; Mitchell 1981; Usdan, Minar, and Urwitz 1969; Wirt 1976). The federal withdrawal in the eighties from a role emphasizing programs and funding stimulated enlarged state involvement in education, just as it stimulated enlarged state involvement in other public policy domains (Nathan 1993). State government became the target of expectations, demands, and interests that could count on little but symbolic fulfillment from the Reagan administration. Nonetheless, the mushrooming of state education policy that occurred in the 1980s grew from well-established roots.

Nor does it appear accurate to portray *A Nation at Risk* and other national forces as triggering the 1980s reform movement. Four states—Mississippi in 1982 and Florida, California, and Arkansas in 1983—had either passed sweeping reform legislation or were well on the way to enactment before the release of that report (Jenkins and Person 1991; Alexander 1986; Massell and Kirst 1986; Osborne 1988). And for several other bellwether states, notably Tennessee and South Carolina which adopted big legislative packages in 1984, the antecedents of reform clearly traced back to earlier state events (Achilles, Lansford, and Payne 1986; Chance 1986). Thus, it seems fair to conclude, with Pipho (1986, p. K1), that *A Nation at Risk* "fell in at the head of a parade that had already begun to take shape." This is not to say, of course, that the national commission reports were unimportant. These reports, to extend Pipho's metaphor, did more than merely report on the reform parade's triumphal march through state capitals; they, along with pulpit and network urging, accelerated the pace, expanded the venues, attracted new marchers, and provided the score for many a musician.

It also adds historical perspective to note that efficiency and productivity concerns, concerns that fueled much of the 1980s school reform effort, were not new arrivals on the state policy scene. "Accountability" for education—and educators—had been the subject of extensive legislative and regulatory action throughout the seventies. Only school finance reform was a bigger issue across the states. Thirty-five states were reported as having adopted accountability legislation by 1975, with emphasis being on comprehensive planning and statewide assessment programs (Kirst 1990; Timpane 1976). As enthusiasm for these approaches waned, another movement rapidly took hold: minimum competency testing. By the end of the decade, 39 state legislatures were reported as having passed bills requiring such testing (Pipho 1979). In California and Florida, in particular, educational accountability became a recurrent policy theme right into the early 1980s (Herrington, Johnson, and O'Farrell 1992; Kirst 1990). By that time, these states had, as Guthrie and Koppich (1988, p. 46) note, "pioneered many of the proposals contained in *A Nation at Risk* prior to its publication."

THE REFORMIST SOUTH

The first wave of the education excellence movement crested in mid-decade and by 1987 had largely spent its force (Kirst 1988). During this initial surge of policy activism, some one-third of the states enacted sweeping, multiple-initiative reforms which closely paralleled many of the recommendations being publicized in the national commission reports. And other states adopted in a more restricted, incremental fashion a number of the same measures (Pipho 1986). These commonalities gave support to the observation that a national education agenda was being implemented in the United States, an agenda being forged into policy not through federal law but through state legislation and regulation (Spring 1988). But similar language did not necessarily translate into the similar meaning or consequence, as each state's policy response was situated in its own unique political context (Fuhrman 1989; Marshall, Mitchell, and Wirt 1989). There was, moreover, a distinct regional cast to the start and early spread of the reform movement. Nor was the movement quite so national in its policy legacy as many commentators made it appear.

With the notable exception of California, long a pacesetter in education, the leaders in instituting first-wave reforms were all southern states (Pipho 1986). And, after two years of activity, these states remained at the top in nationwide surveys taken of reform accomplishments, as measured by *A Nation at Risk* prescriptions. Plank's (1988) quantification across 16 policy areas of 1983–85 state initiatives discloses marked regional differences. His data indicate that the only region which had adopted reform measures in more than half the 16 policy areas was the South, with a mean score of 9.2 (Plank 1988, p. 147). By way of contrast, mean scores for the states in New England, Upper Midwest, and Rocky Mountains were in the 3- to 4-point range. If a "national agenda" was clearly manifest in states such as

South Carolina (14), Tennessee (12), North Carolina (12), Florida (12), and Louisiana (11), it was certainly muted in states such as Massachusetts (2), Michigan (2), Minnesota (2), Wyoming (2), and Colorado (1).

In explaining the South's enthusiasm for the education excellence movement, scholars emphasize the link between economics and education. Timar and Kirp (1988), for example, argue that it was "regional competition for high technology firms and recognition that the region's economic future depended on a skilled work force and good educational system [which] spurred a dramatic school reform movement throughout the South" (p. 97). Vold and DeVitis (1991) also underscore the "popular assumption [in the South] that a region's economic achievement is determined by its educational achievement" (p. 2). But they maintain that there was a further—and mighty—spur to southern activism: "discomfort with the role of perennial underachiever" (p. 2). The economics-education linkage was unusually motivating in the southern states because public schools there were seen as lagging behind the rest of the nation in support, standards, and attainment. The growing mood of dissatisfaction created a rare opportunity for reformers; there might be "no better time...to make Southern schools as good as—or better than—those found in other parts of the country" (Vold and DeVitis 1991).

Along with the economic imperative, as it pressed against perceived educational deficiency, there were other factors conducive to the South's taking a prominent role in first-wave school reforms. It was the most conservative region of the country, one likely to be particularly receptive to the ideology permeating the national commission reports and Reagan administration advocacy. This might explain why, for example, *A Nation at Risk* became the template for policy in conservative Alabama (Rudder 1991), while it was virtually ignored by state lawmakers in liberal Minnesota (Mazzoni and Sullivan 1986). Also, the southern states had typically evolved a more centralized approach to school governance than had other regions of the country (Wirt 1976). Despite localism always being present—and intense in some southern states, such as Texas and Georgia—it was not as much of a political constraint in the South generally as it was, for example, in the New England and Rocky Mountain states.

Besides ideological preference and governance tradition, the differential impact of the 1980–82 national recession contributed to the South's being more able than other regions to focus on—and fund—costly school reform initiatives. Although not spared, the southern states were not hit nearly as hard economically as many states in the Frost Belt. And the fiscal rebound came much later in these northern states than in the South. In such states as Massachusetts, Michigan, and Minnesota, pressing economic issues dominated policy agendas into the mid-1980s (Mazzoni and Sullivan 1986; Osborne 1988).

Finally, the adoption of school reform legislation within the South appeared to fit the regional diffusion model of policy innovation, a model in which a state's policymaking is assumed to be strongly influenced by the actions of its immediate neighbors (Gray 1994). That such emulation and competition were important as southern states decided upon school reforms is suggested in the interview data presented by Chance (1986). For example, a South Carolina official commented: "We got a lot of help from Mississippi, even though their reforms are much different...the process we used [local forums] was similar" (p. 53). And a Florida legislator reported that "people in the state joked about contests between Tennessee and Florida as to who would come out first with a merit pay plan" (p. 83). In addition, the southern states had regional forums, notably the Southern Regional Education Board, that facilitated the sharing of ideas, proposals, and strategies.

ENABLING AND ENERGIZING FORCES

The education reform movement swelled, of course, far beyond its original moorings in California and the South. By 1990, comprehensive policies had been legislated in states as diverse as Kentucky, Missouri, Illinois, New Mexico, Ohio, Iowa, and Washington (Alexander 1990; Pipho 1986; Kirst 1988). Commission reports, pulpit exhortations, media publicity, and high-profile advocates, when taken together, were certainly a contributing—probably a necessary—cause for the nationwide diffusion of innovation. Still, they were not sufficient; at least four other forces enabled and energized the process.

The most basic enabling force was the institutional capacity that had been steadily developing in state governments for two decades. Modern, responsive, and capable political institutions were generally to be found in the American states by the early 1980s (Mitchell 1981; Murphy 1982; Rosenthal 1990). Strengthened institutional capacity was essential to the emergence of what Van Horn (1993) calls the "entrepreneurial states," governments able to innovate across a range of complex issues, in which K–12 education was simply one locus of intense activity. That this capacity existed was evident in the scores of legislative initiatives enacted in the eighties by state governments in such areas as water quality, air pollution, technology development, and energy conservation (Doyle and Hartle 1985; Nathan 1993; Van Horn 1993). State capability might not have been up to the challenge of producing "coherent policy" for upgrading education (Fuhrman 1993); and the intensification of pluralistic politics, another long-term trend, worked against such coherence (Johnson 1993; Mazzoni 1993). But state capability was up to the challenge of enabling lawmakers to respond to—or seize upon—demands for school reform with an unprecedented volume and variety of policy initiatives.

A second enabling factor was the return by the mid-1980s of economic prosperity. The national recession of the early eighties had been deep and prolonged. Although state governments in 1980–1982 could undertake innovations in such areas as teacher competency testing and high school graduation requirements, budgetary surpluses were not available to bear the policy and political costs of big-ticket reforms. Fiscal year 1984 saw a rebound in state revenues as the national economy improved and state taxes—36 states had to hike taxes during the recession—generated ample new monies (McDonnell and Fuhrman 1986). A growing economy and state fiscal surpluses permitted reformers to pump enough money into the bargaining arena to accommodate conflicting interests. The something-for-everyone compromise, a hallmark of omnibus bills that often were vehicles for school legislation, was made possible on a broad scale by the flow of surplus revenues into state coffers.

A pervasive energizing factor was the escalating competition among American states in the 1980s to attract or retain economic resources. In this competition, having good schools—or, at least, the reputation for them—was perceived as a vital asset. As has been described, this sense of competition, and of losing out if one's schools were labeled as inferior, was a powerful spur to education reform in the South. Yet the motivation was hardly exclusive to that region. State after state trumpeted the virtues of its schools as each sought to gain an edge in the new global marketplace (Doyle and Hartle 1985). Economic competition was a powerful contextual dynamic contributing to the diffusion of state education reforms, a dynamic that illustrates what Dye (1990) has proclaimed to be the new "competitive federalism model" of policy innovation in the United States.

A second energizing force was judicial intervention, largely through the resurgence at the end of the decade of school finance lawsuits and court rulings. The court order had been a prime mover of policy activism for many states during the nationwide movement in the seventies to redress disparities in school funding (Fuhrman 1979; Odden and Wohlstetter 1992). Then, for a decade, these "equity" concerns were submerged —though not completely displaced (West Virginia, for example, had to respond to a sweeping school finance decision)—by the "excellence" impulse of first-wave reforms. In 1989, however, unequal funding systems in Kentucky, Montana, and Texas were struck down by the courts. In the early 1990s, the litigation momentum continued to build, with school finance systems in New Jersey, Tennessee, Massachusetts, Alabama, Missouri and Kansas being overturned for violating state constitutional provisions.

Unlike the press of economic competition, the intervention of the court was not an all-encompassing energizing force. While most states since 1970 had experienced school finance litigation—42 as of late 1993—plaintiffs in these cases had not been much more successful than defendants—15 rulings for plaintiffs and 13 for defendants, with 13 cases pending, as of late 1993 (Harp 1993). Still, when a plaintiff's challenge was upheld, it established an agenda priority for the policy system to which state lawmakers had to respond, however grudgingly and minimally. The court order, along with its attendant publicity and pressures, triggered a process of policy revamping—sometimes even policy redesigning—and political accommodation. In some states, notably in New Jersey and Texas, this process proved to be protracted and its outcome problematic. But in Kentucky, where the state supreme court in 1989 declared the entire public school system to be unconstitutional, judicial intervention combined with gubernatorial leadership to produce in 1990 the most comprehensive approach to school reform legislated in any American state (Alexander 1990).

"WINDOWS" AND "ENTREPRENEURS"

Contextual pressures did more than reconfigure the demands, resources, and incentives that impinged on—or were inputs for—state education policy systems. They reconfigured the opportunity structure for individual system actors. These pressures opened up, in Kingdon's (1984) terms, "policy windows"; and there were a host of strategically placed "policy entrepreneurs" in and out of government ready, willing, and able to seize the moment to "hook solutions to problems" and "proposals to political momentum" (p. 191).

Some policy entrepreneurs were charismatic leaders, strong-willed individuals whose ambition and abilities could infuse institutional roles with extraordinary vitality. Predominant among these individuals were elected officials, especially a "new breed" of state governors who were hailed by the media and depicted by scholars as pivotal actors in promoting education reforms (Chance 1986; Fuhrman 1989; Mueller and McKeown 1986; Osborne 1988; Rosenthal 1990; Timar and Kirp 1988). Southern governors captured the limelight, but activist governors were found outside the South as well. Chief state school officers (CSSOs) were prominent in several states (Chance 1986; Layton 1986; Massell and Kirst 1986; Prestine 1989). In one state—Texas—an individual businessman appears to have forcefully stamped his priorities and management philosophy on school reform legislation (Lutz 1986a; McNeill 1988).

Visible leaders were not, however, the only policy entrepreneurs pushing for school reform. Individual legislators, whose activity generally received far less media coverage than governors, were influential across the states; indeed, their overall impact probably exceeded that of any other single class of actor (Fuhrman 1990; Marshall, Mitchell, and Wirt 1986). Along with lawmakers, there were behind-the-scenes policy entrepreneurs among officials, managers, and specialists in state education agencies. In some states, these "bureaucrats" took advantage of the agenda prominence of school reform to put forward their preferred solutions and maneuver them into enactments (Chance 1986; Layton 1986; Holderness 1992; Mazzoni and Sullivan 1986).

Besides government insiders, there were individuals outside of government infusing their policy systems with entrepreneurial energy. Some were linked to—and drew their influence from—national networks that had formed around such reform issues as curriculum standards, educational choice, and school-based management (Kaplan and Usdan 1992; Kirst 1984; Ogawa 1993). Others were more homegrown in origin, such as the individual policy entrepreneurs in Minnesota who working with and through a public interest group—the Citizens League—were a catalyst in moving that state along a restructuring agenda for school reform (Mazzoni 1993).

THE POLITICS OF REFORM POLICYMAKING

PROCESS CHARACTERISTICS

State policymaking in the 1980s on education excellence issues was not politics as usual, at least not in the states where a sweeping array of reform initiatives was undertaken. In such "high-change" states, "much of the tactical plan," Chance (1986, p. 29) observes, "was intended to limit, control, surmount, circumvent, or avoid the constraints of more conventional processes." Reform politics, usually in a short burst of extraordinary policy energy, supplemented or supplanted regular politics. Education policymaking transcended traditional subsystem arenas—and their specialized and established legislator, bureaucrat, and lobbyist actors—and was played out in broader, more public arenas.

In reform politics, top-level leaders—governors, legislators, and CSSOs—took charge. Blue ribbon commissions were formed. Change initiatives of every sort were put forward, sometimes dozens were combined and compromised into a single omnibus package. High cost and redistributive proposals were mostly siphoned out (Firestone, Fuhrman, and Kirst 1991). In Chance's words, "Political imperatives demand[ed] slogans and easily described, cost-contained, and symbol-accommodating solutions" (1986, p. 29). Historic political alignments were often bypassed. New advocacy coalitions were forged, with the weighty influence of business groups adding impressive clout. "Standards," "excellence," and "quality" provided unifying, motivating, and legitimating symbols. Persuasion, bargaining, and trade-offs—and, on occasion, arm-twisting pressure—mobilized supporters and neutralized opponents. The most formidable potential resisters, the big education groups, were brought aboard, bought off, or brushed aside (McDonnell and Pascal 1988). Policy visibility attracted and was expanded by media publicity. Popular support was assured; political credits were amassed; policy—and personal—agendas were attained. And a "juggernaut" of education reforms rolled through many a state legislature (Chance 1986).

Any composite picture of reform policymaking must be qualified by a recognition of interstate differences, differences which existed even among the high-change states. Governors and legislators usually were in the lead—but not always. In New York, for example, the 1984 "Action Plan" for education reform came from the Board of Regents, the result of a participatory process "designed and orchestrated by officials of the State Education Department, and notably [the] Commissioner of Education…" (Layton 1986, p. 9). Business executives and groups usually were central actors—but not always. In Missouri, for example, the business community was not actively involved; in that state, Hall (1989, p. 16) writes, "the theme of reform was never strongly tied to the need for economic development or the attraction of new business as in the Southern states."

The scope, composition, and unity of the education reform movement varied. In some states—for example, Georgia and Missouri—the reform coalition reflected essentially an elite consensus (Fuhrman 1989; Hall 1989). In other states—for example, Florida, Illinois, and California—highly pluralistic politics had to be accommodated (Alexander 1986; Chance 1986; Massell and Kirst 1986). In a few states—notably Mississippi and South Carolina—coalitional efforts went beyond alignments among state-level actors and extended significant political interaction to grassroots participants (Jenkins and Person 1991; Timar and Kirp 1988). In some states—for example, California, Illinois, Georgia, and Missouri—agreement was reached among the major interests; all embraced the final compromise. Yet in other states—for example, Tennessee, Texas, and Arkansas—reform politics proved to be polarizing as political leaders and their business allies squared off in abrasive confrontation against the teacher unions and other education groups over such divisive issues as merit pay, career ladders, "no pass/no play" rules, and teacher testing (Achilles, Lansford, and Payne 1986; Fowler 1988; Lutz 1986a; McNeil 1988).

Differences among the high-change states were relatively minor compared with differences across the other two-thirds of the American states as they experienced the nationwide impulse to improve public schools. Several states in which CSSOs and education departments played a decisive role—for example, Colorado, Washington, Wisconsin, and New Mexico—took a critical, cautious, or containment approach to education reform (Chance 1986; Cibulka and Derlin 1992; Holderness 1992). In other states—for example, Arizona and Pennsylvania—governors developed and pressed for sweeping changes; but only modest departures were adopted by their legislatures (Karper and Boyd 1988; Osborne 1988; Sacken and Medina 1991). In still other states, governor-led reform coalitions came to focus largely on a particular initiative—for example, career ladders in Utah and educational choice in Minnesota—and succeeded, despite sometimes powerful opposition, in passing breakthrough legislation (Malen and Campbell 1986; Mazzoni 1988). And, finally, there were some states where the waves of reform washed over the education policy system with little discernable impact on decisionmaking processes other than those associated with temporary commissions, expanded conversation, and modest innovation (Chance 1986).

Mainstream Politics

The reform movement of the 1980s plunged education ever more into the political mainstream (Fuhrman 1987). While there also was an escalation in the policy activity of state boards of education—and, in some states, they took a proactive role (Chance 1986; Layton 1986)—the arenas for action were typically the legislature and the governor's office. Reform proposals by the many hundreds were picked up, packaged, and promoted by elected officials across the country. Some of these officials, most notably governors, regularly campaigned on educational issues, then emphasized them in new initiatives. Their intentions and influence decisively shaped state policymaking, a process in which "politics" as played out in general governance arenas through symbol manipulation, interest representation, coalition building, and give-and-take bargaining loomed large.

That politicization had come to characterize education policymaking did not represent a deviation from prior trends. Politicization of this process had become obvious in many states during the preceding decade (Campbell and Mazzoni 1976; Geske 1977–78; Lehne 1978; Rosenthal and Fuhrman 1981; Rost 1979). It was most evident on the issue of school finance reform (Fuhrman 1979; Brown and Elmore 1983). On that 1970s reform issue—just as with the 1980s excellence reforms—politicians were in the lead, consensus-building commissions were utilized, advocacy coalitions were constructed, and legislative compromises were hammered out through political processes. There were, to be sure, some noteworthy differences—for example, in precipitating events, patterns of alignment, and participating states (Odden and Wohlstetter 1992). Yet, overall, the basic processes of education policymaking were strikingly similar between the two movements, both being embedded in mainstream politics.

Continuity did not mean the absence of change. Education being politicized in the 1980s was not the same as it being politicized in the 1970s. Among the changes in state school politics associated with the school reform movement, three stand out: (1) the activism of governors, (2) the involvement of big business, and (3) the influence of national organizations and networks.

GUBERNATORIAL ACTIVISM

The education reform movement afforded the nation's governors a unique opportunity as well as motivating incentive to overcome policymaking fragmentation and to marshal broad-based support for innovative legislation. A sense of crisis, and of being a part of a nationwide movement, contributed to cooperation. So, too, did the shared belief among power holders that they had to pull together if their states—or region—were to contend educationally and economically with other states. Many reform proposals, such as student testing and high standards, were enormously popular; lawmakers could readily agree on the political merits of these initiatives, even as they publicly vied for credit. There was also an undergirding flow of surplus revenues, a surge of dollars that encouraged a surge of policy by fostering mutually acceptable compromises among competing interests.

A group of able, ambitious, and pragmatic governors—mainly but not solely in the South—took the spotlight as "policy chiefs" (Caldwell 1985). Focused and determined, the activist governors persisted, frequently in the face of initial setbacks, in pressing for education reform legislation. More than any other state actor, they had the institutional authority, organizational resources, and media access to dramatize need, frame issues, and set agendas. Concentrating their policy arguments on the link between a state's school system and its economic competitiveness, governors made education reform their number one legislative priority, ahead even of tax, economic, and environmental concerns (Beyle 1990).

To pave the way for their education priorities, governors appointed blue-ribbon commissions. Such a commission could serve many functions. For example, as Malen and Campbell (1986) report for Utah, it could "mute executive-partisan tensions by becoming an umbrella organization" where proposals could be formulated and consensus forged; it could help fix public attention on and inspire support for education reforms; and, when key lawmakers were commission members, it could establish effective linkages between itself and the legislative process (pp. 265–66). Malen and Campbell point to the commission they studied as having had a "central role...in the policy-making process" (p. 266). Other analysts have arrived at the same judgment about governor-appointed commissions (e.g., Chance 1986; Fuhrman 1989). "In many of the states that underwent reforms," Rosenthal (1990, p. 111) concludes, "commissions spearheaded the drive."

To buttress the work of commissions, activist governors adopted other strategies. Many engaged in high-powered "issue campaigns" to arouse popular sentiment (Durning 1989). Conducted like an election campaign, these gubernatorial efforts sought to expand grassroots pressure for reform initiatives. The issue campaign, as delineated by Beyle (1993, p. 96), usually consisted of "a campaign organization, a campaign kickoff, a series of campaign speeches, a campaign tour, and a panoply of campaign slogans, endorsements, advertisements, and materials." The strategy, even when cast as an all-out appeal, was not always successful. Governor Perpich, for example, lost in his first run at public school choice in Minnesota (Mazzoni 1989); and Governor Schaefer could not secure legislative approval for a special math and science high school in Maryland (Rosenthal 1990). Yet other governors—for example, Winter in Mississippi, Alexander in Tennessee, Clinton in Arkansas, and Riley in South Carolina—engendered widespread popular and legislative support with their issue campaigns (Durning 1989).

Effective education governors were not only front-stage actors, using their command of media and the techniques of public relations to reach mass constituencies, they were back-stage actors as well, drawing upon the tactics of insider politics to strike accords with other influentials—or to persuade or pressure them into cooperating. Building policy ownership by inviting legislator participation and broadly distributing political credit for policy achievements were widely employed. Governors engaged, too, in political bargaining. For instance, Governor Clinton of Arkansas often followed through on his grassroots campaigns by applying a "full court press" in the legislature, cutting deals and negotiating compromises (Ehrenhalt 1993, p. 123). And some governors were willing to bring to bear a repertoire of power moves. Said Governor Babbitt of Arizona:

"In any given year, I have selected...issues and used everything at my disposal—initiative, referendum, the bully pulpit, the press, browbeating, trade-offs, threats, rewards—to get what I needed" (Osborne 1988, p. 140).

Gubernatorial involvement in the 1980s certainly exceeded that in past decades. Moving beyond budgetary responsibilities and fiscal concerns, governors took on the education quality issue and, in so doing, thrust state policy deep into the core of traditional schooling concerns (Kirst 1984). On reform initiatives to which they assigned top priority, governors usually had great influence, especially when they were committed, tenacious, and accommodating (Rosenthal 1990). Yet the impact of governors should not be overstated. Visibility on an issue did not necessarily mean influence over an issue; credit for an enactment was not the same as creating an enactment. State policy actors were well aware of the governor's political need for visibility and credit; and if these actors received much of the policy substance, they might well have been willing to concede to the governor many of the political symbols. There were, moreover, a number of very tangible constraints on the governor's initiating role.

In the first place, gubernatorial activism was complemented —or countered—by legislative activism. Governors were not the only source of major policy initiatives in education. Many came from legislators—primarily from committee chairs, other education policy specialists, and, in some states, house and senate leaders (Hamm 1989). Case study data portray legislators as the "active pilots" in the reform process in a number of states (Fuhrman 1990). A strategically placed and politically skilled legislator often functioned as the chief policy entrepreneur. Such, for example, was the case for House Majority Leader Connie Levi on the postsecondary choice option in Minnesota (Mazzoni 1993); for Senator Anne Lindeman on career ladders for teachers in Arizona (Firestone 1989); and for House Speaker Vera Katz on the comprehensive redesign of K–12 education in Oregon (Clark 1993). Furthermore, legislators tended to become involved in the whole spectrum of K–12 concerns, while governors targeted their power on a relatively few themes (Rosenthal 1990). Legislators did most of the steady work in shaping education policy; governors did the high-profile policy work, exerting a more showy influence on selected issues.

Secondly, governors were not the only executive officials advancing major proposals to reform the schools. Chief state school officers were among the key actors in many states—for example, in California, Illinois, New York, South Carolina, and Wisconsin (Chance 1986; Layton 1986; Massell and Kirst 1986; Prestine 1988). In at least a few states CSSOs openly contested governors for policy leadership. This was especially true when these agency heads were elected officeholders—in 15 states as of 1992 (McCarthy, Langdon, and Olson 1993). Having their own political constituencies, support groups, and regime interests, elected CSSOs had the resources and incentives to set an independent policy course. And these powerful actors in several states, notably in California and Wisconsin, publicly clashed with governors over issues of school funding and reform (Cibulka and Derlin 1992; Kirst and Yee 1994).

A third factor constraining governors was their need for legislator backing to get bills enacted. No matter how powerful they were, governors could not simply command policy into being. They had to anticipate legislative reactions in formulating programs and to adapt to legislative resistance in bargaining for enactments. Political feasibility considerations had to enter into a governor's policy calculations from the beginning to the end of the legislative process; they restricted governors in what they attempted and what they attained. Conflict with legislatures, which escalated markedly during the latter part of the decade, further constrained governors in their education policy role.

Executive-legislative conflict became so bitter by the end of the 1980s that it constituted in some states a political "war between the branches" (Rosenthal 1990, p. 200). Conflict escalation was fueled by the growing assertiveness of legislatures, intensification of interest group pressures, media reporting focused on controversy, candidate-driven election campaigns, abrasive partisanship, and divided government (Rosenthal 1990). The last of these—divided government—had come to affect most American states. As Beyle (1993, p. 91) summarizes: "Since the mid-1980s, about three-fifths of the states had 'powersplits' [i.e., governorship and legislature not controlled by the same party]; 30 states [had such splits] following the 1991 elections."

Besides legislative and partisan politics, there were other conditions that limited the capacity of governors to act as innovators in education, particularly when they sought to sustain a policy departure over an extended period of time. There was the constant press of other state issues—for example, taxes, jobs, crime, welfare, health care, and the environment—any one of which, if it became "hot," could marginalize education reform on a governor's policy agenda. Health care certainly had this potential in the 1990s. Along with its growing public saliency, it was a source of soaring costs in state budgets and had the prospect by the mid-1990s of soaking up much of the anticipated growth in state revenues (Beyle 1993, p. 192). Another front-burner issue was criminal violence, with "safe streets"—and "safe schools"—being a recurrent theme in governors' 1994 state-of-the-state speeches (Harp 1994).

Another cause of issue displacement was economic downturn. National recession and state revenue shortfalls marked the early 1990s just as they had the early 1980s (Raimondo 1993). Budget issues, tax and spending decisions, and adversarial politics dominated policy processes—and governors were centrally involved in these processes (Beyle 1992). In some states, like Massachusetts and Michigan, issues of school reform and funding became embroiled in legislative and partisan strife (Pipho 1993), with these issues becoming a political vehicle for more overarching power struggles. Hard times made for hardball politics, and education in the early 1990s was sometimes caught squarely in the middle among the contending powers.

Yet despite all the pressures, problems, and politicization, education reform did not disappear from gubernatorial agendas. Governors had showed much more staying power on that issue than would have been predicted from past performances, though they remained more episodic actors than were committee chairs and other education policy specialists in state legislatures. In some states, such as Georgia and Florida, governors spearheaded in the early 1990s another surge of reform initiatives (Kirst and Carver 1994; Wohlstetter 1994). In other states, including Massachusetts and Michigan, governors and legislatures were able to hammer out political accommodations on comprehensive K–12 policies. And in still other states there were promises by governors of ambitious moves forward once prosperity returned (Harp 1994).

BIG BUSINESS INVOLVEMENT

The most dramatic political change associated with the 1980s reform movement was the emergence of corporate executives, organizations, and networks as education policy actors. Big business, prior to 1980, had not sought such policy involvement. Participation was largely confined to school finance issues, with the typical reaction being one of opposition to "expensive" state reforms. Business interests also were active in pressing for tax limitation measures, which in states like Massachusetts crippled public school support (Timpane 1984). But in the 1980s big business entered state education policy arenas in full force. Whether motivated by self-interest related to workforce needs, by a sense of crisis rooted in vulnerability to global economic competition, or by a belief in corporate civic responsibility (McGuire 1990), big business suddenly became a big player, working in tandem with governors and other political leaders in pressing for K–12 reform initiatives.

State Business Roundtables, or like organizations, set up task forces, special commissions, and study committees across the country (Borman, Castenell, and Gallagher 1993). Corporation executives also served on these bodies when they were created by political leaders. Business-sponsored studies were conducted, proposals were put forward, money was solicited, lobbying was undertaken, and public relations campaigns were mounted. The business community in many states became a core member of the coalition advocating education reform and a central contributor to that coalition's political influence.

That big business was a new and significant actor in state school policymaking during the 1980s and into the 1990s is hardly to be doubted. The evidence for such an influence assessment is compelling (Berman and Clugston 1988; Borman, Castenell, and Gallagher 1993; Chance 1986; Fuhrman 1989; Massell and Fuhrman 1994; Mueller and McKeown 1986). Yet just as with governors, the impact of business as an education policy actor should not be exaggerated. These interest groups were not uniformly influential on K–12 policy issues across the states, nor were they as unified or powerful in comparison to other system actors as might be supposed, given the tremendous resources and privileged access of corporate enterprise within the American polity (Lindblom 1977).

In a few states, the power of big business does appear to have decisively shaped K–12 reform legislation. In Texas, this influence largely emanated from computer executive H. Ross Perot who steered—or steamrollered, depending on the account—that state's 1984 school reform package into law (Chance 1986; Lutz 1986a; McNeil 1988). In Georgia, business officials representing the state's multinational corporations were portrayed as exercising dominant influence on the governor-appointed commission which paved the way for that state's 1985 Quality Basic Education Act (Fuhrman 1989, pp. 66–67). Still, these were not typical patterns. Even in states such as Arizona, Arkansas, Kentucky, Florida, and South Carolina where business influence was clearly very substantial, it was hardly controlling (Alexander 1986; Collins 1990; Hatic and La Brecque 1989; Osborne 1988; Timar and Kirp 1988). This was even truer in states with intensely pluralistic politics like California and, on a much smaller scale, Minnesota. The California Business Roundtable and the Minnesota Business Partnership were certainly among the key actors in moving their states toward K–12 reform (Berman and Clugston 1988). They operated, however, in intensely competitive systems where all manner of executive, legislative, agency, and interest group actors contended for policy influence (Kirst 1983; Mazzoni and Clugston 1987). In still other states analyzed by scholars—for example, Missouri, New York, and Wisconsin—the role of big business in the 1980s reforms seems to have been quite modest, at least until near the end of the decade (Cibulka and Derlin 1992; Farnham and Muth 1989; Hall 1989; Layton 1986).

Constraints on corporate influence in education policymaking were many and serious. The most basic was the lack of legislative authority. As with any lobbying group, big business had to have the backing of governors and key lawmakers for its initiatives to gain agenda status and to have any prospect of passage. State political leaders were generally welcoming and supportive when it came to corporate involvement in education reform—and close working relationships, particularly with governors, were established. Political leaders were not, however, the captives or pawns of business interests. Governors and legislators could—and often did—select, adapt, and reformulate proposed innovations to suit their own policy and political requirements (e.g., see Mazzoni and Clugston 1987). Political leaders, not business leaders, held the policy reins.

Nor were state business interests as broadly representative or politically cohesive as "the business community" label implies. While corporation executives acting through Business Roundtables and other organizations sought to rally business around the cause of reforming public education—and enjoyed considerable success—some business interests were not well represented. In particular, as McGuire (1990, p. 114) observes, "small businesses and small business organizations have not become major players." And more marginalized groups—for example, women and nonwhite business owners—were reported to have had little voice in the councils of business elites (Borman, Castenell, and Gallagher 1993, p. 69). The elites who counted most were those representing America's big multinational corporations, the business sector most closely linked to the competitive demands of the global marketplace.

As a state policy actor, the business lobby was fragmented, "even Balkanized" (Rosenthal 1993, p. 151). A state's business community consisted of a number of distinct interests, often in conflict and competition with one another (Thomas and Hrebenar 1990). In some states, a broad consensus was forged around a school reform plan. In other states, however, different business groups put forward different—and rival—proposals, with one important line of cleavage being over whether or not business should throw its political weight behind privatization, vouchers, and public funding of private schools (Weisman 1991a). And in still other states, business interests divided sharply over whether school reform justified tax increases. Such was the case, for example, in Florida when its 1983 reform package was at issue in the legislature (Alexander 1986).

Along with being internally split along interest fissures, state business lobbies in pursuing their vision of school reform had to operate in highly pluralistic political environments. By the mid-1980s, state education policy systems had become congested with individuals and groups trying to set agendas and shape decisions. The mainline K–12 groups representing teachers, administrators, and boards had been joined over the decades by a myriad of other organized interests in education. In addition, noneducation groups other than business—for example, parent, civic, urban, labor, farm, and foundation groups—wanted to have a crack at changing schools. Crowded arenas and competitive politics constrained the influence of any particular group. "There are so many interests and so much pressure in the statehouses that only a few demands go unopposed," observes one scholar of state politics. "Policymaking in many places is more pluralistic than before and any single interest is less likely to dominate" (Rosenthal 1993, p. 216).

Finally, for all its impressive resources—wealth, status, organization, access, and "strategic position," among them (Hayes 1992, p. 49)—big business was not generally the most influential interest group operating in state education policy systems. If big business appeared by mid-decade to be in the ascendancy in these systems (McDonnell and Pascal 1988), it was largely because powerful political leaders had aligned with corporate interests in many states to produce school reform legislation. When it got down to head-to-head conflict in the legislature, as it occasionally did on such issues as career ladders, testing of teachers, and school choice, the countervailing power of the teacher unions and other education interest groups significantly constrained the policymaking influence of big business as well as that of other reform proponents (Cibulka and Derlin 1982; Fiore 1990; Fowler 1988; Mazzoni 1988; Rudiak and Plank 1992).

Two major studies done in the 1980s provide attributional data as to the relative influence of big business, teacher unions, and other interest groups in state policymaking. Comparative research by Marshall, Mitchell, and Wirt (1986) in Arizona, California, Illinois, Pennsylvania, West Virginia, and Wisconsin involved extensive interviews with education policy actors—legislators, executive members, agency administrators, lobbyists, and so on. As part of the study, respondents rated the education policy influence of 18 state actors. The overall assessments for 1982–85, when put into rank orders, portrayed "all education interest groups combined" (ranked fourth) and "teachers' organizations" (ranked fifth) as being in what the study authors call the Near Circle of power (pp. 351–52). These groups ranked behind only legislators and CSSOs as policy influentials and ahead, surprisingly, of governors (ranked sixth). As for business organizations, they were considered under the rubric "non-education groups," a category of actor which in the composite rankings finished a distant 14th. In just one of the six states—Arizona—was there a ranking (fifth) which placed business interests in the Near Circle (p. 355).

The second study offering comparative evidence was a national survey conducted in the latter part of the 1980s by Thomas and Hrebenar (1990, p. 144–145), updated for each state in 1989. In this reputational study, which was of a general nature and did not specify any particular policy domain, the "school teachers' organizations" were more frequently identified by the participating political scientists in each of the 50 states as belonging in the "most effective" category (in 43 states) than any other interest group. Ranked second were "general business organizations," being placed in the most effective category in 31 states. Study authors (Thomas and Hrebenar 1991) conclude that business, "despite its fragmentation," was the "most widespread and powerful interest active at both the national and state levels" in the United States (p. 74). They go on to add, however, that "overall in the 50 states the most prevalent, active, and influential interest is education, especially…the state-level education association" (p. 75).

NATIONAL ORGANIZATION AND NETWORK INFLUENCES

State education policy systems by the 1990s had become enveloped and interpenetrated by national organizations and connecting networks. Their pervasiveness represented an expansion of influences that had been evolving for decades. The professional associations, the oldest networks, had sustained impact on K–12 policymaking dating back into the last century (Iannaccone 1967). And a school finance network of "academic scribblers" was pointed to some three decades ago by researchers as having "enormously influenced the course of educational policy throughout the Northeast—and beyond" (Bailey and others 1962, p. 24). In the mid-1960s the first nationwide compact for education—the Education Commission of the States—was formed; and this "network of networks" (Kaplan and Usdan 1992, p. 671), though rarely a major state-level policy influence, had fostered much dialogue and many connections over the years among its political and education constituencies (Layton 1985). In the early 1970s, an amply funded and tightly organized advocacy network was created by the Ford Foundation, working with the federal government's National Institute of Education, to champion school finance reform in targeted states across the country (Kirst, Meister, and Rowley 1984). By the end of the seventies the "equity network" was identified as an actor in 11 of the 28 states which overhauled their school funding formulas (Odden 1981). Other national organizations and networks were also pointed to during that decade as exerting agenda-setting influence on the issues of collective bargaining, minimum competency testing, and scientific creationism (Kirst, Meister, and Rowley 1984). During 1980s there was continued proliferation of these organizations and networks, constituting by the close of that decade a "web of coalitions and advocacy groups...ubiquitous in shaping public policy" (Kaplan and Usdan 1992, p. 666).

In the first rank of national organizations and networks were those containing state political leaders. Along with the Education Commission of the States, the National Conference of State Legislatures, the Council of Chief State School Officers, and other such organizations accelerated their education policy activities in the 1980s. Still, the one that clearly moved to the front in that decade—and stayed there—was the National Governors' Association (NGA). Indeed, it was the use by state governors of a collective policy voice through the NGA that most clearly distinguished their activism on school reform issues in the 1980s from any previous period of involvement. In 1985, under the leadership of Governor Alexander of Tennessee, the

NGA began for the first time to concentrate on public policy issues, with the first such issue to receive in-depth attention being education. The NGA's report *A Time for Results* (1986) gave a strong nationalizing impetus to second-wave reforms by disseminating "restructuring" proposals across the states, by emphasizing their priority—and providing rationales—for individual governors willing to champion the cause, and by putting the staff resources as well as the prestige resources of the NGA behind them. As Massell and Fuhrman (1994, p. 18) observe: "NGA can take ideas in good currency among policy specialists and professionals and grant them widespread political legitimacy. National action can be used as potential leverage for change within states."

Along with consensus-building, disseminating, and legitimating functions, the NGA grasped the opportunity afforded by President Bush's 1989 Education Summit to gain greatly enhanced visibility and policy influence in setting a national education reform agenda. While it is hard to say whether, in Pipho's (1989, p. 182) words, "the President took his cue from governors or whether key governors were able to make their agendas overlap with the White House," agreement was reached at the Summit on the need for national goals in education. And it was an NGA-created task force that fashioned the six basic goals, which along with a set of 21 related objectives—and after "tough negotiations" between White House officials and key governors, Clinton of Arkansas and Campbell of South Carolina—were embraced by both the President and the governors (Walker 1990, p. 17). The NGA also declared the commitment of each governor to review state goals and education performance "in light of these national goals" (National Governors' Association 1990, p. 39). Finally, governors were well represented on the National Education Goals Panel which was to prepare annually a report on goal achievement. By 1990, then, America's 50 governors had projected their collective power on education issues into national as well as state policy arenas, an expression of influence that would have been unthinkable at the decade's outset.

A second major nationalizing force was big business. No set of individuals and groups was more "networked" than was the

corporate sector—and education became in the 1980s a mobiliz-
ing focus for these relationships. National business organizations and their executive heads played a highly visible role in
stimulating, defining, and expanding the movement for school
reform (McGuire 1990, pp. 112–13). By 1990, the most powerful
of these groups—the Business Roundtable (representing CEOs
from the nation's largest private corporations), the National Alliance of Business, the National Association of Manufacturers,
and the U.S. Chamber of Commerce, among other business organizations—had come together to form a coalition to promote
education reform nationwide. Business Roundtable executives
made it clear that they intended to make a long-term commitment; that they sought fundamental change in America's
schools; and that they wanted to cultivate linkages to—and en-
large their influence in—state policy arenas. The primary strategy for doing the last was to have Roundtable CEOs contact
governors in all the states in which their businesses had close
ties, with the intent of forging relationships, discussing issues,
and formulating plans of action (Pipho 1990). The Business
Roundtable also set forth nine criteria for identifying "essential
components of a successful education system," and urged local
business leaders to apply these as a standard in conducting
"gap" analyses in their states (Borman, Castenell, and Gallagher
1993).

After a decade of effort, big business and its expanding networks seemed more determined than ever in the early 1990s to
be "movers and shakers in school policy" (Kaplan and Usdan
1992, p. 667). But, as has been emphasized earlier, big business
organizations confronted pluralistic state systems in which they
were only one of many influences at play. Unsurprisingly, the
initial efforts to undertake gap analyses, which took place in
Connecticut and Iowa, encountered political difficulty. It was
reported that in both states "the public and the education community were unenthusiastic or hostile" (Weisman 1991b, p. 22).
Moreover, in recession-depressed Connecticut "the ambitious
analysis was quickly blown aside by the fury of the state's bitter
budget battle" (p. 22). While business leaders, following an extensive publicity and grassroots effort, could claim impact on
Iowa's strategic plan, they were not the only force shaping it.

And the independent power of gap analyses as a lever for changing education policy remained an open question as this Roundtable initiative spread to other states.

The activism of political and business networks was matched by that of the educational associations; for they, too, stepped up their policy involvement in the 1980s. The most powerful were the national teacher unions—NEA and AFT—which for years had sought to influence state-level issues. In the 1960s and 1970s, for example, these two organizations led a nationwide push to have state governments enact collective bargaining legislation. Their advocacy, according to Kirst, Meister, and Rowley (1984, p. 14), resulted in "the popularity and spread of collective bargaining statutes in the states." In the 1980s, the teacher unions moved to the forefront in promoting teacher professionalism, school-based management, and other teacher-empowering components of school restructuring (Ogawa 1993).

A quite different manifestation of the influence of professional associations was that exerted by subject-matter organizations of educators. These organizations, like other education groups, were caught in a reactive mode by the first wave of school reforms. They had relatively little influence on its policy direction. But starting in the mid-1980s with the pioneering work of the National Council of Teachers of Mathematics (NCTM), this began to change. NCTM's curriculum and evaluation standards for mathematics were published in 1989; and, by 1993, they were reported as having widespread impact on state policies relating to curriculum content and teacher preparation (Massell and Fuhrman 1994). Following the lead of NCTM, other professional associations began the process of developing and disseminating curriculum and evaluation standards for their respective subject matters. This development, which Massell and Fuhrman (1994, p. 14) attribute partly to "NCTM's success" and partly to "the rise of systemic reform ideas on the public issue-attention cycle," created another access channel for professional as well as nationalizing influences on state education policy systems.

Besides the standards-raising thrust, organizations and individuals came together in national networks during the 1980s to champion other policy initiatives—for example, networks promoting America 2000 (the Bush administration's school reform plan), public school choice, outcome-based education, and school-based management. The last of these was examined in a revealing study by Ogawa (1993) who found that "a relatively small set of actors shaped and promoted school-based management in the national arena" (p. 39). The key actors were four organizations "linked by a network...if only loosely so" (p. 40). The chief initiator of this network was a private foundation, the Carnegie Corporation, and its creation, the Carnegie Forum on Education and the Economy (CFEE). Joining forces with CFEE was a political association (NGA), a teacher union (AFT), and a policy research center (CPRE). These organizations could draw upon ample, diverse, and complementary resources; and they were energized by highly motivated and politically skilled policy entrepreneurs. Network activists, among their many influence tactics, publicized reports, convened meetings, sponsored research, cultivated personal relationships, and lobbied state lawmakers. While the bulk of network activity in "spreading the word" about school-based management was aimed at local school districts and schools, information-sharing was employed, primarily through the NGA connection, to persuade state policy actors as well.

National organizations and networks as influences on state education policy systems continued to surface in the 1990s, pushing sometimes for reforms and sometimes against them. One focal issue for contending influences were state ballot or legislative initiatives which sought to provide public funding through "vouchers" for parents of private school students. On this issue, a new national advocacy organization was formed in late 1993, just before California voters by a large margin rejected a hotly contested school-voucher ballot initiative. (Voucher proposals had also been voted down in 1990 in Oregon and in 1992 in Colorado.) Political linkages for the new organization—Americans for School Choice—were mirrored in its board of directors, which included two former secretaries of education, three governors, and several state legislators, among its prestigious and well-connected members (Olson 1993b). The organization's stated mission was to build state-level advocacy groups, either by establishing them or by linking to existing groups. Warned its executive director: "The California initiative will be the last time school choice will be fought on a single battlefield" (Olson 1993a, p. 17). Americans for School Choice planned by 1996 to have mobilized proponents around either ballot initiatives or legislative lobbying in 25 states. On the other side of the voucher issue, education interest groups and their allies had already put together blocking coalitions of formidable strength, coalitions which not only could draw upon the resources of state education organizations, particularly the powerful teacher unions, but also—if pressed—upon the financial and political resources of their national associations and networks.

Another focal issue for contending national forces was "outcome(s)-based education" (OBE). The idea of redesigning K–12 systems around challenging outcomes and high standards for student performance had come by the close of the decade to hold great appeal for reformers, with such influential organizations as the NGA and Business Roundtable, plus many federal and state officials, calling for systemic approaches to school reform. By the early 1990s, legislative and state board initiatives to translate this idea into policy were underway in a variety of forms and under a variety of rubrics across the country. But in some states, beginning with Pennsylvania in 1992 (McQuaide and Pliska 1993), the specification of outcomes as the drive elements in proposed OBE systems became engulfed in heated public controversy.

Criticisms of outcome-based education (e.g., Schlafly 1993) ranged over a wide spectrum, from language vagueness and implementation costs to bureaucratic intrusiveness. Proposed outcomes that touched upon the ethics, character, or attitudes of students sparked the angriest outcry. Deep divisions surfaced, often in polarizing confrontations, over what values the schools should teach and who—government officials, professional educators, or parents of students—should determine these values (McQuaide and Pliska 1993). Much of the opposition seemed to be homegrown, reflecting varied constituencies and concerns within a particular state. But national religious and conservative groups, linked through extensive networks, also became visible and vocal participants in fanning the fires of populist discontent. Outcome-based education became targeted for counter-mobilization in more than a dozen states by Religious Right and conservative "pro-family" organizations, such as the Citizens for Excellence in Education, the Christian Coalition, and the Eagle Forum (Olson 1993c; Schlafly 1993; Simonds 1993). The pressures generated were apparently widespread and inhibiting. Leading the charge for outcomes-based systems suddenly became politically hazardous for elected officials, some of whom were reported to be "backpedaling" in reaction to grassroots contacts and vociferous criticism (Olson 1993c). As assessed by the director of a national OBE network, there was "intense political pressure—organized political pressure—being placed on many, many districts in many, many states not to do this" (Spady as quoted in Olson 1993c).

To point to the growing involvement of national organizations and networks in state education policymaking is not to say that they eclipsed the power of more proximate actors. Governors, legislators, bureaucrats, and interest groups exercised preponderant influence over most issues and over most stages of policymaking (Marshall, Mitchell, and Wirt 1986; Massell and Fuhrman 1994; Rosenthal 1990; Rosenthal 1993). Moreover, these actors generally welcomed—and often actively sought out—ideas, information, and proposals from outside their borders: from other states, from their political and professional associations, and from broader policy networks. There were, of course, marked variations in all of this. There was no uniform pattern for networks; they differed in size, composition, resources, leadership, and other policy-relevant dimensions. And the states, themselves, varied on a host of dimensions that affected their permeability to external influences. A state's political culture was probably the most salient of these. This culture and the "assumptive worlds" of its policymakers (Marshall, Mitchell, and Wirt 1989) fundamentally shaped the impact that national organizations and networks could have on a particular state education policy system (Kirst, Meister, and Rowley 1984).

CONTINUITY AND CHANGE

Looking back over the ten-year period of state activism on school reform issues suggests five concluding observations. *The first is that this activism, for all its remarkable sweep and intensity, did not mark an abrupt break with the past.* It built on decades of more gradual state involvement, involvement which cumulatively had evolved to the point where, a full ten years before *A Nation at Risk,* a 50-state survey of formal enactments revealed a "massive structure" of state education policy (Wirt 1977, p. 186). And the 1970s, most notably in extensive state policymaking on accountability and minimum competency issues, provided more immediate precursors for the 1980s reform thrust. Nor were the basic processes of state education policymaking transformed by the education excellence movement. Pluralistic, politicized, and open policy systems had emerged by 1980 in many—probably most—American states (Murphy 1982; Rosenthal and Fuhrman 1981).

A second observation is that the policy eruption of the 1980s accelerated as well as reflected the pluralism, politicization, and openness of state education policy systems. Pluralism grew with the infusion of new activists around reform issues, big business in particular becoming widely and powerfully represented on these issues. Previously stable systems were penetrated by new interests, giving rise to more complex, participatory, and public decision-making in which a multiplicity of actors sought to command influence over outcomes. National organizations and networks added to the volatility of the mix by putting their causes on state policy agendas and by pressing for their passage—or defeat.

Politicization became more marked as governors and legislators became deeply involved in policy decisions about school quality as well as about school funding. Education became a focus for political competition, a process intensified by dispersed institutional power, high career stakes, short-term orientations, and ongoing media scrutiny. Divided government, mounting partisanship, and executive-legislative rivalry injected additional turbulence and contentiousness into education policymaking, particularly when revenues became tight and competing policy issues pressed hard.

Openness expanded as policymaking processes became more accessible, as education reform became a front-burner media topic, and as state actors became more and more linked to broader organizations and networks. System openness enhanced system responsiveness to the mounting press of external demands. Reform "waves" and "mini-waves" (Cuban 1990), shifts in the federal stance and its political ideology, court rulings on school finance and education reform, promotional activities of national organizations and networks—among other outside forces—left an ever-growing legacy and layering of policy in state statutes and regulations.

A third observation is that governors and big business, usually as coalitional partners, took on a vastly expanded initiating role in state education policy systems. Though they did not typically dominate or control these systems—and their influence was often much constrained by competing actors and countervailing power, especially that of legislators and education interest groups—governors and big business were constantly at the forefront during the eighties in pushing for K–12 reforms. And to the surprise of many observers they stuck with that issue, both at the state level and through their influential national organizations, into the 1990s. Interstate and global economic competition proved to be a compelling dynamic in motivating sustained attention and policy-oriented activity.

A fourth observation is that nationalizing influences increasingly shaped state education policymaking. These influences took varied forms. The most obvious was the push and pull of federalism. Federal "push," symbolic as well as substantive, persuaded, induced, or pressured states into enlarging their policy activism on federal priorities. Federal "pullback" also could stimulate this activism, since interests not satisfied at the federal level often turned their lobbying energies to the state level. The Reagan and Bush administrations strategically combined both push (bully pulpit exhortations) and pull (federal devolution) to become a political source of nationalizing influence, an influence that was abetted and amplified by national commission reports and media publicity.

Another powerful nationalizing influence was to be found in state fiscal dependence on the health of the national economy.

When it surged, state treasuries overflowed with revenues; and expensive school reform initiatives could be undertaken—or enlarged. When it stumbled, budgetary shortfalls prevailed; and the tide of education reform ebbed, with activity being mostly restricted to low-cost initiatives, regulatory adjustments, and symbolic posturing. State education policy systems had no control over the occurrence or amplitude of the boom-and-bust cycles on which their fiscal condition heavily depended. Their capacity for policy innovation became energized or enervated by the cyclical health of the national economy.

National organizations and networks were yet another source of nationalizing influence. Though these forces appear to have had a telling impact on the enactment stage of the OBE issue—at least in some states—the greatest impact of national organization and networks was usually on the early stages of policymaking. Collectively, they helped define issues, configure public debate, and set agendas for governmental action. They could—and did—make extensive use of the amplifying power of mass media and the linking power of computer-based communications technology. Through their promotional activities, national organizations and networks contributed to the rapid circulation of policy proposals through state capitals and to the accelerated as well as the nationwide diffusion of policy innovations. Increasing economic competition among the American states heightened their receptivity to network-promoted policy initiatives, as did mounting political competition within states among elected officials who often saw in these initiatives the opportunity to gain credit, acquire status, and retain office—as well as the opportunity to solve problems and realize ideals.

A fifth observation is that state education policy systems became arenas for political confrontation between contending national organizations and networks. By early 1994, these mobilized forces were embroiled in conflict with one another in a number of states over several explosive issues. One was outcome-based education which pitted, at the network level, national reform advocates of diverse sorts and linkages against the Religious Right and its conservative allies. Another was the school voucher issue where newly formed organizations were being geared up to fight for ballot or legislative initiatives on dozens of state battlefields, efforts that were certain to encounter all-out opposition from other organizations, especially those representing the education associations. The issues involved in these network confrontations cut deep; they raised questions of values as well as of interests. They promised—or threatened—to institute basic structural changes, changes widely perceived as having profound redistributive implications. They could be couched in evocative, motivating symbols and slogans. Outcome-based education and vouchers were, in short, the kind of reform issues around which broad-based networks could be mobilized and their partisans propelled into the political arena. That such mobilization was occurring nationwide was clear by the end of 1993; that it would make a decisive difference for both politics and policies on these issues—and, perhaps, on the course of education reform generally in the United States—seemed likely given the increasing openness of state education policy systems to outside influences, and the scope, power, and zeal of the contending organizations and networks.

REFERENCES

Achilles, C. M., Lansford, Z., and Payne, W. H. (1986). Tennessee educational reform: Gubernatorial advocacy. In V. D. Mueller and M. P. McKeown (Eds.), *The fiscal, legal, and political aspects of state reform of elementary and secondary education* (pp. 223–244). Cambridge, MA: Ballinger.

Alexander, K. (1986). Executive leadership and educational reform in Florida. In V. D. Mueller and M. P. McKeown (Eds.), *The fiscal, legal, and political aspects of state reform of elementary and secondary education* (pp. 145–168). Cambridge, MA: Ballinger.

Alexander, K. (1990). The courts and the governor show the way in Kentucky. *Politics of Education Bulletin, 16*(3), 1–3.

Astuto, T. A., and Clark, D. L. (1986). The effects of federal education policy changes on policy and program development in state and local education agencies (occasional paper #2). Bloomington, IN: Policy Studies Center.

Bailey, S. K. et al. (1962). *Schoolmen and politics.* Syracuse, NY: Syracuse University Press.

Beyle, T. L. (1990). Governors. In V. Gray, H. Jacob, and R. B. Albritton (Eds.), *Politics in the American states*, 5th ed. (pp. 201–251). Glenview, IL: Scott, Foresman.

Beyle, T. L. (1992). *Governors and hard times*. Washington, DC: CQ Press.

Beyle, T. L. (1993). Being governor. In C. E. Van Horn (Ed.), *The state of the states*, 2nd ed. (pp. 79–114). Washington, DC: CQ Press.

Berman, P., and Clugston, R. (1988). A tale of two states: The business community and educational reform in California and Minnesota. In M. Levine and R. Trachtman (Eds.), *American business and the public schools* (pp. 121–149). New York: Teachers College Press.

Borman, K., Castenell, L., and Gallagher, K. (1993). Business involvement in school reform: The rise of the business roundtable. In C. Marshall (Ed.), *The new politics of race and gender* (pp. 69–83). London: Falmer Press.

Boyd, W. L. (1988). How to reform schools without half trying: Secrets of the Reagan administration. *Educational Administration Quarterly, 24*(3), 299–309.

Bracey, G. W. (1991). Why can't they be like we were? *Phi Delta Kappan, 73*(2), 105–117.

Brown, P. R., and Elmore, R. F. (1983). Analyzing the impact of school finance reform. In N. Cambron-McCabe and A. Odden (Eds.), *The changing politics of school finance* (pp.107–138). Cambridge, MA: Ballinger.

Burlingame, M., and Geske, T. (1979). State politics and education: An examination of selected multiple state case studies. *Educational Administration Quarterly, 15*(2), 50–79.

Caldwell, P. (1985, February 6). Governors: No longer simply patrons, they are policy chiefs. *Education Week, 4*(20), 1, 34.

Campbell, R. F., and Mazzoni, T. L. (1976). *State policy making for the public schools*. Berkeley, CA: McCutchan.

Chance, W. (1986). *The best of educations, reforming America's schools in the 1980s*. Olympia, WA: MacArthur Foundation.

Cibulka, J. G., and Derlin, R. L. (1992). State leadership for education restructuring: A comparison of two state policy systems. Paper presented at the annual meeting of the American Educational Research Association, San Francisco.

Clark, D. L., and Astuto, T. A. (1987). Federal education policy in the United States: The conservative agenda and accomplishments. *Educational Policy in Australia and America*, 47–76.

Clark, S. M. (1993). Higher education and school reform. *The Review of Higher Education, 17*(1), 1–20.

Collins, T. (1991). Reform and reaction: The political economy of education in Kentucky. Paper presented at the annual meeting of the Rural Sociological Society, Columbus, OH.

Cooper, B. S. (1988). School reform in the 1980s: The new right's legacy. *Educational Administration Quarterly, 24*(3), 282–298.

Cuban, L. (1990). Reforming again, again, and again. *Educational Researcher, 19*(1), 3–13.

Cuban, L. (1992). The corporate myth of reforming public schools. *Phi Delta Kappan, 74*(2), 157–159.

Doyle, D. P., and Hartle, T. W. (1985). *Excellence in education.* Washington, DC: American Enterprise Institute.

Durning, D. (1989). Governors' issue campaigns: An exploration. Paper presented at the annual meeting of the Southern Political Science Association, Memphis, TN.

Dye, T. R. (1990). *American federalism: Competition among governments.* Lexington, MA: Lexington.

Ehrenhalt, A. (1993). What if a real governor became president? In T. L. Beyle (Ed.), *State government* (pp. 121–124). Washington D.C: CQ Press.

Farnham, J., and Muth, R. (1989). Who decides, the politics of education in New York. Paper presented at the annual meeting of the American Educational Research Association, San Francisco.

Fiore, A. M. (1990). The efforts of educational interest groups to defeat merit pay for teachers in Pennsylvania: 1983–1986. Paper presented at the annual meeting of the Eastern Educational Research Association, Clearwater, FL.

Firestone, W. A. (1989). Educational policy as an ecology of games. *Educational Researcher, 18*(7), 18–24.

Firestone, W. A., Fuhrman, S. H., and Kirst, M. W. (1991). State educational reform since 1983: Appraisal and future. *Educational Policy, 5*(3), 233–250.

Fowler, F. C. (1988). The politics of school reform in Tennessee: A view from the classroom. In W. L. Boyd and C. T. Kerchner (Eds.), *The politics of excellence and choice in education* (pp. 183–198). London: Falmer Press.

Fuhrman, S. H. (1978). The politics and process of school finance reform. *Journal of Education Finance, 4*(4), 158–178.

Fuhrman, S. H. (1979). *State education politics: The case of school finance reform*, with contributions by J. Berke, M. Kirst, and M. Usdan. Denver: Education Commission of the States.

Fuhrman, S. H. (1987). Educational policy: A new context for governance. *Publius: The Journal of Federalism, 17*(3), 131–143.

Fuhrman, S. H. (1989). State politics and education reform. In J. Hannaway and R. Crowson (Eds.), *The politics of reforming school administration* (pp. 61–75). London: Falmer Press.

Fuhrman, S. H. (1990). Legislatures and education policy. Paper presented for the Symposium on the Legislature in the Twenty-First Century, Williamsburg, VA.

Fuhrman, S. H. (1993). The politics of coherence. In S. H. Fuhrman (Ed.), *Designing coherent education policy* (pp. 1–34). San Francisco: Jossey-Bass.

Geske, T. G. (1977–78). State educational policy-making: A changing scene? *Administrator's Notebook, 26*(2), 1–4.

Ginsburg, M. B. (Ed.) (1991). *Understanding educational reform in global context: Economy, ideology, and the state.* New York: Garland.

Gray, V. (1994). Competition, emulation, and policy innovation. In L. C. Dodd and C. Jillson (Eds.), *New perspectives on American politics* (pp. 230–248). Washington DC: CQ Press.

Guthrie, J. W., and Koppich, J. (1988). Exploring the political economy of national educational reform. In W. L. Boyd and

C. T. Kerchner (Eds.), *The politics of excellence and choice in education* (pp. 37–47). London: Falmer Press.

Hall, P. M. (1989). Policy as the transformation of intentions, act 1: Missouri's 1985 excellence in education act. Paper presented at the annual meeting of the American Educational Research Association, San Francisco.

Hamm, K. E. (1989). The evolution of state legislative education committees: Independent sources of power or parts of cozy triangles. Paper presented at the annual meeting of the American Educational Research Association, San Francisco.

Harp, L. (1993, September 22). Momentum for challenges to finance systems still seen strong. *Education Week, 13*(3), 22.

Harp, L. (1994, January 26). Running on hope. *Education Week, 13*(18), 27–29.

Hatic, H., and La Brecque, R. (1989). State education reform: Crisis and consensus. *Educational Policy, 3*(3), 217–231.

Hayes, M. T. (1992) *Incrementalism and public policy.* New York: Longman.

Herrington, C. D., Johnson, B., and O'Farrell, M. (1992). A legislative history of accountability in Florida: 1971–1991. Unpublished paper, Learning Systems Institute, The Florida State University.

Hilgartner, S., and Bosk, C. L. (1988). The rise and fall of social problems: A public arena model. *American Journal of Sociology, 94*(1), 53–78.

Holderness, S. T. (1992). The politics of state educational policymaking: Usefulness of the Kingdon model. In F. C. Wendel (Ed.), *Issues of professional preparation and practice* (pp. 17–31). University Park, PA: The Pennsylvania State University.

Iannaccone, L. (1967). *Politics in education.* New York: Center for Applied Research in Education.

James, T. J. (1991). State authority and the politics of educational change. In G. Grant (Ed.), *Review of Research in Education 17* (pp. 169–224). Washington DC: American Educational Research Association.

Jenkins, R. L., and Person, W. A. (1991). Educational reform in Mississippi: A historical perspective. In D. J. Vold and J. L. DeVitis (Eds.), *School reform in the deep south* (pp. 75–108). Tuscaloosa, AL: University of Alabama Press.

Johnson, B. L., Jr. (1993). In search of coherent reform policy at the state level: A longitudinal study. Paper presented at the annual meeting of the University Council for Educational Administration, Houston.

Jung, R., and Kirst, M. (1986). Beyond mutual adaptation, into the bully pulpit: Recent research on the federal role in education. *Educational Administration Quarterly, 22*(1), 80–109.

Kaplan, G. R. (1992). *Images in education: the mass media's version of America's schools.* Washington, DC: Institute for Educational Leadership and National School Public Relations Association.

Kaplan, G. R., and Usdan, M. D. (1992). The changing look of education's policy networks. *Phi Delta Kappan, 73*(9), 664–672.

Karper, J. H., and Boyd, W. L. (1988). Interest groups and the changing environment of state educational policymaking: developments in Pennsylvania. *Educational Administration Quarterly, 24*(1), 21–54.

Kingdon, J. (1984). *Agendas, alternatives, and public policy.* Boston: Little, Brown.

Kirst, M. W. (1983). The California business roundtable: Their strategy and impact on state education policy. Paper prepared for the Committee for Economic Development, New York.

Kirst, M. W. (1984). *Who controls our schools?* New York: Freeman.

Kirst, M. W. (1988). Recent state education reform in the United States: Looking backward and forward. *Educational Administration Quarterly, 24*(3), 319–328.

Kirst, M. W. (1990). *Accountability: Implications for state and local policymakers.* Washington D.C: Office of Educational Research and Improvement, U.S. Department of Education.

Kirst, M. W. (1994). A changing context means school board reform. *Phi Delta Kappan, 75*(5), 378–381.

Kirst, M. W., and Carver, R. (1994). School reform in Florida: A decade of change from 1983–1993. In D. Massell and S. Fuhrman, *Ten years of state education reform, 1983–1993: Overview with four case studies* (pp. 105–135). New Brunswick, NJ: Consortium for Policy Research in Education.

Kirst, M. W., Meister, G., and Rowley, S. (1984). Policy issue networks: Their influence on state policymaking. *Policy Studies Journal, 13*(1), 247–264.

Kirst, M. W., and Yee, G. (1994). An examination of the evolution of California state educational reform, 1983–1993. In D. Massell and S. Fuhrman, *Ten years of state education reform, 1983–1993: Overview with four case studies* (pp. 67–103). New Brunswick, NJ: Consortium for Policy Research in Education.

Layton, D. H. (1985). ECS at 20: New vitality and new possibilities. *Phi Delta Kappan, 67*(4), 272–276.

Layton, D. H. (1986). The regents action plan: New York's educational reform initiative in the 1980s. *Peabody Journal of Education, 63*(4), 6–22.

Lehne, R. (1978). *The quest for justice: The politics of school finance reform*. New York: Longman.

Lehne, R. (1983). Research perspectives on state legislatures and education policy. *Educational Evaluation and Policy Analysis, 5*(1), 43–54.

Lindblom, C. E. (1977). *Politics and markets: The world's political-economic systems*. New York: Basic Books.

Lutz, F. W. (1986a). Education politics in Texas. *Peabody Journal of Education, 63*(4), 70–89.

Lutz, F. W. (1986b). Reforming education in the 1980s. *Peabody Journal of Education, 63*(4), 1–5.

Malen, B., and Campbell, R. F. (1986). Public school reform in Utah: Enacting career ladder legislation. In V. D. Mueller and M. P. McKeown (Eds.), *The fiscal, legal, and political aspects of state reform of elementary and secondary education* (pp. 245–276). Cambridge, MA: Ballinger.

Marshall, C., Mitchell, D., and Wirt, F. (1986). The context of state-level policy formation. *Educational Evaluation and Policy Analysis, 8*(4), 347–378.

Marshall, C., Mitchell, D., and Wirt, F. (1989). *Culture and education policy in the American states.* London: Falmer Press.

Massell, D., and Kirst, M. W. (1986). State policymaking for educational excellence: School reform in California. In V. D. Mueller and M. P. McKeown (Eds.), *The fiscal, legal, and political aspects of state reform of elementary and secondary education* (pp. 121–144). Cambridge, MA: Ballinger.

Massell, D., and Fuhrman, S. (1994). *Ten years of state education reform, 1983–1993: Overview with four case studies.* New Brunswick, NJ: Consortium for Policy Research in Education.

Mazzoni, T. L. (1988). The politics of educational choice in Minnesota. In W. L. Boyd and C. T. Kerchner (Eds.), *The politics of excellence and choice in education* (pp. 217–230). London: Falmer Press.

Mazzoni, T. L. (1989). Governors as policy leaders for education: A Minnesota comparison. *Educational Policy, 3*(1), 79–90.

Mazzoni, T. L. (1993). The changing politics of state education policy making: A 20-year Minnesota perspective. *Educational Evaluation and Policy Analysis, 15*(4), 357–379.

Mazzoni, T. L., and Clugston, R. M. Jr. (1987). Big business as a policy innovator in state school reform: A Minnesota case study. *Educational Evaluation and Policy Analysis, 9*(4), 312–324.

Mazzoni, T., and Sullivan, B. (1986). State government and educational reform in Minnesota. In V. D. Mueller and M. P. McKeown (Eds.), *The fiscal, legal, and political aspects of state reform of elementary and secondary education* (pp. 169–202). Cambridge, MA: Ballinger.

McCarthy, M., Langdon, C., and Olson, J. (1993). *State education governance structures.* Denver: Education Commission of the States.

McDonnell, L., and Fuhrman, S. (1986). The political context of reform. In V. D. Mueller and M. P. McKeown (Eds.), *The fiscal, legal, and political aspects of state reform of elementary and secondary education* (pp. 43–64). Cambridge, MA: Ballinger.

McDonnell, L. M., and Pascal, A. (1988). *Teacher unions and educational reform*. New Brunswick, NJ: Center for Policy Research in Education.

McNeil, L. M. (1988). The politics of Texas school reform. In W. L. Boyd and C. T. Kerchner (Eds.), *The politics of excellence and choice in education* (pp. 199–216). London: Falmer Press.

McGivney, J. (1984). State educational governance patterns. *Educational Administration Quarterly, 20*(2), 43–63.

McGuire, K. (1990). Business involvement in the 1990s. In D. E. Mitchell and M. E. Goertz (Eds.), *Education politics for the new century* (pp. 107–117). London: Falmer Press.

McQuaide, J., and Pliska, A. (1993). The challenge to Pennsylvania's education reform. *Educational Leadership, 51*(4), 16–21.

Mitchell, D. E. (1981). *Shaping legislative decisions: Education policy and the social sciences*. Lexington, MA: Heath.

Mitchell, D. E. (1988). Educational politics and policy: The state level. In N. J. Boyan (Ed.), *Handbook of research on educational administration* (pp. 453–466). New York: Longman.

Mueller, V. D., and McKeown, M. P. (Eds.) (1986). *The fiscal, legal, and political aspects of state reform of elementary and secondary education*. Cambridge, MA: Ballinger.

Murphy, J. T. (1982). Progress and problems: The paradox of state reform. In A. Lieberman and M. W. McLaughlin (Eds.), *Policy making in education* (pp. 195–214). Chicago: National Society for the Study of Education.

Murphy, J. (Ed.) (1990). *The educational reform movement of the 1980s*. Berkeley, CA: McCutchan.

Nathan, R. P. (1993). The role of the states in American federalism. In C. E. Van Horn (Ed.), *The state of the states*, 2nd ed. (pp. 15–29). Washington D.C: CQ Press.

National Governors' Association (1990). *Educating America: State strategies for achieving the national education goals*. Washington, DC: National Governors' Association.

Odden, A. (1981). School finance: An example of redistributive policy at the state level. Paper prepared for the School Finance Project, National Institute of Education.

Odden, A., and Wohlstetter, P. (1992). The role of agenda setting in the politics of school finance: 1970–1990. *Educational Policy, 6*(4), 355–376.

Ogawa, R. T. (1993). The institutional sources of educational reform: The case of school-based management. Unpublished paper.

Olson, L. (1993a, November 10). Novel voucher plan suffers resounding defeat in California. *Education Week, 13*(10), 1, 17.

Olson, L. (1993b, November 17). Choice for the long haul. *Education Week, 13*(11), 27–29.

Olson, L. (1993c, December 15). Who is afraid of OBE? *Education Week, 13*(15), 25–27.

Osborne, D. (1988). *Laboratories of democracy.* Boston: Harvard Business School Press.

Pipho, C. (1979). *State activity: Minimum competency testing.* Denver: Education Commission of the States.

Pipho, C. (1986). Kappan special report: States move closer to reality. *Phi Delta Kappan, 68*(4), K1–K8.

Pipho, C. (1989). Can the states agree to national performance goals? *Phi Delta Kappan, 71*(4), 182–183.

Pipho, C. (1990). Coming up: A decade of business involvement. *Phi Delta Kappan, 71*(8), 582–583.

Pipho, C. (1993). Taxes, politics, and education. *Phi Delta Kappan, 75*(1), p. 6.

Plank, D. N. (1988). Why school reform doesn't change schools: Political and organizational perspectives. In W. L. Boyd and C. T. Kerchner (Eds.), *The politics of excellence and choice in education* (pp. 143–152). London: Falmer Press.

Plank, D. N., and Adams, D. (1989). Death, taxes, and school reform: Educational policy change in comparative perspective. *Administrator's Notebook, 33*(1), 1–4.

Prestine, N. A. (1989). The struggle for control of teacher education. *Educational Evaluation and Policy Analysis, 11*(3), 285–300.

Raimondo, H. J. (1993). State budgeting in the nineties. In C. E. Van Horn (Ed.), *The state of the states*, 2nd ed. (pp. 31–50). Washington D.C: CQ Press.

Ravitch, D. (1990, January 10). Education in the 1980s, a concern for quality. *Education Week, 9*(2), 48, 33.

Rosenthal, A. (1990). *Governors and legislatures: Contending powers*. Washington D.C: CQ Press.

Rosenthal, A. (1993). *The third house: Lobbyists and lobbying in the states*. Washington D.C: CQ Press.

Rosenthal, A., and Fuhrman, S. (1981). *Legislative education leadership in the states*. Washington D.C: Institute for Educational Leadership.

Rost, J. C. (1979). The times are changing in educational politics. *Thrust, 8*(5), 4–8.

Rudder, C. F. (1991). Educational reform in Alabama: 1972–1989. In D. J. Vold and J. L. DeVitis (Eds.), *School reform in the deep South* (pp. 109–130). Tuscaloosa, AL: University of Alabama Press.

Rudiak, B., and Plank, D. N. (1992). The politics of choice in Pennsylvania. Paper presented to the annual meeting of the American Educational Research Association, San Francisco.

Sacken, D. M., and Medina, M. Jr. (1990). Investigating the context of state-level policy formation. *Educational Evaluation and Policy Analysis, 12*(4), 389–402.

Schlafly, P. (1993). What's wrong with outcome-based education? *The Phyllis Schlafly Report, 26*(10), 1–4.

Simonds, R. L. (1993). A plea for the children. *Educational Leadership, 51*(4), 12–15.

Spring, J. (1988). *Conflict of interests: The politics of American education*. New York: Longman.

Thomas, C. S., and Hrebenar, R. J. (1990). Interest groups in the states. In V. Gray, H. Jacob, and R. B. Albritton (Eds.), *Politics in the American states*, 5th. ed. (pp. 123–157). Glenview, IL: Scott, Foresman.

Thomas, C. S., and Hrebenar, R. J. (1991). Nationalizing of interest groups and lobbying in the states. In A. J. Cigler and B. A.

Loomis (Eds.), *Interest group politics*, 3rd ed. (pp. 63–80). Washington D.C: CQ Press.

Timar, T. B., and Kirp, D. L. (1988). *Managing educational excellence*. London: Falmer Press.

Timpane, M. (1984). Business had rediscovered the public schools. *Phi Delta Kappan, 65*(6), 389–392.

Timpane, M.(1988). Some political aspects of accountability mandates. In E. K. Mosher and J. L. Wagoner, Jr. (Eds.), *The changing politics of education* (pp. 181–186). Berkeley, CA: Mc-Cutchan.

Tyack, D. (1993). School governance in the United States: Historical puzzles and anomalies. In J. Hannaway and M. Carnoy (Eds.), *Decentralization and school improvement* (pp. 1–32). San Francisco: Jossey-Bass.

Usdan, M. D., Minar, D. W., and Hurwitz, E. Jr. (1969). *Education and state politics*. New York: Teachers College Press.

Van Horn, C. E. (1993). The quiet revolution. In C. E. Van Horn (Ed.), *The state of the states,* 2nd ed. (pp. 1–14). Washington D.C: CQ Press.

Vold, D. J., and DeVitis, J. L. (1991). Introduction. In D. J. Vold and J. L. DeVitis (Eds.), *School reform in the deep south* (pp. 109–130). Tuscaloosa, AL: University of Alabama Press.

Walker, R. (1990, March 7). With goals in place, focus shifts to setting strategy. *Education Week, 9*(24), 1, 17.

Weisman, J. (1991a, September 18). In Indiana, business groups not talking as one on reform. *Education Week, 11*(3), 1, 18.

Weisman, J. (1991b, November 20). Business roundtable assessing state progress on reform. *Education Week, 11*(11), 22.

Wimpelberg, R. K., and Ginsberg, R. (1989). The national commission approach to educational reform. In J. Hannaway and R. Crowson (Eds.), *The politics of reforming school administration* (pp. 13–25). London: Falmer Press.

Wirt, F. M. (1977). State policy culture and state decentralization. In J. Scribner (Ed.), *Politics of education* (pp. 164–187). Chicago: National Society for the Study of Education.

Wohlstetter, P. (1994). Georgia: Reform at the crossroads. In D. Massell and S. Fuhrman, *Ten years of state education reform, 1983–1993: Overview with four case studies* (pp. 137–151). New Brunswick, NJ: Consortium for Policy Research in Education.

PART IV

LOCAL AUTONOMY IN THE LATE TWENTIETH CENTURY

7

CREATING "A NEW SET OF GIVENS"? THE IMPACT OF STATE ACTIVISM ON SCHOOL AUTONOMY[1]

Betty Malen
and
Donna Muncey
University of Maryland

Previous chapters in this volume demonstrate that since the 1970s, states have substantially, at times dramatically, increased

---

1 The phrase "creating a new set of givens" was coined by Tim Mazzoni in a telephone conversation about this chapter. We are grateful to Patricia Marin, who diligently tracked, secured and organized much of the literature we read to prepare this chapter. We thank Ed Andrews, Sydney Farivar, Barbara Finkelstein, Frances Fowler, Tim Mazzoni, Lise Reilly, and Jennifer Rice for their helpful comments on earlier versions of this chapter.

their involvement in education while simultaneously endorsing notions of local control. This chapter focuses on the impact of such persistent and pervasive state activism on school autonomy. Our purpose is to describe how the proliferation and accumulation of education policies enacted at the state level may be affecting organizational discretion at the site level. We begin with a brief discussion of the conceptual perspectives and data sources that undergird our analysis and the major limitations of our approach. Then we provide an overview of how this topic has been treated in the literature, illustrate how prominent characterizations may underestimate the power of the state, outline an alternative hypothesis, assess it, and highlight the implications of this analysis for future research. In essence, the chapter suggests why we should and how we might revisit the relationship between state activism and school autonomy.

CONCEPTUAL PERSPECTIVES, DATA SOURCES, AND LIMITATIONS

Our analysis reflects a set of assumptions about the nature of power, the ability of institutional actors to exert influence on units of the system, the indicators used to gauge the autonomy of schools, and the scope of judgements rendered. First, power is viewed as multidimensional. That is, it may be exercised through fairly direct and highly visible regulatory strategies (e.g., establishing rules, allocating or withholding resources, applying sanctions) and through less direct or more subtle symbolic processes (e.g., controlling agendas, shaping expectations, altering perceptions of problems, priorities, and possibilities).

Second, the relative power of actors at the state and site level is manifest in their ability to exercise influence on education policy. It is evidenced by their ability to initiate as well as react to, advance as well as constrain, actions during the various stages of policy articulation, formulation, and implementation (Mazzoni 1991; Malen and Ogawa 1988; Kingdon 1984). In other words, the relative power of actors can be gauged in part by the roles they assume, or prompt others to assume, during various phases of policymaking.

Third, the autonomy afforded organizations like schools can be assessed in a variety of ways (Boyne 1993; Davies and Henschke 1991). Given the complexity of the phenomenon, we incorporate multiple indicators. These include (a) the degree of formal authority site actors have to make binding decisions about critical aspects of their organization; (b) the web of rules embedded in the federal, state, or district policies, a web that encompasses the obligations as well as the regulations that circumscribe what individual schools may or must do (Boyne 1993); (c) the availability of resources at the disposal of site actors; and (d) the strength of various rewards or sanctions that individual schools may anticipate or higher authorities may impose. Taken together, these indicators help reveal whether and how schools may set their own directions as well as deliver required services.[2]

Fourth, the autonomy afforded organizations, like schools, is contingent on many contextual and institutional factors, including policies emanating from various levels of the system. Simply put, schools are nested in complex social, cultural, and political contexts that can reinforce or counteract the power of state policies. Schools are also subject to a host of federal and district policies that may complement or contradict state policies and may operate to enhance or restrict site autonomy. These factors complicate efforts to gauge the impact of state activism on site autonomy.

Fifth, assessments of the relative power of institutional actors and the potential impact of these power configurations on school autonomy are confined to the nature, not the merits, of these arrangements. Our intent is to characterize rather than

---

2 When compared with other organizations, public schools have less to say about key aspects of organizational life such as "decisions about the business to be in...the kinds of labour to be employed and how that labour is compensated...[and] the clients to be served..." (Davies and Hentschke 1994, pp. 99–101). However, when focusing on autonomy of interdependent units in the education system, it's hard to tell where decisions are really lodged. Still, these indicators help detect the discretion schools possess and track if/how that discretion has changed over time.

criticize or justify the governance dimensions of the state-site relationship.

Our analysis is necessarily suggestive. It relies heavily on a systematic review of articles based on case studies of state education policy implementation conducted from the late 1970s to the mid-1990s, as well as in-progress studies of the implementation of various education reforms. While case study data can reveal the multiple, often subtle ways state influence may be exercised or circumscribed, they cannot capture universal trends. Since some settings have been studied rather extensively while others have not, it is hard to know what patterns may be typical and what patterns may be exceptional.[3] And, since there are few multi-level, longitudinal studies, the ability to track state influence on sites over time is constrained. It is difficult to discern, for example, whether state influence may be episodic or enduring, incidental or incremental.

Further, states differ in their approaches to education reform (Mazzoni 1994; Fuhrman 1988). Their reform initiatives embody diverse priorities and strategies.[4] They vary in their comprehensiveness and aggressiveness as well as in their consistency,

---

3 Even where careful, longitudinal studies have been conducted, it may be difficult to sort out the key actors involved in creating policies, let alone the major effects of those policies on site autonomy. As Danielson and Hochschild (1998), in their summary interpretation of seventeen case studies of education reform in urban and metropolitan settings, express it: "...school boards have relatively minor policy roles everywhere, as do parents and community organizations. But other interactions follow no common patterns; the roles of superintendents, teachers' unions, legislative bodies, corporations, mayors, federal courts, and state education officials range from featured player to bit part in different places and at different times in the same place" (1998, p. 277). How such fluid political contexts shape school autonomy is rarely the major focus of education policy studies.

4 The reasons for the variance in state policymaking are not addressed here. Our point is simply that "No two states are likely to have identical experiences [in either the selection or implementation of education policies]. While patterns exist, variation in policy and process persists" (Fuhrman 1988, p. 64).

prescriptiveness, and persuasiveness (Tyree 1993). Insofar as the features of policy affect the strength of policy, different packages of state policies may have quite different consequences for site autonomy.

Moreover, the literature documents considerable variation in local responses to state actions (Fuhrman and Elmore 1995; Fuhrman 1994; McLaughlin 1987). In so doing, the literature often blurs the distinctions between district and site reactions to state policies. Although scholars acknowledge the "profound differences in how local schools make sense of [and respond to] state initiated changes" (Rossman and Wilson 1996, p. 416), it is difficult to distinguish between district and site reactions to state policies, especially when reports of case studies combine them under the generic category of "local responses." The detailed description required to differentiate district and site responses is often not available in the published pieces. For that reason, we sometimes refer to districts and sites as objects of state activity and examine the more generic "local responses" to state policy. However, the literature also portrays the district as a pivotal actor that can align with the state to restrict (or expand) site autonomy. Thus we also treat districts as arms or extensions of the state where that appears to be their major role.[5]

Finally, interpretations of power depend, in part, on one's vantage point. For example, state governments lament their inability to control sites while local agents resent the intrusion of the state. Both "takes" seem to "ring true" for actors in different positions of the system. Because this chapter focuses on studies of policy implementation, it tends to see power from the ground

---

5 We are indebted to Frances Fowler for pointing out that at times we situate the district with the site as if these levels were both elements of local control, and, at other times we situate the district with the state as if they were both elements of centralized control. While conceptually slippery, our treatment of the district reflects the multiple, pivotal roles districts may play. It also illustrates the importance of developing a stronger basis for clarifying the role of the district in education policy initiation and implementation (Spillane 1996; Drury 1999). But that task falls well beyond the scope of this chapter.

up, that is, from the vantage point of site actors. Hence it may be more sensitive to perceptions of state invasiveness than accounts of local evasiveness.

PROMINENT VIEWS OF STATE ACTIVISM AND SITE AUTONOMY

While writings on this topic contain diverse findings and interpretations, a central thesis in the literature is that state activism does not constitute a credible threat to local autonomy. For example, policy implementation studies carried out over the last three decades often indicate that educators at the district and site have the opportunity, inclination, and ingenuity required to effectively insulate the school and the people who work in it from a host of policies imposed from afar. The idea that "street-level bureaucrats" (Lipsky 1980) could unmake or remake policy faster than policy could influence organizational priorities and practices seems to capture the realities and, for some, the frustrations of state attempts to influence schools (Weatherly and Lipsky 1977; Elmore 1983; Malen and Hart 1987; Rossman and Wilson 1996). Whether the source of directives is federal, state, or district officials, it appears, to some, that the school site may be virtually untouchable. As Schon put it, when "outsiders" attempt to gain control through regulatory means, the efforts usually precipitate "games of control and escape from control...[wherein] locals are always able to foil or transform...distort or resist [the directives]" (1981, p. 59). Other scholars reach similar conclusions, albeit for different reasons.

For instance, Cohen and Spillane, relying less on individual gamesmanship and more on organizational structures to account for the preservation of local autonomy amidst intensified policy activity in the broader system, write that "the US political system was specifically designed to frustrate central power. Authority in education was divided among state, local and federal governments by an elaborate federal system and it was divided within governments by the separation of powers" (1992, p. 5). Commenting on federal and state policy activity in the 1960s and 1970s, they add:

New educational policies expanded central authority and drew the agencies of policy and practice
closer together. But these policies did not commensu-
rately reduce the autonomy of "lower level" agencies
[particularly in the domains of curriculum and in-
struction]. The flood of state and federal policies and
programs coursed through a large and loosely
jointed governance system, and agencies throughout
the system retain much of their operating independence. ...Despite the increasing flow of higher-level
requirements, advice and inducements, lower level
agencies have much room to interpret and respond
(Cohen and Spillane 1992, pp. 8–9).

Others like Rossman and Wilson point to the strength of local cultures, deeply ingrained norms, rituals, and "sacred" values to explain why "feisty, challenging responses to state-initiated mandates are alive and well in the local schools" (1996,
p. 417). The idea that various combinations of "local forces" can
overwhelm state policies has been broadly endorsed and essentially cast as a "lesson" that policymakers ought to heed (Mc-
Laughlin 1987).

Although many policy implementation studies offered different explanations for findings, they documented and at times
bemoaned the apparent inability of state governments to effectively influence school systems. As these writings accumulated,
it seemed that state efforts to reform schools by "remote control" (Cuban 1984) were doomed to modest, if not minuscule,
impact. The various combinations of wit and wizardry site actors used to duck and dodge directives, to create the appearance
of compliance, or to convert new initiatives into conventional
practices lent credence to observations that "schools change reforms as much as reforms change schools" (Cuban 1998, p. 453).

The power of the state has been open to question not simply
because studies of local responses to state initiatives tend to emphasize "the power of the bottom over the top" (Elmore 1983).
Various analyses of state actions revealed that states were not
deploying the full range of strategies required for policy initiatives to take hold (McDonnell and Elmore 1987) or aligning policies in ways that would allow them to complement and rein-

force rather than undermine or offset each other (Smith and O'Day 1991; O'Day and Smith 1993; Fuhrman 1993). But even when states adopted more comprehensive, and purportedly more coherent, approaches to education policy, the pattern of local responses suggested that both district and site actors made selective use of state policies. Local units embraced some initiatives and ignored others. While some state policies (most notably high-stakes testing and related accountability policies) penetrated the boundaries of school systems, others did not (Firestone et al. 1992).

The intriguing cases of creative defiance, the recurrent patterns of uneven implementation, the perennial problem of "local variation" (McLaughlin 1987; Fuhrman and Elmore 1995) and the apparent tendency of districts "to use policies that fit their own plans and fight the reforms that did not" (Firestone et al. 1992, p. 271) suggested that although states might have become involved in education policy, districts and sites tended to retain a protective armor that enabled them to deflect, diffuse, and otherwise diminish the influence of state actions. The findings of early implementation studies have been reiterated as scholars continued to report that, for a host of reasons, "authoritative direction and responsive compliance turn out to be the exception. The best that can usually be expected of efforts to get districts [and, by extension, sites] to implement state and federal policy is mutual adaptation through which central expectations adapt to local preferences at least as much as the opposite occurs" (Firestone et al. 1992, p. 257).

The power of the state was further challenged by findings that suggest local actors may have initiated education reforms quite apart from the pressure or persuasion of the state (F. M. Hess 1999; Fuhrman and Elmore 1990). For example, F. M. Hess argues that local districts have adopted "an endless stream of policy initiatives" (1999, p. 52) for reasons more closely associated with "professional reputation" and "community prestige" than state activism.[6] Other scholars point to settings where local

---

6 The conclusion that state policies were not very influential in these contexts may be in part, an artifact of how questions were asked.

action preceded state action, to districts that exceeded state expectations for compliance, and to situations where state policy may have been issued top-down, but was effectively crafted "bottom-up," because local actors provided ideas for and exercised considerable influence on the design of state reforms (Hertert 1996; Elmore and Sykes 1992; Firestone 1989). Using these sorts of developments to gauge the impact of state activism on local autonomy, some scholars conclude that state policy has "left not only considerable room for [local] flexibility but also enhanced local activism....The busier states became, the busier local districts became; everyone made more policy, and the arena of governance expanded" (Fuhrman and Elmore,1990, p. 82). In this view, state activity has not substantially eclipsed local autonomy as the "zero sum model" of inter-governmental relations might predict; rather, the state-local relationship is judged to be one of "mutual influence" (Fuhrman and Elmore 1990, p. 83; Elmore and Fuhrman 1995; Kirst 1995a; Spillane 1996).

POTENTIAL LIMITATIONS OF THE PROMINENT THESIS

While the prominent thesis is persuasive, it may represent a limited, potentially distorted characterization of the state-local relationship. Indications of mutual influence do not necessarily translate into patterns of symmetrical influence or even meaningful influence. Indeed, patterns of reciprocal influence, mutual adaptation, intensified action, and "street-level" transformation of policy may understate, even obfuscate, the manner in which state activism may be substantially constraining site autonomy. We focus on four ways the prominent view may be minimizing the power of the state.

For example, informants were asked to discuss the two most important local issues and the greatest local success that had occurred over the previous three years (Hess 1999, p. 90, 92).

UNDERESTIMATING THE
IMPACT OF AGENDA CONTROL

Over the last three decades, state officials have often dominated if not essentially controlled the education reform agenda
(McDonnell and Fuhrman 1986; Mazzoni 1994). While "setting
the agenda is not the same as getting one's way" (Kingdon 1984,
p. 24), the "ability to determine the official organizational
agenda is one of the most important sources of institutional
power" (Fischer 1990, p. 288). Indeed, those who control the
agenda may well wield the "supreme instrument of power," the
ability to define the issues and alternatives that will get governmental attention, consideration, and support (Schattsneider
1960). While it may be true that "[a]dministrators and teachers
usually can tailor higher level programs to local purposes and
conditions, if they have the will and take the time" (Cohen and
Spillane 1992, p. 11), the focus is on accommodating state priorities and "correcting" state policies more than determining
school priorities and creating site policies.

EQUATING INGENUITY
WITH AUTONOMY

Accounts of how site actors subvert state initiatives or accounts of how state policies spawn local activity may be a reflection of the ingenuity more than the autonomy of local actors.
The ability of local actors, notably teachers, to convert merit pay
and career ladder policies into uniform salary increases and familiar staffing practices is a telling case in point (Malen and
Hart 1987). In this case, state officials in Utah controlled the
agenda. Educators had very little influence on reform inputs. A
merit pay/career ladder statute was initiated, promoted and enacted despite the resistance of local educators (Malen and
Campbell 1985). While educators, notably teachers, secured
some concessions and inserted some protections that enabled
them to substantially influence reform outcomes during the implementation phase, they were in a reactive posture, maneuvering within the narrow parameters set by the new state rules and
the limited state funds. The state policy spawned a lot of local
activity, but much, if not most, of that activity was in anticipa-

tion of or in reaction to state overtures. The fact that site actors had some opportunity to remake policy turned out to be an indication of their limited, and arguably endangered, autonomy. Considerable energy was devoted to sorting through the confusion, figuring out how to address the goals set by others, searching for ways to accommodate the policy or remedy the problems attached to (or associated with) it. In short, the "opportunity" and, in the minds of some site actors, the necessity of remaking state policy can divert attention from and undermine the ability to advance site level initiatives (Malen and Hart 1987). Apparently this case is not unique (Kirp and Driver 1995).

CASTING THE EXCEPTION
AS THE RULE

Accounts of "assertive districts" (Hertert 1996, p. 383) that influence the development of state education policies or seemingly progressive districts that "take pride in being ahead of the state on most reforms" (Hertert 1996, p. 384) can make the exception appear to be the rule. In one study, more than 80 percent of the districts in the sample were not able to either "influence state policies or to insulate themselves from their effects....[The majority of districts] perceive state policies as having a significant impact on their daily operations and priorities" (Hertert 1996, p. 384). Other studies indicate that since the early 1980s, state governments have enacted education reforms without the endorsement and, in many instances, despite the objections of local units (McDonnell and Fuhrman 1986; Mazzoni 1991; Mazzoni 1994; Pipho 1991). These findings cast doubt on the ability of a vast number of local units to effectively direct or redirect state initiatives or to otherwise secure the legislative influence that select "assertive districts" may have exercised.

OVERLOOKING THE POSSIBILITY
OF IMPLICIT INFLUENCE

In settings where state action did not appear to stifle local activity or where local districts appeared to be charting the course for state education reform, the state could have been wielding considerable "implicit influence" (Dahl 1980, p. 25). That is, local units may have been developing policies in *antici-*

pation of state action, if not in response to state action. Either way, the state may be exercising influence in ways that effectively narrow the range of local options and ultimately restrict site autonomy. As earlier noted, local activity around the career ladder reform in Utah was both in anticipation of and in response to state action. Perhaps that explains some, if not all, the activity in districts that appear to be initiating their own reforms.

In these four ways, and perhaps in other ways, prominent views of the relationship between state activism and site autonomy may be underestimating the power of the state. Thus, we explore an alternative view.

AN ALTERNATIVE HYPOTHESIS

Recognizing that state activism is not necessarily equivalent to state influence (Fuhrman and Elmore 1990), that intergovernmental relationships need not fit a zero-sum scenario, and that the prominent thesis may underestimate the power of the state, we examine an alternative hypothesis—that state activism may constitute a credible threat to local autonomy. We probe the available evidence in an effort to determine whether the state may be influencing schools in multiple ways which, when taken together, significantly restrict the options open to and the degree of discretion available to site actors. This interpretation is cast as a hypothesis to be tested because the available evidence does not warrant a more definitive position. We explore this alternative hypothesis by using two general trends in state education policymaking as windows for looking at state-site governance relationships. Ironically, the first trend encompasses efforts to "relinquish" state control through various decentralization and deregulation policies. The second trend encompasses efforts to "reclaim" control, largely, but not solely, through performance standards and related testing requirements and accountability provisions.

APPARENT RELINQUISHING OF POWER:
DECENTRALIZATION AND DEREGULATION

Resurrected, in part, to correct the imbalance created by the rapid-fire expansions of rules and regulations that marked state responses to the "first wave" of education reform in the early 1980s, efforts to decentralize decisionmaking authority regained prominence in the "second wave" of education reform that occurred in the mid-1980s (Mazzoni 1994; Fuhrman and Elmore 1995; Wells and Oakes 1996) Whether nested in plans to redefine professional roles, in mandates to establish school-improvement teams, or in calls to institute site-based governance councils, state governments permitted, encouraged, or required schools to establish site-based governance bodies (Malen and Ogawa 1988; James 1991). Presumably, these bodies would be granted greater decisionmaking authority in the central domains of budget, personnel, and program. Even though their formal authority would be circumscribed by the web of rules embedded in existing statutes, regulations, accountability requirements, and/or contractual agreements as well as by the availability of resources, the promise was that site actors would have much greater discretion over key aspects of their organization.

In many instances, however, it was extraordinarily difficult to determine what if any new authority sites were granted, let alone whether that newfound authority translated into meaningful increases in organizational discretion (Bimber 1993; Malen, Ogawa, and Kranz 1990; Whitty, Power, and Halpin 1998). In other instances, the scope of authority delegated was modest, piecemeal, and temporary. In most if not all cases, site autonomy was sharply circumscribed by higher-level rules and scarce resources (Drury 1999). State policies that promised to deregulate schools or to move toward more flexible application of regulation were also weak in scope and impact (Fuhrman and Elmore 1995). Since demands for school improvement intensified, in part through legislative packages that exacted a price— stronger accountability for the promise of increased autonomy —the "bottom line" seemed to be a substantial, sustained increase in site responsibility but not a substantial, dependable expansion of site autonomy (Malen et al. 1990; Whitty et al. 1998). These broad claims are briefly illustrated.

SCOPE AND STABILITY OF "NEW" AUTHORITY

Since site autonomy is contingent, in part, on the formal policymaking authority granted schools in key domains of organizational decisionmaking, it is important to sift through the vague and varied efforts to decentralize decisionmaking and to map what "new" authority may have been delegated (Malen et al. 1990). When such an analysis is carried out, it appears that most moves to decentralize decisionmaking authority to the school level through various site-based management policies made minor changes in select domains of decisionmaking (Malen et al. 1990; Elmore 1993; Drury 1999).

For example, under site-based management plans, schools might be given authority over discretionary funds but were rarely given authority over their operating budgets[7] (Odden and Busch 1998). Likewise, schools might be given some latitude in how existing personnel positions could be allocated but they were rarely given additional posts and were typically required to hire from pre-approved lists. Save for settings that permit school councils to hire and fire their principals, evidence of a fundamental shift in decisionmaking authority in any, let alone all, the critical areas of budget, personnel, and instructional programming is rare. Even in reputedly exemplar cases such as Kentucky, the "far-reaching policymaking authority"

---

7 Writing about site-based management, Odden and Busch noted that "No state, even of the several that have endorsed strong school-based management, has proposed...that the bulk of education funds be budgeted to the school in a lump sum or described how such a new education finance structure would work..." (1998, p. 131). Information shared at a School Development Conference held in New York in July of 1999 indicates some New Jersey schools may be given the responsibility for their operating budgets. It is also possible that some charter schools may have more budgetary authority than was typically granted schools under site-based management plans.

(Russo 1995, p. 407; Sandridge et al. 1996) attributed to schools is more a lengthy list of topics school councils might consider than a clear indication these bodies have significant authority, particularly given the term limits and other dictates that make it hard for site actors to develop any real momentum and that make it clear that their primary role is to advise and recommend actions to others.

Whatever the degree of "new" authority sites may have been granted, the enabling legislation makes it clear that the state (or its designate) can retract powers delegated to schools or otherwise intervene to "apply remedial measures" on schools (Leithwood and Menzies 1998, p. 333; Weiss 1995). In June of 1995, the Illinois legislature did just that when it enacted a law that "gave sweeping new powers to a school district management team" (Shipps 1998, p. 161; Katz, Fine and Simon 1997). This team works with the mayor and a board of trustees appointed by the mayor, to "determine which schools require intervention; to dismiss, lay off, or reassign any and all personnel in them; and to dissolve elected Local School Councils. They are also empowered to cut costs, privatize work usually performed by employees, and abrogate many collective bargaining agreements" (Shipps 1998, p. 161). With this action, the "most radical" decentralization experiment in the nation, (i.e., the Chicago school reform) became a most poignant reminder of the ability of the state to institute a re-centralization model. As such, it underscores the temporary and dependent nature of state efforts to decentralize decisionmaking authority. Because decisionmaking authority that has been delegated can be retracted, school autonomy is always contingent on the will of the state.

RULE AND RESOURCE CONSTRAINTS

Since site autonomy is shaped by the web of rules and the availability of resources in the broader context, efforts to decentralize decisionmaking need to be scrutinized to see whether the rules and resources provide opportunities for, or operate as constraints on, site discretion. In some cases, state mandates or district regulations appeared to severely restrict site autonomy. As one review concluded, "for certain schools, increased authority consists solely of being permitted to make recommendations to the central administration" (Summers and Johnson 1996, p. 76). While there was some evidence of greater autonomy in other instances, even in reputedly exemplar sites and even under "ideal" conditions (White 1992), the actual authority afforded the site was highly circumscribed by the rules set elsewhere and by the limited money available for technical assistance and program enhancements (White 1992; Geraci 1995–96; Sandidge et al. 1996; Whitty et al. 1998; Drury 1999).

For example, studies of decentralization in Chicago revealed that even though site actors "were working very hard with insufficient resources and authority," the base level of funding for schools was cut. The persistent fiscal crises did "undermine much of the discretionary budget power of the [local school councils]" (Handler 1998, p. 10) and "forced schools to divert resources from planned improvements into maintenance of previously existing programs" (G. A. Hess, Jr. 1999, p. 81). In other settings schools were granted the power to manage budget reductions, not initiate school improvements (Malen 1994b).

Since proposals to delegate decisionmaking to school sites tend to be revived during times of intense fiscal stress, decentralization, at least in some contexts, appeared to be a "budget cutting exercise masquerading under the banner of schools getting more control of their own affairs" (Smyth 1995, p. 172; Malen 1994b). Further, since these proposals often failed to "fundamentally alter the web of policies, many of which originate not from the local districts but from the state and federal levels within which schools operate, the idea that [site-based management] involves decentralization of authority...to 'the school' was characterized, by some, as "a convenient fiction that masks considerable ambiguity and disagreement over...what decisions are supposed to be made at the school-site level" (Elmore 1993, p. 45; see also Malen et al. 1990, Malen 1994a, and Drury 1999). In short, the rule and resource constraints, coupled with the modest delegation of authority, suggest that efforts to decentralize decisionmaking did little to enhance site autonomy. As one review put it, "the locus of power remained where it has always been—with school boards, central office staffs, and state authorities" (Paik et al. 1999, p. 8)

To be sure, there have been some efforts on the part of state governments to "lift" state rules and regulations, at least for some schools (notably those deemed to be performing well), or to engage in forms of "differential regulation" that could range from rule waivers to school takeovers (Firestone and Nagle 1995). Generally viewed as limited initiatives, these state-level exemptions have not significantly enhanced site autonomy for a number of reasons, including that schools may be required to go through a fairly labor-intensive, time-consuming process of initiating and justifying requests for exemptions from state regulations (Fuhrman and Elmore 1995).

Whether other forms of deregulation such as charter schools or choice plans will significantly enhance school autonomy remains an open question.[8] The autonomy granted charter schools varies substantially within districts and across states (Wohlstetter, Wenning, and Briggs 1995; Wells and Associates 1998; Berman et al. 1998). Since charter schools, at least in theory, trade greater autonomy for stricter accountability (Bierlien and Mulholland 1994; Whitty et al. 1998), it will be important to track the manner in which state accountability requirements constrain charter school autonomy.[9] One of the stark realities is that states can influence site autonomy by the obligations as well as by the regulations imposed on schools (Boyne 1993). Insofar as charter schools are held to stringent standards defined by the broader system, they, like other schools, may be confined to figuring out the means to realize ends established elsewhere. As subsequent sections will make clear, such a constriction relegates schools

---

8 While we do not review the data on charter schools and choice plans, we think it is important to examine the actual autonomy schools have under these arrangements. In some cases "educational choice policy, although touted as 'deregulating' education—that is substituting the discipline of market incentives for external regulation—actually is a substitution of one regulatory regime for another" (Handler 1998, p. 110).

9 We are indebted to Jennifer Rice for helping us see that the literature on charter schools does not critically appraise the trade-off between autonomy and accountability or focus on the crux of the issue—that strict accountability constrains site autonomy.

and those who work in them to a subservient rather than an autonomous position (Bullough and Gitlin 1994; Strike 1998).

DELEGATION OF RESPONSIBILITY
VERSUS EXTENSION OF AUTONOMY

While efforts to decentralize decisionmaking did little to enhance site autonomy, they did a lot to shift responsibility for educational improvements from the state, and at times from the district, to schools. For example, schools were given various assignments, such as developing school improvement plans, organizing inservice sessions, revising report cards, sponsoring student recognition programs, arranging tutorial services, implementing curricular frameworks and the like (Malen et al. 1990). Since these sorts of tasks, and other responsibilities associated with decentralized decisionmaking came in addition to, not in lieu of, their prior professional responsibilities, site actors reported being more overpowered than empowered.

Given these developments, it is not surprising that observers of decentralization raised critical questions about "what is being devolved—is it real power, or merely the responsibility for implementing a bigger agenda decided elsewhere, far removed from schools?" (Smyth 1995, p. 172). Nor is it surprising, given the concurrent state policymaking actions in the areas of curriculum, assessment, and accountability, that some observers maintained that "far from shifting power from the center, the reverse is actually happening. Central policymaking groups are actually acquiring more power to determine policy centrally, through guidelines, frameworks and directions documents, with responsibility being shunted down the line to schools" (Smyth 1995, p. 172; see also Weiler 1993 and Whitty et al. 1998).

This interpretation is more stark, certain and monolithic than one we would render, particularly given the variance in state authority structures and local traditions that can interact to create a "crazy quilt of different degrees of state control" (Pipho 1991, p. 67). Still, it crystallizes a key contention that we examine more closely as we move from our discussion of the relatively modest state efforts to relinquish power to their more aggressive efforts to reclaim power.

AGGRESSIVE RECLAIMING OF POWER: STANDARDS AND ASSESSMENTS

In the United States as well as in other countries, "decentralization tends to be accompanied by renewed efforts by central state organizations to control schools through both managerialist policies and processes of accountability" (Gordon 1995, p. 54). That general tendency is one of the hallmarks of the education reform movement of the 1980s and 1990s. Although states passed and publicized various decentralization and deregulation policies, they also expanded and intensified efforts to strengthen their control of schools. Through an "extraordinary eruption" of policy activity (Mazzoni 1994, p. 53), states added to the volume of obligations and expectations, rules and regulations imposed on schools.[10] Whether they were scooping up ideas from "lighthouse districts" (Pipho 1991), capitalizing on proposals advanced by issue networks (Mazzoni 1994; Kirst 1995b), or importing ideas from other sources, states continued to take an active hand, at times a heavy hand, in virtually every domain of education policy, including curriculum and instruction, assessment, and accountability (McDonnell and Fuhrman 1986; Airisian 1988; Pipho 1991; Kirst 1995a, 1995b). States extended their reach, intensified their rhetoric and bolstered their strategies for "getting results."

To illustrate, many states asserted their interest in domains that had been the province of individual schools and school districts or professional organizations. States chose to hold schools accountable to *state-articulated* standards through an array of monitoring and sanctioning tactics such as publicizing test scores, labeling and ranking schools, issuing bonuses to "high-performing" schools, placing struggling schools on watch-lists, and threatening reconstitution or privatization (Cohen 1996; El-

---

10 States had been "on the move" in education policymaking for some time (Kirst 1995b, p. 45). Still, the scope and degree of involvement picked up noticeably as states experienced a host of pressures to make schools work (Mazzoni 1994).

more, Abelmann, and Fuhrman 1996).[11] Whether large numbers
of states would actually level the ultimate assault on site autonomy and take over large numbers of individual schools or
school districts was not entirely clear.[12] But their right to do so
was. Thus states sent strong signals. They also took dramatic actions. Under the auspices of stronger accountability and coherent policy, states became more directly and aggressively involved in hiring and firing educators (Manzo 1998); articulating
curriculum content through various requirements, frameworks,
and tests (Odden and Marsh 1988; Toch 1991; Sheldon and
Biddle 1998); defining school programs through mandates to select from fairly short lists of state-approved options for at-risk
students (an action which in turn, regulates the professional development school staffs receive) (Hendrie 1999a; Johnston and
Sandham 1999); and by issuing sanctions often through publicity but at times through takeovers.[13]

To be sure, not all states were equally active in all aspects of
education. But many states were certainly intent on exercising

---

11 For a very concrete example, see the Maryland State Department of
Education advertisement in Education Week, May 17, 1999, page 9.
This ad seeks to identify vendors interested in assuming "third
party management" roles in schools the state may reconstitute.

12 In several states (e.g., New Jersey, Connecticut, California), select
school districts were "taken over" by the state. About 21 districts
"have had control transferred from an elected board and its choice
of a superintendent to a mayor, a state legislature or an appointed
oversight board" (Green 1999, p. 4). In other states (e.g., Maryland),
no schools have been taken over but many are designated as "reconstitution eligible" sites. About 23 states have laws that explicitly
call for the state, or its designate to take control of low-performing
schools; about 11 states have "made good on their promise to do so"
(White 1999, p. 11).

13 At times local actors challenge state actions. For example, when two
teachers were "fired by the state board after a state assistance
team...found their performance inadequate" local authorities re-
hired the teachers but assigned them to other schools (Manzo 1998,
p. 9). Still, such dramatic examples illustrate how state governments have been crossing conventional boundaries of professional
discretion, limited intervention, and local control.

greater control over schools through policies that combined the persuasiveness of high academic standards, and the prescript-iveness of curricular frameworks and guidelines, with the pressures of high-stakes assessments (Airisian 1988; McDonnell 1994; Madaus and O'Dwyer 1999; Darling-Hammond 1990). The policies were often packaged and promoted as a form of performance-based accountability wherein states specify the desired outcomes, set the standards of acceptable performance, select the assessment instruments, and determine the rewards and sanctions that could be issued or imposed on schools to engender compliance. At this time, virtually all states are in the process of developing their own renditions of performance-based accountability (Fuhrman 1999).

Since "demanding particular levels of system wide outcomes has been shown to be an especially effective means of exercising power over organizational action" (Corbett and Wilson 1991, p. 106), these developments may be telling indicators of how state activism may affect site autonomy. A small but growing body of evidence suggests that the state standards, curricular guides, testing requirements, and accountability policies may be constraining site autonomy in numerous direct and indirect ways (e.g., Tyree 1993; Page 1995; Firestone et al. 1998; Finkelstein et al. 1998; Malen, Finkelstein, Croninger, and Rice 1999). For example, state policies may be influencing the content of the curriculum, the allocation of time, the deployment of personnel, the focus of professional development, the substance and structure of site-level deliberations and decisions, the conceptions of the educational purposes, and the conceptions of legitimate governance roles and relationships. In these, and perhaps other ways, states may be, in Mazzoni's words, "creating a new set of givens" that site actors accede to, but do not agree with. These general observations are briefly illustrated.

CONTENT OF CURRICULUM

Although state-initiated curriculum reforms and testing requirements receive mixed reviews,[14] there is reason to believe that the combination of curricular standards or frameworks and publicly disseminated test scores do penetrate schools and precipitate adjustments in schools and classrooms (Odden and Marsh 1988; Berliner and Biddle 1995). While the effects are not straightforward or uniform, state-mandated "instructional policy makes a difference" (Cohen and Ball 1990, p. 331) for individual teachers (Borko and Elliott 1999; Cohen 1991; Wolf and McIver 1999) and for schools and school districts.

Some teachers adjust their practice, though not always in ways that are congruent with the particular policy (Cohen and Ball 1990; Sykes 1990) or in ways that conform to their views (or researchers' views) of best practice (Corbett and Wilson 1991; Koretz et al. 1996a 1996b). Some schools and school districts revise their policies to secure "topical alignments" with state standards (Spillane and Thompson 1997, p. 187; Firestone et al. 1998) and/or adjust practices in ways that quickly improve or artificially inflate their test scores (Corbett and Wilson 1991; Darling-Hammond 1994; Berliner and Biddle 1995).[15] Those adjust-

---

14 Many discuss a range of issues associated with testing policies and practices through studies, commentaries, and histories. See, for example, Sheldon and Biddle (1998), Baron and Wolfe, (1996), Berliner and Biddle (1995), Page (1995), Darling-Hammond (1994), Madaus and O'Dwyer (1999), and Resnick and Resnick (1985).

15 To elaborate, "Schools where test scores are used for making decisions about rewards and sanctions have found ways to manipulate their test taking population in order to inflate artificially the school's average test scores. These strategies include labeling large numbers of low-scoring students for special education placements so that their scores won't 'count' in school reports, retaining students in grade so that their relative standing will look better on 'grade-equivalent' scores, excluding low-scoring students from admission to 'open enrollment' schools, and encouraging such students to leave schools or drop out" (Darling-Hammond 1994, p. 15). In some settings, "pressures of accountability have led some educators to cheat"—be that through administrators "quietly distributing

ments occur primarily but not solely in the subject areas and grade levels that state testing programs target (Elmore, Adelman, and Fuhrman 1996). Over time, these individual and organizational adjustments can substantially alter the content of the curriculum made available to students (Archbald and Porter 1994; Berliner and Biddle 1995).

Whether curriculum standards, guidelines, and related testing policies can also alter instructional strategies is less clear (Firestone et al. 1998). Some case studies of site responses to state policies suggest that "teachers believe they have near total control over their pedagogy but generally lower and more varying control over content" (Archbald and Porter 1994, p. 30). These data are generally consistent with surveys wherein principals acknowledge the influence of the state, as well as other parties, on curriculum (Ingersoll and Rossi 1995) and surveys wherein teachers report modest and at times diminishing control over curriculum policies but considerable discretion over classroom strategies (Anderson 1994). Other surveys and case studies suggest that "teachers will gear their teaching methods and strategies to the types of performance elicited by standardized tests, particularly when the tests are the basis for important decisions about students or schools" (Darling-Hammond 1990, p. 343; see also Berliner and Biddle 1995; Corbett and Wilson 1991; Smith 1991; Stetcher and Baron 1999).

Although the impact of externally mandated curricular standards, frameworks and assessments can vary within and across schools, there is evidence that these policies, particularly the high-stakes testing policies, precipitate changes (for better or worse) in schools and classrooms (McDonnell 1994; McMillan et al. 1999). The most common effects are changes in the content of the curriculum (Darling-Hammond and Wise 1985; Firestone et al. 1998; McMillan et al. 1999) and, in high-stakes settings, changes in the balance of power between state and local units. As Madaus, quoted by McClellan (1989), summarized:

tests to teachers ahead of time," or through other questionable practices such as teaching a restricted curriculum, exempting low-achieving children and reporting fraudulent results (Berliner and Biddle 1995, p. 198).

"… when you have high-stakes test, the tests eventually become the curriculum.…Items that are not emphasized in the test are…not emphasized in school. That's a fundamental lesson that cuts across countries and across time… (1989, p. 644; see also Madaus and O'Dwyer 1999). For that reason, "the administrative mechanism [an external test] used to ensure that standards are met…greatly diminishes cherished local control over what is taught and how it is taught and learned" (Madaus 1988, p. 111).

Given the power of tests, states may be able to wield influence not only by what they require, but also by what they do not require. The recent decision to eliminate theories of evolution from state tests in Kansas provides a telling opportunity to see whether states significantly influence curriculum by what they omit, as well as by what they include in their required tests (*Washington Post* 1999).

Yet another opportunity for states to influence the content of curriculum may occur when states require that schools select textbooks from a state-approved list (Pipho 1991). Writing about textbook adoptions processes in Texas and California, Delfattore points out that "Requiring publishers to produce charts showing how each textbook correlates with [state] guidelines… puts publishers on notice that their books had better conform as closely as possible to the curricula of those states" (1992, p. 123). Publishers respond to these pressures because Texas and California are the nation's two most lucrative textbook markets. Accommodations made for these states have ramifications for curriculum content in other states because more often than not, companies publish only one edition of a major text (Delfattore 1992; Cooper 1999). Thus, state influence on curriculum may be quite subtle, but it may also be quite extensive.

ALLOCATION OF TIME

One of the recurring effects of the state mandated standards and testing policies seems to be shifts in the use of time—by teachers, administrators and support staff. Some teachers reportedly invest considerable time preparing for and teaching to tests, particularly in high-stakes settings (Firestone et al. 1998; McMillan et al. 1999). Surveys and observations of elementary teachers in Chicago demonstrate that increasing numbers of teachers (from 44 percent in 1994 to 65 percent in 1997–98) are spending increasing amounts of time (from about 12 hours in 1994 to over 50 hours in 1997–98) on preparation for the state standardized tests (Smith 1998; see also Wong et al. 1999; Hendrie 1999b). These teachers reallocate their preparation and teaching time even though they are concerned about the ability to cover the required curriculum, let alone deal with what we term the "preferred curriculum," that is, what teachers would like to teach and view as important to teach. In Florida, administrators talk about getting their teachers to spend about six weeks each year "prepping" or coaching students for the state's standardized examination (Toch 1991, p. 221). Although educators in these and other settings may question the wisdom of such adaptations, they seem less inclined to question the necessity of them (Toch 1991; Firestone et al. 1998; McMillan et al. 1998).

These examples parallel the findings of surveys and interviews of administrators and teachers in Maryland. Here surveys indicate that schools and schools districts "seemed to be devoting more administrative and teacher time to devising strategies to improve scores [on the state tests]" (Corbett and Wilson 1988, p. 34). Follow-up visits corroborate that administrators in some settings "were planning expedient strategies for improving the test scores quickly," even though they resented having to do so and were concerned that "what they were doing was compromising a standard of good professional practice" (Corbett and Wilson 1991, p. 96). These patterns suggest that "the opportunity costs of time spent testing and preparing students for tests are considerable" (Madaus, in McClellan 1989, p. 643), even in settings where site actors may be acceding to the pressures for improved test scores rather than agreeing with those priorities (Corbett and Wilson 1991; Toch 1991; Finkelstein et al. 1998; Malen, Finkelstein, Croninger, and Rice 1999).

DEPLOYMENT OF PERSONNEL

The combination of state policies, particularly standards and accountability policies, not only prompts adjustments in the content of curriculum and the allocation of time inside and outside the classroom, but also precipitates changes in how human resources are configured and utilized. For example, an in-progress study of site responses to reconstitution illustrates how state testing and accountability pressures are contributing to changes in the work assignments and priorities of employees. Here, a district, under intense pressure from the state to improve its performance, as measured by the state's tests, launched a reconstitution initiative of its own. In this context, pressure to perform well on state assessments is intense (Finkelstein et al. 1998). Some reconstituted schools have responded to that pressure by (a) dedicating positions to testing coordinators and to persons who might be especially skilled in helping teachers prepare students for the tests; (b) using substitute teachers to relieve classroom teachers so they can develop practice packets and conduct practice sessions with groups of students in hopes that they will be more ready for the state tests; and (c) making improvement of test scores a main, if not the main, priority for resource teachers and specialists as well as for classroom teachers and school principals (Malen, Finkelstein, Croninger, and Rice 1999; Malen, Croninger, Redmond, and Muncey 1999). Other studies also document how schools can be persuaded and pressured to "redirect personnel and...[target] resources on activities specifically linked to raising test scores," even in settings where site educators resist and resent these reallocations (Wong and Anagnostopoulos 1998, p. 46; Stetcher and Baron 1999).

FOCUS OF PROFESSIONAL DEVELOPMENT

In some contexts, state standards and testing policies may be shaping how professional development resources are configured and invested. The in-progress study of site responses to reconstitution suggests that issues associated with the state testing program permeate the professional development agenda and consume much of the available time set aside for inservice sessions (Finkelstein et al. 1998; Malen, Croninger, Redmond, and Muncey 1999). These findings echo the observations of others who report that "Districts in Maryland focused their professional development resources on helping teachers align their instruction with the [state assessments]" (Firestone et al. 1998,

p. 110) or claim that "Most of their [local educators'] professional time became devoted to test-related activities, to the exclusion of other staff development and improvement initiatives" (Corbett and Wilson 1991, p. 103). While that tendency was more widespread in some contexts than others, it was evident in both high-stake and lower-stake states (e.g., Maryland, a high-stakes setting, and Pennsylvania, a lower-stakes setting).

As earlier noted, some states are beginning to require schools to select programs for at risk students from lists of approved vendors. These choices often determine who will provide professional development services at the site. As the early Rand study demonstrated, external consultants can be influential orchestrators of organizational change processes (McLaughlin 1990). Insofar as states directly or indirectly limit the list of approved vendors to agents that reinforce state policies and priorities, they may be carving out another channel for exercising influence on the site and creating another mechanism for reducing the degree of discretion afforded the site.

SUBSTANCE AND STRUCTURE OF SITE-LEVEL DELIBERATIONS AND DECISIONS

Analyses of school improvement plans and observations of schoolwide planning activities suggest that site-level deliberations focus on and are framed by templates that are clearly rooted in and reflective of state requirements (Advocates for Children and Youth 1998; Finkelstein et al. 1998). Site participants tend to accept the items on the template as the topics they ought to consider. Thus the template becomes a vehicle for pre-structuring conversations, for creating the impression that the template is what they must rely on in their planning and decisionmaking, even though it fails to capture aspects of school improvement that teachers and administrators identify in private interviews as more salient to them and more sensible for their school.

Insofar as state policies are wending their way to schools through various templates and guidelines that define the topics and terms of professional discussions, determine the parameters and priorities of professional deliberations, and shape the premises and pre-conditions for collective decisions, the state is exercising considerable power over the site. As Morgan explains, "...much unobtrusive control is built into vocabularies, structures of communication, attitudes, beliefs, rules and procedures that, though unquestioned, exert a decisive influence on decision [premises and] outcomes" (1986, p. 166). And, as Pfeffer makes clear in his discussion of sources of power in organizational decisionmaking, "decisions are, in large measure, determined by the premises used in making them." The agents that can establish the premises can "in effect determine the decision" (1981, p. 116).

CONCEPTIONS OF THE PRIMARY PURPOSES OF SCHOOLING

Studies of responses to state standards and accountability policies illustrate how these policies may take on a normative force that affects not only the content of the curriculum and the allocation of resources but also conceptions of the primary purposes of schooling. Beyond becoming "the Bible on what we have to teach" (Firestone et al. 1998, p. 108), these policies may alter views about even more foundational aspects of the organization. In one study, for example, "a shift occurred from educators viewing the test as one indicator among many to their treating the next set of test results as the most important outcome of schooling....Thus, the indicator of performance becomes the goal itself" (Corbett and Wilson 1991, pp. 104, 105). Whether this sort of goal transformation or goal substitution is prevalent or inevitable is an empirical question. What the "threads of evidence" (Knapp 1997, p. 227) suggest is that state policies, particularly testing and accountability policies, may be intentionally or inadvertently altering site actors' conceptions of the primary purposes of schools.

Some argue that is precisely what ought to occur. The state should be determining the ends and the standards by which those ends are assessed, while districts and sites should be determining the means through which those goals and objectives can be realized. While that is not the only view of educational governance that is being promoted, it is a prominent one that serves to illustrate yet another avenue through which the state may be influencing schools in ways that constrain the autonomy of the site.

CONCEPTIONS OF LEGITIMATE ROLES AND RELATIONSHIPS

As policy analysts and actors sought to reconcile or rationalize how states could be simultaneously promoting and passing centralizing and decentralizing reforms, one definition of state and local authority relationships became fairly prevalent. As Wells and Oakes (1996) described the process, states would be creating *"centralized* standards, curricular frameworks, and assessment programs while encouraging *decentralized* decision-making through which local schools design and implement strategies for teaching the frameworks and meeting the standards for student outcomes" (Wells and Oakes 1996, p. 135). Upper-level governments (federal and state) were to set standards, disseminate frameworks, and develop assessments, and "schools and their communities were to be granted the autonomy to implement the frameworks as they saw fit while being held accountable for student outcomes as measured against the standards, frameworks, and tests" (Wells and Oakes 1996, p. 135). Presumably such a division of responsibility would engender greater coherence in the education policy system and improve the performance of schools (Smith and O'Day 1991; O'Day and Smith 1993).

While judging the merits of this definition of intergovernmental relations falls beyond the scope of this chapter, gauging its impact on site autonomy does not. What seems clear is that, under this definition, site autonomy is severely constrained because all schools have the freedom to do is to figure out how to meet the goals set elsewhere and measure up to the standards set elsewhere (Bullough and Gitlin 1994). As Strike writes:

> [Under such an arrangement] the what of education...is determined largely by the state....[Such an approach] substantially restricts the opportunities for local schools to amend centrally defined curricula or to engage in local deliberations about their content. Moreover, the deliberations of local schools

become focused on implementation of state curricula, on means, not ends (1998, p. 209).

A "NEW SET OF GIVENS"

When we array the multiple ways that state policy may be influencing critical aspects of schools, it seems that states may be creating what Mazzoni has called a "new set of givens." This "new set of givens" may be influencing what site actors think as well as what they do. As the preceding paragraphs suggest, state policies along with the district reactions they spawn may be influencing the orientations and actions of site participants by persuading or pressuring schools to make adjustments in core aspects of the organization; by shaping, if not fully framing, site actors' perceptions of problems, priorities, and possibilities; and by modifying their responses to them. There is evidence that state policies may be able to infiltrate, if not fully control, the agendas at the site; to define the decision situation in ways that site actors reluctantly, at times inadvertently, accept; and to extract concessions even though site actors may openly express their displeasure with, at times disdain for, the accommodations they make.[16] These patterns suggest that the aggregate effect of state policies, particularly in the area of standards and accountability, may be to rewrite "the rules of the game" (Mazzoni 1991, p. 116).

Insofar as the state policies are precipitating adjustments not only in key aspects of the organization but also in underlying constructions or "visions of what the problems and issues are and how they can be tackled" (Morgan 1986, p. 166), the state has secured a potent power advantage, because the underlying views "often act as mental straitjackets that prevent us from seeing other ways of formulating our basic concerns and the alternative courses of action that are available" (Morgan 1986, p. 116). Insofar as the organizational and conceptual adjustments mirror

---

16 The concerns expressed by site actors go beyond irritation and frustration. Some question whether state standards and assessments are appropriate for their students and resent what they view as state "intrusion" on professional autonomy (Toch 1991; Malen et al. 1999; Firestone et al. 1998; Corbett and Wilson 1991).

the preferences embodied in state policies, the state may be infusing and reinforcing a "new set of givens" that directly and indirectly restrict the degree of autonomy afforded site actors.

A PROVISIONAL REAPPRAISAL OF STATE ACTIVISM AND SITE AUTONOMY

Our analysis suggests that one of the major, cumulative effects of the proliferation and intensification of state policymaking may well be to substantially constrain site autonomy. Our review of state efforts to "relinquish" power and strengthen the autonomy of schools indicates that the formal authority delegated to sites was at best modest and temporary; that the web of rules and regulations, the intensification of expectations and obligations, and the limited availability of resources interacted to further constrain the discretion afforded schools. Ironically, despite the state emphasis on decentralization and deregulation, it seems that sites inherited a great deal of responsibility, but they did not secure additional autonomy. Our review of state efforts to "reclaim" power and exert greater control over schools illustrates that states have repeatedly and resolutely crossed the boundaries of modest and intermittent involvement in select domains of education and moved toward aggressive and persistent intervention in multiple domains of education, including those traditionally seen as falling within the purview of local units. At least in some contexts, state policies appear to be penetrating schools, shaping site priorities and practices, and precipitating changes despite site actors' reluctance, resentment, and resistance. Through various combinations of symbols, sanctions, rules, regulations, and exhortations, state policies seem to be creating "a new set of givens" that limit the latitude of site actors.

Taken together, the illusion of relinquishing power and the pattern of reclaiming power lend credence to the idea that education policymaking may be largely "rigged from the top" (Fischer, 1990, p. 288). While that interpretation stands in sharp contrast to the prevalent view that education policy is essentially "made" or "remade" at the bottom, it is a plausible, albeit provisional, interpretation that captures key features of what seems to be an emerging redefinition of state-local roles, relationships, and responsibilities.

In part because states have essentially controlled the education reform agenda and effectively concentrated their symbolic, regulatory and fiscal resources on "results-based" accountability ventures, sites have been relegated to a reactive, arguably subservient role in that they are being required to meet the goals developed elsewhere with the resource allocations determined elsewhere or experience the sanctions set elsewhere. Although some schools may still be able to insulate themselves from the influence of state policies, it appears that the balance of power has shifted. Schools are the clear targets and the reluctant recipients of a host of state initiatives that tend to make schools assume substantial responsibility for reform outcomes but grant them little opportunity to influence reform inputs. While sites may appear to be ingeniously eluding or defying the steady influx of state directives, they also appear to be maneuvering within the relatively narrow and apparently narrowing parameters set by the states.

To be clear, we are not arguing that the broad array of forces which can intervene to dilute or derail policies as they move from state enactment to site implementation no longer comes into play. In all likelihood, organizational layers, local cultures, policy features, actor dispositions, and other factors such as the complexity of educational problems will continue to complicate and confound state efforts to control schools. What we are suggesting however, is that states may be consolidating their power —controlling organizational agendas, reconstructing the rules of the game, and otherwise influencing site-level decisions and operations in multiple, consequential ways which, when taken together, significantly restrict the options open to and the degree of discretion available to site actors.

While our analysis provides support for this alternative hypothesis, our interpretation must be seen as tentative on several counts. First, our analysis concentrates on only two broad trends in education policymaking. While developments in these prominent domains of education policy can be instructive, they are not conclusive. The relationship between state activism and site autonomy may look quite different when examined through the window of education policy developments in other domains such as teacher education, professional development and licensure requirements, and education finance legislation and litigation.

Second, our analysis recognizes that state policy is only one of many forces that can enhance or restrict site autonomy. But we do not elaborate how these "other factors" operate or how they might mediate the influence of state policies on the "degrees of freedom" found in schools. As earlier noted, schools are nested in multi-level governmental systems and complex social, cultural, and political contexts that can reinforce or counteract state policies. Given data and space limitations, we do not explicitly address the forces that may be magnifying or minimizing the impact of state policies. For that reason, our analysis may distort the impact of state policy on site autonomy (Boyne 1993).

Third, our analysis focuses only on the nature of the state-site governance relationship. We sought to uncover the potential connections between state activism and site autonomy, not weigh all the conceivable consequences of them. The emphasis was on understanding if and how state activism may be affecting the balance of power between states and sites, not assessing how changes in that balance might affect other important matters, such as the prospects for educational improvements or the distribution of educational benefits.

IMPLICATIONS FOR FUTURE RESEARCH

The shortcomings in our analysis that we have noted, as well as others that could be added, indicate that there is considerable work to be done if we want to get a clearer understanding of the relationship between state activism and school autonomy. To begin, we need to develop a stronger data base. We need more multi-level, longitudinal looks at how state education policies make their way to and through the system, interact with other forces and operate, over time, to shape the autonomy of schools. Mapping these dynamics across levels and over time is an essential step in "developing a reasonable web of causal influences that help us understand not only what happened but why it happened that way" (Huberman and Miles 1984, p. 1).

We also need more integrated looks at how state actions within and across key domains of education policy play out in various contexts. Such work could reveal how clusters of policies combine and interact to shape the opportunity structure within which site actors make decisions and take actions. In addition, we need more penetrating looks that get at the obvious and the unobtrusive, the regulatory and the symbolic processes that may be operating as states actively and aggressively seek to influence schools. And, we need more comprehensive looks that get at how changes in governance relationships may affect the capacity and the resolve required to improve the quality of life and learning for those who live and work in our schools.[17] While such a program of research would be conceptually, empirically, and logistically ambitious, it could enable us to get a more complete picture of the aggregate and cumulative impact of state activism on site autonomy.

---

[17] Scholars who have pursued this line of work offer different judgments. Some suggest that state education policy is misguided; that it has adopted the wrong strategies. They argue that the illusion of greater autonomy and the intensity of performance-based accountability create a context wherein schools are allocated "the blame for failure rather than the freedom to succeed" (Whitty et al. 1998, p. 12). Others suggest state education policy misses the mark, that it fails to address underlying conditions of racial, social, and economic equity that must be ameliorated in order to secure meaningful and enduring improvements in education (e.g., Anyon 1997; Lipman 1997). Others add that state education reforms may direct attention away from those critical issues (Anyon 1997; Lewis and Nakagawa 1995; Hess 1999). On a more hopeful note, some argue that education reforms can be integrated into a blend of state direction and site discretion that will ultimately engender school improvement (e.g., Smith and O'Day 1991; Fuhrman,1993).

REFERENCES

Advocates for Children and Youth (1998). *Making accountability work: An initial assessment of Maryland's school reconstitution program.* Unpublished report.

Anderson, J. (1994). *Who's in charge? Teachers' views on control over school policy and classroom practices.* Research report, Office of Educational Research and Improvement, Washington, DC. (ED 376 240).

Anyon, J. (1997). *Ghetto schooling: A political economy of urban educational reform.* New York: Teachers College Press.

Archbald, D. A., and Porter, A. C. (1994). Curriculum control and teachers' perceptions of autonomy and satisfaction. *Educational Evaluation and Policy Analysis, 16,* 21–39.

Airasian, P. W. (1988). Symbolic validation: The case of state-mandated, high-stakes testing. *Educational Evaluation and Policy Analysis, 10,* 301–313.

Baron, J. B., and Wolf, D. P. (Eds.) (1996). *Performance-based student assessment: Challenges and possibilities.* Chicago: The University of Chicago Press.

Berliner, D. C., and Biddle, B. J. (1995). *The manufactured crisis: Myths, fraud, and the attack on America's public schools.* New York: Longman.

Berman, P., Nelson, B., Ericson, J., Perry, R., and Silverman, D. (1998). *A national study of charter schools: Second-year report.* Washington, DC: Office of Educational Research and Improvement.

Bierlein, L. A., and Mulholland, L. A. (1994). The promise of charter schools. *Educational Leadership, 52*(1), 34–40.

Bimber, B. (1993). *School decentralization: Lessons from the study of bureaucracy.* Santa Monica, CA: Rand.

Borko, H., and Elliott, R. (1999). Hands-on pedagogy versus hands-off accountability: Tensions between competing commitments for exemplary math teachers in Kentucky. *Phi Delta Kappan, 80,* 394–400.

Boyne, G. A. (1993). Central policies and local autonomy: The case of Wales. *Urban Studies, 30*(1), 87–101.

Bullough, R. V. Jr., and Gitlin, A. D. (1994). Challenging teacher education as training: Four propositions. *Journal of Education for Teaching, 20*(1), 67–81.

Cohen, D. K. (1991). Revolution in one classroom. In S. H. Fuhrman and B. Malen (Eds.), *The politics of curriculum and testing* (pp. 103–123). Bristol, PA: Falmer Press.

Cohen, D. K. (1996). Standards-based school reform: Policy, practice, and performance. In H. F. Ladd (Ed.), *Holding schools accountable: Performance-based reform in education* (pp. 99–127). Washington, DC: The Brookings Institution.

Cohen, D. K., and Ball, D. L. (1990). Relations between policy and practice: A commentary. *Educational Evaluation and Policy Analysis, 12,* 331–338.

Cohen, D. K., and Spillane, D. K. (1992). Policy and practice: The relations between governance and instruction. *Review of Research in Education, 18,* 3–49.

Cooper, K. J. (1999, September 5). Education standards gaining momentum. *Washington Post*, A3, A20.

Corbett, H. D., and Wilson, B. (1988). Raising the stakes in state-wide mandatory minimum competency testing. *Journal of Education Policy, 3*(5), 27–39.

Corbett, H. D., and Wilson, B. (1991). *Testing, reform and rebellion.* Norwood, NJ: Ablex.

Cuban, L. (1984). School reform by remote control: SB 813 in California. *Phi Delta Kappan, 66,* 213–215.

Cuban, L. (1998). How schools change reforms: Redefining reform success and failure. *Teachers College Record, 99,* 453–477.

Dahl, R. (1984). *Modern political analysis.* Englewood Cliffs, NJ: Prentice-Hall.

Danielson, M. N., and Hochschild, J. (1998). Changing urban education: Lessons, cautions, prospects. In C. N. Stone (Ed.), *Changing urban education* (pp. 277–295). Lawrence, KS: University Press of Kansas.

Darling-Hammond, L. (1990). Instructional policy into practice: "The power of the bottom over the top." *Educational Evaluation and Policy Analysis, 12,* 339–347.

Darling-Hammond, L. (1994). Performance-based assessment and educational equity. *Harvard Educational Review, 64*(1), 5–30.

Darling-Hammond, L., and Wise, A. E. (1985). Beyond standardization: State standards and school improvement. *The Elementary School Journal, 85,* 315–336.

Davies, B., and Hentschke, G. C. (1994). School autonomy: Myth or reality—developing an analytical taxonomy. *Educational Management and Administration, 22*(2), 96–103.

Delfattore, J. (1992). *What Johnny shouldn't read: Textbook censorship in America.* New Haven, CT: Yale University Press.

Drury, D. W. (1999). *Reinventing school-based management.* Alexandria, VA: National School Boards Association.

Elmore, R. (1983). Complexity and control: What legislators and administrators can do about implementing policy. In L. S. Shulman and G. Sykes (Eds.), *Handbook of Teaching and Policy.* New York: Longman.

Elmore, R. (1993). School decentralization: Who gains? Who loses? In J. Hannaway and M. Carnoy (Eds.), *Decentralization and school improvement* (pp. 33–54). San Francisco, CA: Jossey-Bass.

Elmore, R. F., Abelmann, C. H., and Fuhrman, S. H. (1996). The new accountability in state education reform: From process to performance. In H. F. Ladd (Ed.), *Holding schools accountable: Performance-based reform in education* (pp. 65–98). Washington, DC: The Brookings Institution.

Elmore, R. F., and Fuhrman, S. H. (1995). Opportunity-to-learn standards and the state role in education. *Teachers College Record, 96,* 432–457.

Elmore, R., and Sykes, G. (1992). Curriculum policy. In P. Jackson (Ed.), *Handbook of Research on Curriculum* (pp. 185–215). New York: Macmillan.

Finkelstein, B., Malen, B., Croninger, R. C., Rice, J. K., Mourad, R. F., Snell, J., and Thrasher, K. (1998, October). *In the early states of reform: A composite profile of three twenty-first century schools.* A report available through the Department of Education Policy, Planning and Administration, University of Maryland, College Park.

Firestone, W. A. (1989). Using reform: Conceptualizing district initiative. *Educational Evaluation and Policy Analysis, 11,* 151–164.

Firestone, W. A., Bader, B. D., Massel, D., and Rosenblum, S. (1992). Recent trends in state educational reform: Assessment and prospects. *Teachers College Record, 94,* 254–277.

Firestone, W. A., Mayrowetz, D., and Fairman, J. (1998). Performance-based assessment and instructional change: The effects of testing in Maine and Maryland. *Educational Evaluation and Policy Analysis, 20,* 95–113.

Firestone, W. A., and Nagle, B. (1995). Differential regulation: Clever customization or unequal interference? *Educational Evaluation and Policy Analysis, 17,* 97–112.

Fischer, F. (1990). *Technocracy and the politics of expertise.* Newbury Park, CA: Sage Publications.

Fuhrman, S. H. (1988). State politics and education reform. *Journal of Education Policy, 3*(5), 61–75.

Fuhrman, S. H. (Ed.) (1993). *Designing coherent education policy: Improving the system.* San Francisco, CA: Jossey-Bass Publishers.

Fuhrman, S. H. (1994). *Challenges in systemic education reform.* CPRE Policy Briefs. New Brunswick, NJ: Consortium for Policy Research in Education. (ED 377 562)

Fuhrman, S. H. (1999, January 27). *The new accountability.* CPRE Policy Briefs. Philadelphia, PA: Graduate School of Education, University of Pennsylvania.

Fuhrman, S. H., and Elmore, R. F. (1990). Understanding local control in the wake of state education reform. *Educational Evaluation and Policy Analysis, 12,* 82–96.

Fuhrman, S. H., and Elmore, R. F. (1995). Ruling out rules: The evolution of deregulation in state education policy. *Teachers College Record, 97,* 279–309.

Geraci, B. (1995–1996). Local decision making: A report from the trenches. *Educational Leadership, 53*(4), 50–52.

Gordon, L. (1995). Controlling education: Agency theory and the reformation of New Zealand schools. *Educational Policy, 9*(1), 54–74.

Green, R. L. (1999). A reform strategy for troubled times: Takeovers of urban school districts in the 1990s. Paper presented to the Leadership Policy Institute of the National Alliance for Black School Educators, April 24, 1999.

Handler, J. F. (1998). Chicago school reform: Enablement or empowerment? *The Good Society, 8*(2), 9–14.

Handler, J. F. (1996). *Down from bureaucracy: The ambiguity of privatization and empowerment.* Princeton, NJ: Princeton University Press.

Hendrie, C. (1999a). N. J. schools put reform to the test: Verdict still out on "whole school" model. *Education Week, 28*(32), 1, 13–14.

Hendrie, C. (1999b). Researchers see some progress in Chicago high schools. *Education Week, 28*(35), 12.

Hertert, L. (1996). Systemic school reform in the 1990s: A local perspective. *Educational Policy, 10,* 379–398.

Hess, F. M. (1999). *Spinning wheels: The politics of urban school reform.* Washington, DC: The Brookings Institution.

Hess, G. A., Jr. (1999). Understanding achievement (and other) changes under Chicago school reform. *Educational Evaluation and Policy Analysis, 21,* 67–83.

Huberman, M., and Miles, M. (1984). *Innovation up close.* New York: Plenum Press.

Ingersoll, R., and Rossi, R. (1995). *Who influences decisionmaking about school curriculum: What do principals say?* Issue Brief, National Center for Education Statistics, Washington, DC. (ED 384 989)

James, T. (1991). State authority and the politics of educational change. *Review of Research in Education, 17,* 169–224.

Johnston, R. C., and Sandham, J. L. (1999). States increasingly flexing their policy muscle. *Education Week, 28*(31), 1, 19–20.

Katz, M. B., Fine, M., and Simon, E. (1997). Poking around: Outsiders view Chicago school reform. *Teachers College Record*, 99, 117–157.

Kingdon, J. W. (1984). *Agendas, alternatives, and public policies.* Boston, MA: Little, Brown and Company.

Kirp, D. L., and Driver, C. D. (1995). The aspirations of systemic reform meet the realities of localism. *Educational Administration Quarterly*, 31, 589–612.

Kirst, M. W. (1995a). Recent research on intergovernmental relations in education policy. *Educational Researcher*, 24(9), 18–22.

Kirst, M. W. (1995b). Who's in charge? Federal, state, and local control. In D. Ravitch and M. A. Vinovskis (Eds.), *Learning from the past* (pp. 25–56). Baltimore, MD: The Johns Hopkins University Press.

Knapp, M. S. (1997). Between systemic reforms and the mathematics and science classroom: The dynamics of innovation, implementation, and professional learning. *Review of Educational Research*, 67(2), 227–266.

Koretz, D. M., Barron, S., Mitchell, K. J., and Stecher, B. M. (1996a). *Perceived effects of the Kentucky Instructional Results Information Systems (KIRIS)* (MR-792.PCTT/FF). Santa Monica, CA: Rand.

Koretz, D., Mitchell, K., Baron., S., and Keith, S. (1996b). *Final report: Perceived effects of the Maryland School Performance Assessment Program* (CSE Tech. Report 409). Los Angeles, CA: UCLA National Center for Research on Evaluation, Standards and Student Testing.

Leithwood, K., and Menzies, T. (1998). Forms and effects of school-based management: A review. *Educational Policy*, 12(3), 325–346.

Lewis, D. A., and Nakagawa, K. (1995). *Race and educational reform in the American metropolis: A study of school decentralization.* Albany, NY: State University of New York Press.

Lipman, P. (1997). Restructuring in context: A case study of teacher participation and the dynamics of ideology, race, and power. *American Educational Research Journal*, 34(1), 3–37.

Lipsky, M. (1980). *Street-level bureaucracy.* New York: Russell Sage Foundation.

Madaus, G. F. (1988). The influence of testing on the curriculum. In L. N. Tanner (Ed.), *Critical issues in curriculum* (pp. 83–121). Chicago: University of Chicago Press.

Madaus, G. F., and O'Dwyer, L. M. (1999). A short history of performance assessment: Lessons learned. *Phi Delta Kappan, 80,* 688–695.

Malen, B. (1994a). Enacting site based management: A political utilities analysis. *Educational Evaluation and Policy Analysis, 16,* 249–267.

Malen, B. (1994b). The micropolitics of education: Mapping the multiple dimensions of power relations in school polities. In J. D. Scribner and D. H. Layton (Eds.), *The study of educational politics* (pp. 147–167). New York: Falmer Press.

Malen, B., and Campbell, R. F. (1985). Public school reform in Utah. In V. D. Mueller and M. P. McKeown (Eds.), *The fiscal, legal and political aspects of state reform of elementary and secondary education* (pp. 245–275). Cambridge, MA: Ballinger.

Malen, B., Croninger, R., Redmond, D., and Muncey, D. (1999, October). Uncovering the potential contradictions in reconstitution reforms. A paper presented at the annual conference of the University Council for Educational Administration, Minneapolis.

Malen, B., Finkelstein, B., Croninger, R., and Rice, J. K. (1999, April). Mandating miracles: The implementation of a district-initiated reconstitution reform. Paper presented at the annual meeting of the American Educational Research Association, Montreal, Canada.

Malen, B., and Hart, A. W. (1987). Shaping career ladder reform: The influence of teachers on the policymaking process. Paper presented at the annual conference of the American Educational Research Association, Washington, DC.

Malen, B., and Ogawa, R. T. (1988). Professional-patron influence on site-based governance councils: A confounding case study. *Educational Evaluation and Policy Analysis, 10,* 251–270.

Malen, B., Ogawa, R. T., and Kranz, J. (1990). What do we know about school-based management? A case study of the literature—a call for research. In W. H. Clune and J. F. Witte (Eds.), *Choice and control in American education, Volume 2: The practice of choice, decentralization and school restructuring* (pp. 289–342). New York: Falmer Press.

Manzo, K. K. (1998). N.C. teachers battle state over firings. *Education Week, 18*(15), 1, 9.

Mazzoni, T. L. (1994). State policy-making and school reform: Influences and influentials. In J. D. Scribner and D. H. Layton (Eds.), *The study of educational politics* (pp. 53–73). New York: Falmer Press.

Mazzoni, T. L. (1991). Analyzing state school policymaking: An arena model. *Educational Evaluation and Policy Analysis, 13,* 115–138.

McClellan, M. C. (1989). An interview with George Madaus: New ways of thinking about testing. *Phi Delta Kappan, 70,* 642–645.

McDonnell, L. M. (1994). Assessment policy as persuasion and regulation. *American Journal of Education, 102,* 394–420.

McDonnell, L., and Elmore, R. (1987). Getting the job done: Alternative policy instruments. *Educational Evaluation and Policy Analysis, 9,* 133–152.

McDonnell, L. M., and Fuhrman, S. (1986). The political context of school reform. In V. D. Mueller and M. P. McKeown (Eds.), *The fiscal, legal and political aspects of state reform of elementary and secondary education* (pp. 43–64). Cambridge, MA: Ballinger.

McLaughlin, M. (1987). Learning from experience: Lessons from policy implementation. *Educational Evaluation and Policy Analysis, 9,* 171–178.

McLaughlin, M. (1990). The Rand change agent study revisited: Macro perspectives and micro realities. *Educational Researcher, 19,* 11–16.

McMillan, J. H., Myran, S., and Workman, D. (1999, April). The impact of mandated statewide testing on teachers' classroom assessment and instructional practices. Paper presented at the annual conference of the American Educational Research Association, Montreal.

Morgan, G. (1986). *Images of organization*. Beverly Hills, CA: Sage.

O'Day, J. A., and Smith, M. S. (1993). Systemic reform and educational opportunity. In S. H. Fuhrman (Ed.), *Designing coherent education policy: Improving the system* (pp. 250–312). San Francisco, CA: Jossey-Bass Publishers.

Odden, A., and Marsh, D. (1988). State education reform implementation: A framework for analysis. *Politics of Education Association Yearbook*, 3(5), 41–59.

Odden, A., and Busch, C. (1998). *Financing schools for high performance: Strategies for improving the use of educational resources.* San Francisco, CA: Jossey-Bass Publishers.

Page, R. (1995). Who systematizes the systematizers? Policy and practice interactions in a case of state-level systemic reform. *Theory into Practice*, 34(1), 21–29.

Paik, S. J., Walberg, H. J., Komukai, A., and Freeman, K. (1998, July). A taxonomy and analysis of decentralization in developed countries. Paper presented at the World Congress of Comparative Education, Capetown, South Africa.

Pfeffer, J. (1981). *Power in organizations*. Marshfield, MA: Pitman.

Pipho, C. (1991). Centralizing curriculum at the state level. In M. F. Klein (Ed.), *The politics of curriculum decision-making: Issues in centralizing the curriculum* (pp. 67–96). Albany, NY: State University of New York Press.

Resnick, D. P., and Resnick, L. B. (1985). Standards, curriculum, and performance: A historical and comparative perspective. *Educational Researcher*, 14(4), 5–20.

Rossman, G. B., and Wilson, B. L. (1996). Context, courses, and the curriculum: Local responses to state policy reform. *Educational Policy*, 10, 399–421.

Russo, C. J. (1995). School based decision making: Councils and school boards in Kentucky: Trusted allies or irreconcilable foes? *West Education Law Quarterly*, 4, 398–412.

Sandidge, R. F., Russo, C. J., Harris, J. J., III, Ford, H. H. (1996). School-based decision making, American style: Perspectives and practices throughout the United States. *Interchange, 27,* 313–329.

Schattschneider, E. E. (1960). *The semi-sovereign people.* New York: Holt, Rhinehart and Winston.

Schon, D. A. (1981). A review of the federal role in curriculum development, 1950–1980. *Education Evaluation and Policy Analysis, 5,* 55–61.

Sheldon, K. A., and Biddle, B. J. (1998). Standards, accountability, and school reform: Perils and pitfalls. *Teachers College Record, 100,* 164–180.

Shipps, D. (1998). Corporate influence on Chicago school reform. In C. N. Stone (Ed.), *Changing urban education* (pp. 161–183). Lawrence, KS: University Press of Kansas.

Smith, B. (1998). *It's about time: Opportunities to learn in Chicago's elementary schools.* Chicago: Consortium on Chicago School Research.

Smith, M. L. (1991). Put to the test: The effects of external testing on teachers. *Educational Researcher, 20*(5), 8–11.

Smith, M. S., and O'Day, J. A. (1991). Systemic school reform. In S. Fuhrman and B. Malen (Eds.), *The politics of curriculum and testing* (pp. 233–268). Bristol, PA: Falmer Press.

Smyth, J. (1995). Devolution and teachers' work: The underside of a complex phenomenon. *Educational Management and Administration, 23*(3), 168–175.

Spillane, J. P. (1996). School districts matter: Local educational authorities and state instructional policy. *Educational Policy, 10*(1), 63–87.

Spillane, J. P., and Thompson, C. L. (1997). Reconstructing conceptions of local capacity: The local education agency's capacity for ambitious instructional reform. *Educational Evaluation and Policy Analysis, 19,* 185–203.

Strike, K. A. (1998). Centralized goal formation, citizenship, and educational pluralism: Accountability in liberal democratic societies. *Educational Policy, 12,* 203–215.

Stetcher, B. M., and Barron, S. (1999, April). Test-based accountability: The perverse consequences of milepost testing. Paper presented at the annual conference of the American Educational Research Association, Montreal, Canada.

Summers, A. A., and Johnson, A. W. (1996). The effects of school-based management plans. In E. A. Hanushek and D. W. Jorgenson (Eds.), *Improving America's schools: The role of incentives* (pp. 75–96). Washington, DC: National Academy Press.

Sykes, G. (1990). Organizing policy into practice: Reactions to the cases. *Educational Evaluation and Policy Analysis, 12,* 349–353.

Toch, T. (1991). *In the name of excellence: The struggle to reform the nation's schools, why it's failing, and what should be done.* New York: Oxford University Press.

Tyree, A. K., Jr. (1993). Examining the evidence: Have states reduced local control of curriculum? *Educational Evaluation and Policy Analysis, 15,* 34–50.

Washington Post (1999). Evolution and Kansas. *Washington Post,* August 16, 1999, A14.

Weatherly, R., and Lipsky, M. (1977). Street-level bureaucrats and institutional innovation: Implementing special education reform. *Harvard Education Review, 47,* 171–197.

Weiler, H. N. (1993). Control versus legitimization: The politics of ambivalence. In J. Hannaway and M. Carnoy (Eds.), *Decentralization and school improvement: Can we fulfill the promise?* (pp. 55–83). San Francisco, CA: Jossey-Bass Publishers.

Weiss, C. H. (1995). The four "I's" of school reform: How interests, ideology, information, and institution affect teachers and principals. *Harvard Educational Review, 65,* 571–592.

Wells, A. S. and Associates (1998). Charter school reform in California: Does it meet expectations? *Phi Delta Kappan, 80,* 305–312.

Wells, A. S., and Oakes, J. (1996). Potential pitfalls of systemic reform: Early lessons from research on detracking. *Sociology of Education,* extra issue, 135–143.

White, K. A. (1999). N. J. plans to end takeover in Jersey City. *Education Week, 18,* (39), 1, 11.

White, P. A. (1992). Teacher empowerment under "ideal" school-site autonomy. *Educational Evaluation and Policy Analysis, 14,* 69–82.

Whitty, G., Power, S., and Halpin, D. (1998). *Devolution and choice in education: The school, the state and the market.* Bristol, PA: Open University Press.

Wohlstetter, P., Wenning, R., and Briggs, K. L. (1995). Charter schools in the United States: The question of autonomy. *Educational Policy, 9*(4), 331–358.

Wolf, S. A., and McIver, M. C. (1999). When process becomes policy: The paradox of Kentucky state reform for exemplary teachers of writing. *Phi Delta Kappan, 80,* 401–406.

Wong, K. K., and Anagnostopoulos, D. (1998). Can integrated governance reconstruct teaching? Lessons learned from two low-performing Chicago high schools. *Educational Policy, 12*(1–2), 31–47.

Wong, K. K., Anagnostopoulos, D., Rutledge, S., Lynn, L., and Dreeben, R. (1999). *Implementation of an educational accountability agenda: Integrated governance in the Chicago public schools enters its fourth year.* Chicago: Department of Education and Irving B. Harris Graduate School of Public Policy Studies, The University of Chicago.

8

SALVAGING FISCAL CONTROL: NEW SOURCES OF LOCAL REVENUE FOR PUBLIC SCHOOLS

Michael F. Addonizio
Wayne State University

During the century-long period ending in 1990, U.S. public elementary and secondary schools enjoyed steady and substantial growth in real aggregate and per pupil resources (Guthrie 1997; Hanushek and Rivkin 1997), with nearly all of this revenue raised from broad-based state and local taxes. Over this period, the relative shares of state and local support changed dramatically. Local shares, raised almost exclusively from property taxes, fell from more than 80 percent in the 1910–1930 period to about 45 percent by the mid-1990s, while state contributions, raised primarily by sales taxes and personal and corporate income taxes, rose from less than 20 percent to nearly 48 percent over this same period[1] (Howell and Miller 1997).

---

1 Federal funding, never a substantial share of total public school revenue, rose from negligible levels during the pre-1930 era to about 7 percent by 1995.

The steady increase in funding underscored the high priority assigned public education in the United States, while the rise in state share followed from state-level concerns about distributional equity across local districts and, more recently, universal educational adequacy. This century-long trend of steady revenue growth, however, came to an abrupt halt in 1990 (Hanushek and Rivkin 1997), while both school enrollments and expectations for academic achievement continued to rise. To meet their students' and communities' expectations in the face of essentially flat real revenues from traditional tax sources, local school districts in recent years have turned increasingly to nontraditional sources of revenue. These non-tax sources of revenue include user fees, developer fees, partnerships with postsecondary schools, government agencies and private businesses, donations, volunteer services, interest earnings on investment of school resources and the creation of educational foundations to promote giving from individuals and businesses. The growth of these nontraditional revenues, however, has raised concerns among policymakers about their potentially disequalizing effects.

This study will examine the sources of these nontraditional revenues, the institutional arrangements by which these revenues are raised, and the legal restrictions placed on these revenue-raising activities. The paper will also assess the extent of public reporting of such revenue and review the proposed reporting standards of the Governmental Accounting Standards Board (GASB) regarding these revenues. Finally, to assess the equity effects of this activity in one particularly active state, local educational foundations in Michigan will be examined and comparisons drawn between foundation and non-foundation districts in terms of educational and socioeconomic characteristics.

NATIONAL TRENDS IN
PUBLIC SCHOOL SPENDING

For the past century, public elementary and secondary education in the United States has enjoyed remarkably steady revenue growth. Hanushek and Rivkin (1997) report that real expenditure per pupil increased at 3.5 percent per year over the entire period of 1890–1990, with total annual expenditures rising from $2 billion to more than $187 billion, in constant 1990 dollars, over this period. This nearly 100-fold increase is more than triple the growth of the U.S. gross national product (GNP) over this period, with K–12 public school expenditures increasing from less than 1 percent of GNP in 1890 to 3.4 percent in 1990. This increased spending resulted from a combination of falling pupil-staff ratios, increasing real wages paid to teachers, the expansion of educational services for handicapped students, and rising expenditures outside the classroom, including spending on central administration, plant maintenance and pupil transportation (Hanushek and Rivkin 1997).

Since 1990, however, the growth rate in per pupil expenditures appears to have fallen precipitously. While real spending per pupil grew at a 3.75 percent rate in the 1980s, the growth rate from 1990 to 1993 was a mere 0.6 percent (National Center for Education Statistics 1995). This lower growth rate is due, in part, to the return of growth in school enrollments, which have been rising nationally since 1981. Further, resulting fiscal pressures on public schools are exacerbated by the steady growth of the special education population, for whom financial support is mandated by federal law. As noted by Meredith and Underwood (1995), cost containment is of only secondary importance in the special education paradigm. Under the Individuals with Disabilities Act (IDEA), school districts must provide every special education child with a free, appropriate education regardless of cost. On average, per pupil expenditures for special education equals approximately 2.3 times per pupil expenditures for regular education (Chaikand, Danielson, and Brauen 1993). Moreover, the special education population continues to grow more rapidly than the general student population, rising from 11.6 percent of total enrollment in 1990 to 11.9 percent in 1992.[2]

These pressures on regular education funding are exacerbated by stringent tax and spending limits enacted in a number

2 Further, because of the mandated status of special education, the expansion of special education in either scope or intensity would take a larger share of any new revenue in times of slow budget growth.

of states (Mullins and Joyce 1996; Mullins and Cox 1995). As of 1994, forty-three states specifically limited local revenues and expenditures by means considered more constraining than full disclosure–truth in taxation measures that require public discussion and specific legislative action prior to enactment of tax rate or levy increases (Mullins and Cox 1995). Twelve states have set overall property tax rate limitations. Thirty states limit tax rates levied by specific types of local governments. Twenty-five states limit local tax levies, six states limit the growth in assessments, three states limit general revenue growth, eight limit expenditure growth and at least seventeen have some form of full disclosure requirement (Mullins and Joyce 1996).[3] Mullins and Joyce (1996) examine the effects of tax and expenditure limitations (TELs) using pooled, cross-sectional, time-series models of state and local spending and observe a diminished use of broad-based taxes at the local level and a "dramatic increase in reliance on user charges and miscellaneous revenue sources from both state and local governments." As revenue growth from broad-based taxes slowed and enrollments grew, public schools increasingly sought revenue from alternative sources.

SOURCES OF
NONTRADITIONAL REVENUE

Public school districts across the United States have long attempted to identify and tap into so-called nontraditional sources of revenue. The term "nontraditional" appears to stem not from a limited history of school revenue raised from sources

---

3 Mullins and Joyce (1996) note the difficulty in assessing the degree of constraint imposed by these limitations. Mechanisms such as local popular or legislative votes, authorization by state tax commissions and state legislatures, and charter and constitutional revisions are provided to suspend the provisions of these constraints and, depending upon their comprehensiveness, circumvention is more difficult in some cases than others. Comparisons across and within states are further complicated by variations in the definition of the property tax base, in assessment practices, and in the exclusion of various revenue and expenditure categories (e.g., long-term debt and fees and charges) from the limitations.

other than broad-based taxes, but from their relatively small magnitude. Research into the collection of these revenues dates to at least the early 1980s. Meno (1984) categorizes these efforts to augment traditional, broad-based tax revenues into three types of activities: donor activities, including the solicitation of goods, services, and money; enterprise activities involving the selling or leasing of services and facilities; and shared or cooperative activities whereby functions are pooled with other agencies or organizations to lower costs. Other nontraditional initiatives include the investment of school resources and the pursuit of new government funds through grant-writing (Pijanowski and Monk 1996). Schools and school districts have enjoyed limited and uneven success in raising revenues from these sources. Potential budget impacts of 7 percent to 9 percent have been reported for public schools in regional studies of alternative revenues (Meno 1984; Picus, Tetreault, and Hertert 1995; Salloum 1985). While the genesis of such revenue-raising efforts is often some degree of fiscal stress, some evidence suggests that relatively wealthy school districts enjoy relatively greater success in tapping into these revenue sources than do their less affluent counterparts. Thus, these revenues may exert a mild disequalizing effect (Addonizio 1998).

DONOR ACTIVITIES

DIRECT DONATIONS

Meno (1984) characterizes donor activities as any activities intended to raise funds, goods, or services from non-government sources. These donations can take the form of direct district fundraising from individuals or from corporations and foundations. Resources raised in this fashion may consist of large single donations for a specific purpose. For example, the Beloit Public Schools in Wisconsin received $440,000 from a local foundation to buy microcomputers as part of an experimental program in computer education (Meno 1984). Other examples of direct donor activity include an enrichment fund established by local businesses and community members in the Tucson (Arizona) Unified School District, the funding of a dental prevention model in the Wichita City Schools by the American Dental Association, and the support of a health education project in the North Glenn (Colorado) School District by the Gates Foundation (Maeroff 1982; Meno 1984).

INDIRECT DONATIONS

SCHOOL DISTRICT FOUNDATIONS

School districts in recent years have turned increasingly to an alternative type of donor activity—the indirect donation of funds through local district educational foundations, nonprofit organizations created to receive donations for the district. For example, in Michigan 153 such nonprofit organizations have been established by local districts to raise revenue for curriculum improvements, enrichment activities, capital projects, and instructional materials and to strengthen links between schools and communities. Further, this activity in Michigan appears to be part of a growing national trend. While reliable national figures are not available, the National Association of Educational Foundations (NAEF) estimates that by the year 2000 there will be 4,000 public school foundations throughout the United States (NAEF 1996).

Districts may create foundations through which money can flow to fund a variety of school activities. Examples of large, urban districts taking this approach include San Francisco, Washington, D.C., Dallas, and Oakland (Meno 1984). Alternatively, foundations may be created for a single purpose. For example, the Escondido County Union High School District in California established a foundation following passage of Proposition 13 to support its interscholastic athletics program (Meno 1984). In New York City, parents in an affluent area raised money to retain a popular teacher whose job was threatened by budget cuts (Anderson 1997).

While the scope of such foundation activity across the United States has yet to be accurately measured, the rise of these organizations is not surprising in light of the slowing of revenue growth for public schools. This development, however, has not been viewed with universal approval. Concern has focused on the possible disequalizing effects of foundation revenue. Virtually every state allocates school aid to local districts by means of equalizing formulas designed to offset disparities in local fiscal resources.[4] Local education foundations have raised concerns that they may exacerbate fiscal disparities. For example, political economist and former U.S. Labor Secretary Robert Reich has characterized these organizations as "another means by which the privileged are seceding from the rest" (Pollack 1992). The impact of local education foundations on school finance equalization efforts in Michigan is examined in section VI, below.

BOOSTER CLUBS

In addition to school district foundations, schools rely on booster clubs to support specific activities. Club members develop fundraising strategies, including networking with local businesses, and coordinate their efforts with the school activities they support. Club activities may focus on a single school or an entire district. School programs enjoying the support of boosters include athletics, band, orchestra, choral, debate, and drama (Meno 1984). Booster volunteers, who are often school parents, frequently obtain donations of school supplies (e.g., equipment, uniforms) from local vendors who are then provided commercial access to the students through advertising in school venues and publications (Pijanowski and Monk 1996). In addition, members often make direct cash or in-kind contributions to support school activities and associated staff (e.g., end-of-season gifts or bonuses for coaches). While anecdotal evidence suggests that booster activities are widespread across U.S. public schools, research in New York State revealed that many school officials were not familiar with booster club activities associated with their schools (Pijanowski and Monk 1996).

---

4 Nationally, states provided 46 percent of K–12 public school revenues in 1993–94, with most aid distributed so as to offset differences among local districts in the ability to finance education. The sole exception is New Hampshire, where state aid comprises a mere 7 percent of K–12 public school revenue. Local property taxes, on the other hand, provide 90 percent of school revenue, while federal sources provide the remaining 3 percent (American Education Finance Association 1995).

ENTERPRISE ACTIVITIES

USER FEES

Under these arrangements, users of school-provided programs or services are required to pay for those services. Examples of fee-based arrangements are driver education programs, swimming instructions, school supplies, athletics, and pupil transportation. However, as a growing number of schools have considered the imposition of fees for educational supplies or services, these fees have been challenged on federal and state constitutional grounds and state statutory provisions.[5] Restrictions on the enforcement of school district fee policies are largely a matter of state law, as federal courts generally defer to state authorities in these matters (Dayton and McCarthy 1992).

According to a 1991 survey of state departments of education, only eight states allow local public schools to charge fees for required textbooks (Hamm and Crosser 1991).[6] Many more states, however, allow fees for general school supplies and services. This same survey found 29 states permitting equipment fees, 20 states permitting lab fees, and 20 states allowing fees for field trips. Other permitted fees included general supplies (12 states), workbooks (15 states), and pencils and paper (11 states) (Hamm and Crosser 1991).

Tuition fees are generally prohibited for required courses offered during the academic year. Further, while fees for elective and summer school courses have been allowed in the past, they have been subject to legal challenge in recent years (Dayton and McCarthy 1992).[7] On the other hand, fees for extracurricular activities have become more widespread in recent years. A total of

---

5 For an analysis of the constitutional challenges to school fee policies, see Dayton and McCarthy 1992.

6 These eight states are Alaska, Illinois, Indiana, Iowa, Kansas, Kentucky, Utah, and Wisconsin.

7 Historically, courts have held that summer school fees were constitutional because summer school was not considered part of a student's entitlement to a free public education. However, as more states establish minimum competency testing programs for promotion and graduation and require summer school attendance for students who fail these exams, summer school may be increasingly

23 states allow fees for participation in school clubs and 21 states allow fees for participation in interscholastic sports (Hamm and Crosser 1991). Finally, 34 states permit fees for pupil transportation, although these fee revenues are relatively small (Wassmer and Fisher 1997). Many local school boards provide fee waivers for children of low-income families.[8] Further, while many states permit the use of fees for "auxiliary" services, local school districts have used them only minimally. User charges provided only 3.2 percent of school district revenue in 1977, and then declined to 2.8 percent of revenue in 1991 (Wassmer and Fisher 1997).[9]

IMPACT OF DEVELOPER FEES

Local governments across the United States have adopted various forms of developer charges as a means of financing the timely installation of public facilities. These charges imposed as a condition of development approval include impact fees, special assessments, development agreements, user fees, and connection fees. Impact fees are imposed on developers to ensure sufficient funding for those capital services and facilities needed to support the new development. Such public services and facilities include roads, parks, police, fire, sewer, water, libraries, and schools (Siemon and Zimet 1992).

The imposition of impact fees for public schools, however, raises an issue not associated with other public services or facilities. Specifically, case law provides that impact fees must be imposed on the basis of actual use. At the same time, virtually every state constitution requires "free" (i.e., tax-supported) public schools. Thus, payment of fees for the use of public schools is ar-

---

viewed as part of a student's entitlement. Further, while fees for elective courses have been upheld by the Supreme Courts of New Mexico and Montana, the Supreme Court of California held that all educational activities must be free (Dayton and McCarthy 1992).

8 As Dayton and McCarthy (1992) note, poor families may choose to withdraw from user financed-activities rather than face the potential embarrassment of seeking a waiver.

9 Wassmer and Fisher (1997) observe that, while U.S. local school districts employ user fees only very minimally, as much as $30 billion in expenditures on auxiliary services could be funded through fees.

guably unconstitutional. The issue is whether or not developers may be required to pay a pro rata share of the cost of additional public school capacity needed to serve new development. The authority of local governments to impose school impact fees was upheld by the Florida Supreme Court in 1991 in *St. Johns County, Florida v. Northeast Florida Builders Ass'n.*[10] This ruling provides persuasive authority for the imposition of such local government fees in other states such as California that are experiencing rapid growth and development.

LEASING OF FACILITIES AND SERVICES

Local school boards often raise revenue by leasing facilities to community organizations or private enterprises. In some instances of severely declining enrollments, districts have leased entire buildings to private tenants (Pijanowski and Monk 1996).[11] Districts also lease excess space to public agencies in exchange for services to be provided to students, school staff and neighborhood residents (Meno 1984). In addition to leasing property, some districts raise revenue by leasing services. Examples include selling food services or computer support (e.g., business services, test scoring) to private nonprofit organizations or private schools, and the sale of transportation services to public nonprofit organizations or government agencies (Meno 1984; Pijanowski and Monk 1996).

SALE OF SCHOOL ACCESS

The sale of access to school markets, generally through advertising on school property or in school publications, is another means by which public schools generate revenue. Examples include the sale of advertising on school buses in New York City and advertising on homework handouts in California (Pijanowski and Monk 1996). School districts also sell conces-

---

10 583 So. 2d 635 (Fla. 1991), 43 ZD 266.
11 Examples include a credit union in Southfield Public Schools (Michigan), a dating service in the Hazelwood School District (Missouri) and the rental of playing fields and locker facilities to professional sports teams for preseason training camp by the Phoenix Public Schools (Meno 1983).

sions to businesses for various services such as student pictures and vending machine operations. Perhaps the most well-known example of the sale of school access is the arrangement between Whittle Communications Channel One and local school districts whereby, in exchange for about $50,000 worth of programming and equipment (including a satellite dish, recorders, and television sets), students are exposed to daily news broadcasts that include some advertisements. In 1995, over 8 million students in approximately 12,000 schools received daily broadcasts from Channel One. This audience comprises approximately 40 percent of the students in the sixth through twelfth grades nationwide (Johnston 1995).[12]

PERSONAL SEAT LICENSES

In 1998, officials at Ravenna High School in Ohio sold personal seat licenses, or the right to purchase tickets to sporting events, to help finance an 8,000-seat football and soccer stadium. This fundraising strategy, initiated in 1995 by professional sports teams to help finance new stadiums, is used by a few colleges and universities nationwide but appears to be new to public high schools with the Ravenna plan (Blair 1998). Under this plan, Ravenna fans may buy two seats with their names inscribed on them at the forty-yard line for $1,500. Inscribed seating elsewhere in the stadium costs $1,000. Both packages include preferred parking and an optional five-year payment plan. The licenses are guaranteed for the patron's lifetime contingent upon the annual $30 purchase of season tickets. (Blair 1998). Whether this practice spreads to other school districts as an alternative to selling bonds remains to be seen, but the Ravenna plan represents a new, and possibly lucrative, enterprise activity for public schools.

---

12 Despite its broad list of subscribers, Channel One is not without its critics, who cite its intrusive nature and the perceived school endorsement of advertised products. As of 1992, the highest subscription rates were found in Michigan, Ohio, Pennsylvania, and Texas. On the other hand, Channel One is banned in California, Massachusetts, New York, North Carolina, and Washington (Greenberg and Brand 1993).

SHARED OR COOPERATIVE ACTIVITIES

Local school districts sometimes seek to share operating costs by establishing cooperative programs with other governmental agencies, private nonprofit or community organizations, colleges or universities, or businesses.

GOVERNMENTAL AGENCIES

Examples of these activities include the use of public buildings for instruction, the shared use and cost of recreational facilities (e.g., pools, gymnasiums) and sharing transportation vehicles with local governmental agencies (Pijanowski and Monk 1996). According to Meno (1984), the most common shared activity between schools and governmental agencies involves the running of local parks and recreation departments, including the shared use and maintenance of playing fields and grounds. While most of the arrangements are intended to be fiscally neutral for both parties, there are exceptions. For example, the Merced City School District (California) provides use of playing fields and grounds to the parks and recreation department. In consideration, the department makes a yearly contribution to the district's capital account for fields and grounds that exceeds the district's additional operating costs (Meno 1984).

HIGHER EDUCATION

These partnerships include opportunities for high school students to take courses at local community colleges or four-year institutions in lieu of high school courses. Under such cooperative arrangements, students would pay no tuition and the college would enjoy free use of school district staff.[13] Meno (1984) identifies a number of school districts that participate in graduate student internship programs with local universities. For example, local colleges may place psychologist interns in public schools, where they perform standard school district

---

13 Such arrangements, of course, may also be competitive. In Michigan, for example, high school students may enroll in courses at community colleges and public universities with tuition paid from a pro rata share of state school aid, in effect, a transfer from the local school district to the postsecondary institution.

functions under district supervision but at a substantially lower cost to the district as compared with regular staff costs.

PRIVATE NONPROFIT AGENCIES

School districts often share excess space with local social service providers. Rather than charge the provider for a share of the cost of facility maintenance, the district makes the space available in return for social services provided to students at no charge. As Pijanowski and Monk (1996) note, the ability of local schools to negotiate such arrangements may assume greater importance as greater demands are placed on local schools for social services.

BUSINESS AND INDUSTRY

Schools often rely on business partnerships to share operational, instructional and programmatic costs. Businesses, in turn, are given an opportunity to enter schools and classrooms. Schools benefit by gaining access to the expertise of business officials who have the opportunity to shape educational programs to meet needs of the business community (Monk and Brent 1997). Such cooperative arrangements date back to at least the 1960s. For example, New York City Schools have long maintained cooperative efforts with local businesses and industry to assist students as they enter the labor force. Activities include work/study, job placement, career guidance, basic skill training, remedial education, and curriculum development (Meno 1984).

A common result of school outreach to the private sector is school adoption. In return for donations of money or service, business employees receive training in teaching techniques, use of athletic facilities, and access to students for marketing research (Pijanowski and Monk 1996).

REPORTING
NONTRADITIONAL REVENUE

While revenue from enterprise, cooperative, and direct donor activities are generally reported in standard local school district financial reports, revenues from indirect donor activities are not. The apparent rise in the number of local education foundations and, to a lesser extent, booster clubs and the dearth of information regarding revenue levels raised from these sources have been noted by the Governmental Accounting Standards Board (GASB 1994). GASB, established as an arm of the Financial Accounting Foundation in 1984 to promulgate standards of financial accounting and reporting with respect to activities and transactions of state and local governmental activities, has noted the rise of "affiliated organizations;" that is, organizations that are not themselves governmental entities but exist for the purpose of raising resources for such entities. According to GASB standards, affiliated organizations should be considered a part of the "financial reporting entity," and subject to the same public reporting requirements that apply to the governmental entity. Examples of such affiliated organizations arguably include school district foundations and, possibly, booster clubs. GASB Statement No. 14, *The Financial Reporting Entity,* defines that entity as consisting of not only the primary government but also "organizations for which the primary government is financially accountable" and "other organizations for which the nature and significance of their relationship with the primary government are such that exclusion would cause the reporting entity's financial statements to be misleading or incomplete" (GASB 1994). The statement cited a nonprofit fundraising corporation affiliated with a college as an example of an organization that should be evaluated as a potential component unit subject to governmental reporting standards that apply to the financial reporting entity. However, the statement did not provide specific guidance for identifying these "affiliated organizations" (GASB 1994).[14]

---

14 This omission is explicitly noted in a subsequent GASB *Proposed Statement*: "Under the financial accountability criteria established in Statement 14, the inclusion of legally separate organizations in the reporting entity is based on either the appointment process or fiscal dependency. Certain entities, however, are affiliated with legally separate organizations, created for the specific purpose of providing financial assistance or other types of support to their programs without meeting the financial accountability criteria defined in

In December 1994, GASB published a draft of a proposed statement that would establish a definition for affiliated organizations and financial reporting guidance for those organizations (GASB 1994). According to the draft, an "affiliated organization" is one that meets the following criteria:

1. The organization has separate legal standing, where neither direct association through appointment of a voting majority of the organization's governing body nor fiscal dependency exists.

2. The affiliation with a specific primary government is set forth in the organization's articles of incorporation—for example, by reference to the name of the primary government in describing the purposes for which the organization was established.

3. The affiliation with a specific primary government is set forth in the organization's application to the Internal Revenue Service for exemption from payment of federal income tax pursuant to Internal Revenue Code (IRC) 501(c)(3)—for example, by

Statement 14. This occurs particularly among colleges and universities; it also occurs among hospitals, museums, elementary and secondary education institutions, and other types of organizations. Because of the methods used to create and administer some of these organizations, the nature of their relationship is different from what has been set forth in the Statement 14 'financial accountability' criteria. The Board believes that, despite the absence of direct association through the appointment process or fiscal dependency, the relationships between the primary government and some of these organizations are such that either financial accountability exists through other means or exclusion would render the statements of the financial reporting entity misleading or incomplete....The Board concluded that in certain circumstances these relationships make an affiliated organization an integral part of the primary government reporting entity. The Board also concluded that financial reporting could best recognize the nature of this relationship (in the absence of direct association through the appointment process of fiscal dependency) through discrete presentation of the affiliated organization on the face of the financial reporting entity's financial statements" (GASB 1994 pp. 7–8).

reference to the name of the primary government in response to any of the questions contained in the exemption application—and the organization has been granted that exemption.

According to the draft, the affiliated organization should be reported as a component unit of the primary government "if the primary government has the ability to *impose its will* on that organization or there is a potential for the organization to provide specific *financial benefits* to, or impose specific *financial burdens* on, the primary government." The draft also states in a footnote that an affiliated organization should be reported as a component unit of the primary government "if the nature and significance of the relationship with the primary government are such that exclusion would cause the primary government reporting entity financial statements to be misleading or incomplete." The draft would require that an affiliated organization component unit be included in the financial reporting entity "by discrete presentation" and provides guidance for reporting transactions between the primary government and the component units of affiliated organizations, based upon the form of those transactions. In response to critical comments from public school booster clubs and parent teacher organizations (PTOs), the exposure draft was withdrawn and, at the time of this writing, is being revised by GASB staff. While the revised statement is expected to exempt small PTOs and booster clubs from the financial reporting requirements, local school district education foundations will likely be subject to new disclosure requirements. Such foundation activity has been particularly widespread in California and Michigan (Brunner and Sonstelie 1997; Addonizio 1998).

PUBLIC SCHOOL REVENUE TRENDS IN MICHIGAN

The development of nontraditional revenue sources in response to slowing growth of broad-based school taxes is illustrated in Michigan, the site of sweeping school finance reform in 1994. The quest for new school revenues, principally through the creation of local education foundations, substantially preceded the state reform and has had a mildly disequalizing effect on the distribution of resources across local districts. While not necessarily representative of a national trend, Michigan's experience as a leader in the foundation movement may signal future trends in other states.

PRE-REFORM PERIOD

Trends in state and local revenue per pupil from 1981–82 through 1992–93, in constant 1992–93 dollars, are presented in Table 8.1 (p. 262).

As Table 8.1 reveals, total per pupil revenue fell in 1982–83 and 1983–84, as Michigan and the United States weathered a recession that began in 1979 and persisted until 1983. Real revenue then rose slowly through 1985–86 and increased a robust 9.6 percent in 1986–87. Following a modest 1.2 percent increase in 1987–88, revenue rose by fully 14.5 percent in 1988–89. The rate of real growth then fell steadily from 1989–90 through 1992–93, turning negative in that year. This decline in real per pupil revenue growth, combined with flat or falling enrollments in many Michigan school districts and increasing academic expectations as reflected by more challenging state assessments of pupil achievement in reading, writing, mathematics and science and an achievement-based school accreditation program created by the legislature in 1994, led some districts to search for nontraditional sources of support.

MICHIGAN SCHOOL FINANCE REFORM

In 1994, the Michigan legislature enacted the state's most sweeping fiscal reforms in more than 20 years, reducing property taxes, increasing the state share of school funding and substantially reducing local discretion regarding school taxation

TABLE 8.1. REAL STATE AND LOCAL REVENUE PER PUPIL, 1981–82 TO 1992–93 IN CONSTANT 1992–93 DOLLARS

Year	Local Revenue	State Revenue	Total Revenue
1981–82	$2,933	$1,577	$4,510
1982–83	2,862	1,452	4,314
1983–84	2,835	1,427	4,262
1984–85	2,884	1,563	4,446
1985–86	2,832	1,654	4,486
1986–87	3,103	1,814	4,917
1987–88	3,114	1,859	4,973
1988–89	3,732	1,963	5,695
1989–90	3,919	2,039	5,958
1990–91	4,065	2,096	6,160
1991–92	4,170	2,154	6,324
1992–93	4,163	2,150	6,313
% change	+41.9	+36.6	+40.0

Source: National Education Association, as reported in American Education Finance Association (1995).

and expenditure decisions. On the allocation side, the new legislation replaced a 20-year-old district power equalizing (DPE) school aid formula and numerous categorical grants with a foundation formula, which closely regulated local per pupil revenue. Each district's 1993–94 combined state and local (base) revenue for school operations became the basis for determining its 1994–95 foundation allowance. The major components of a district's base revenues were local ad valorem property taxes, DPE aid and most state categorical aid.

The new state formula substantially constrained per pupil revenue growth for high-spending districts.[15] Further, the state-imposed constraint on per pupil revenue growth was designed to become binding on more local districts in the 1995–96 fiscal year and beyond. This constraint is imposed on local districts in the form of a state basic foundation allowance set at $5,000 for 1994–95 and indexed annually to nominal school-aid-fund revenue per pupil. This basic allowance has risen slowly, from $5,000 in 1994–95 to $5,153 in 1995–96, $5,308 in 1996–97, and $5,462 in 1997–98. Local districts at or above the basic foundation allowance simply receive an absolute dollar increase in their district foundation allowances equal to the dollar increase in the basic foundation allowance.[16] Districts below the basic foundation allowance in 1995–96 and subsequent years receive increases up to double that amount. As the finance system is

---

15 The foundation formula guaranteed each local district a per pupil allowance that ranged from the $4,200 minimum to a maximum of $6,660, provided the district levies a local property tax rate of 18 mills on nonhomestead property. Specifically, local districts with 1993–94 base per pupil revenue below $4,200 are raised either to $4,200 or to $250 over their 1993–94 level, whichever is greater. Districts between $4,200 and $6,500 in 1993–94 received a per pupil increase varying linearly from $250 at $4,200 to $160 at $6,500. Finally, local districts with 1993–94 base per pupil revenue in excess of $6,500 were allowed an increase of up to $160 per pupil if local voters approved hold harmless millage sufficient to raise the additional revenue. This local millage is levied against homesteads, up to a maximum of either 18 mills or the district's prior year millage vote, whichever is less.

16 The annual change in the basic foundation allowance is determined by a final index, which may be written as follows:

$$I = (R_t/R_{t-1})(M_{t-1}/M_t)$$

where I = final index; R_t = total school aid fund revenue in current year; R_{t-1} = total school aid fund revenue in prior year; M_{t-1} = total pupil membership in prior year; M_t = total pupil membership in current year.

The annual basic foundation allowance is determined by

$$BF_t = BF_{t-1} \times I$$

where BF_t = current year basic foundation; BF_{t-1} = prior year basic foundation.

currently designed, the number of local districts subject to this constraint will rise each year, as relatively low-spending districts are boosted to the basic foundation allowance and then locked in at that level.

AGGREGATE REVENUE TRENDS

The financial position and revenue levels of a local district also depend, of course, on its enrollment levels. Given the universal practice of allocating state aid on a per pupil basis, recipient local districts with excess capacity and rising enrollments enjoy positive marginal revenue and negligible marginal costs, while districts with falling enrollments face declining revenue and the need to lower variable costs, principally staff costs. While aggregate school district revenues and expenditures will differ according to net changes in district fund balances, total operating expenditures provide some indication of the fiscal constraints facing local districts. Nominal and real total current operating expenditures (TCOP) for Michigan's local school districts from 1978–79 through 1996–97 are presented in Figure 8.1. These data indicate a period of fiscal stress well before the implementation of Proposal A in 1994. Beginning in 1979–80, real TCOP declined four consecutive years and did not regain the 1979–80 level until 1991–92. Indeed, over the entire period examined, which begins with the first year of the implementation of Michigan's constitutional tax and expenditure limitation amendment, TCOP rose a mere 1 percent annually in real terms.[17]

The local foundation allowance for an individual district is determined as follows:

$$LF_t = LF_{t-1} + 2b - [(b-\$50) \times (LF_{t-1}-\$4,200)/(c-\$4,200)]$$

where LF_t = district's current year foundation allowance; LF_{t-1} = district's prior year foundation allowance; $b = I \times BF_{t-1}$ = current year increase in basic foundation allowance; $c = BF_t$ = current year basic foundation allowance.

17 Popularly known as the "Headlee Amendment" after its author Richard Headlee, this constitutional amendment limited both local property taxes and total state tax collections.

FIGURE 8.1. TOTAL CURRENT OPERATING EXPENDITURES (TCOP) FOR MICHIGAN SCHOOL DISTRICTS, 1978–79 TO 1996–97

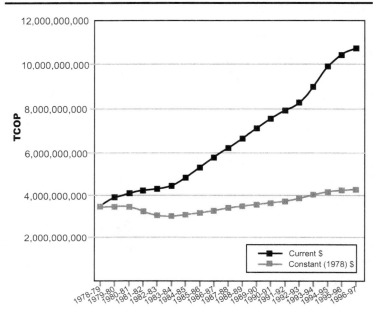

Sources: Expenditure data obtained from the Michigan Department of Education, Local District Financial Reports. TCOP is General Fund Total Expenditures less expenditures for capital outlay and community services. Inflation indices obtained from the State Tax Commission of the Michigan Department of Treasury.

NONTRADITIONAL REVENUES FOR MICHIGAN PUBLIC SCHOOLS

Tracking the growth of nontraditional revenues in Michigan public schools is made difficult by the lack of complete and uniform reporting by local districts and consistent time-series data. One source of consistent, but historically limited, time-series data is Michigan's Common Core of Data (CCD) for school years 1988–89 through 1995–96. These data are summarized in Table 8.2.

TABLE 8.2. SHARE OF NONTRADITIONAL REVENUE IN MICHIGAN, 1988–89 THROUGH 1995–96

Year	Local Revenue ($ million)	Total Revenue ($ million)	Nontraditional Revenue ($ million)	% of Local Revenue	% of Total Revenue
1988–89	$5,190	$7,734	$599	11.5	7.7
1989–90	5,656	8,395	599	10.6	7.1
1990–91	6,099	9,054	628	10.3	6.9
1991–92	6,474	9,659	545	8.4	5.6
1992–93	6,803	10,766	652	9.6	6.1
1993–94	7,210	10,828	639	8.9	5.9
1994–95	3,159	11,925	658	20.8	5.5
1995–96	3,431	12,699	711	20.7	5.6

Source: Michigan Department of Education. "Nontraditional Local Revenue" includes transportation fees, food service revenues, investment earnings, student activity fees, tuition revenue, summer school revenue, community service revenue, rental revenue, and direct donations. It does not include indirect donations, such as those from local education foundations. Note the reduction in "total local revenue" effected by Proposal A, beginning in 1994–95.

As Table 8.2 indicates, reported nontraditional revenue for Michigan school districts has been fairly substantial, accounting for nearly 6 percent of revenue from all sources, down from nearly 8 percent in 1988–89, and more than 20 percent of all local revenue in the post-reform period. Moreover, these reported revenues do not include indirect donations, consisting largely of revenue raised by local education foundations.

LOCAL EDUCATION FOUNDATIONS IN MICHIGAN

Generally, a foundation is a nonprofit, tax-exempt entity with a board of trustees engaged in raising, managing and disseminating resources for one or more designated purposes, such as charitable, religious, literary, scientific or educational. Foundation trustees are generally selected from the local community and focus on raising resources, while directors implement policies and programs.

Creating a local education foundation in Michigan is relatively simple. Organizers file a four-page Articles of Incorporation form, along with a $20 fee, with the Corporation Division, Corporation and Securities Bureau, Michigan Department of Commerce, as required by Michigan's Nonprofit Corporation Act (P.A. 162 of 1982). Foundations generally begin operations within four to six months of filing Articles, and often exist alongside booster and parent groups that also raise funds for the local public schools. Although their fundraising activities may overlap (e.g., raffles, sales, etc.), foundations often focus on developing partnerships with corporations, individual major donors and other foundations, and seek planned gifts through wills and memorials. Grants are often made to teachers for innovative instructional practices, visual arts, and technology, areas seldom supported by booster groups. Further, education foundations usually limit grants to items not normally part of the local school district budget.

Local educational foundations in Michigan were identified through a key word search of files of both the Corporation Division, Corporation and Securities Bureau, Michigan Department of Commerce and the Charitable Trust Division of the Michigan Attorney General's office. A total of 153 local education foundations was identified. A questionnaire was then mailed to each foundation and, as a follow-up, to each associated local school district superintendent. A profile of the foundations and the respondents is presented in Figure 8.2 (p. 268) and Table 8.3 (p. 269).

FIGURE 8.2. EDUCATIONAL FOUNDATIONS IN MICHIGAN

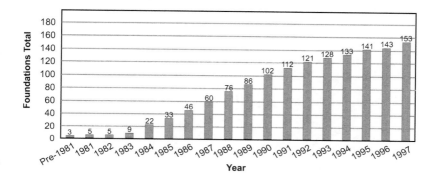

Source: Michigan Department of Consumer and Industry Services.

TABLE 8.3. PROFILE OF LOCAL EDUCATION FOUNDATIONS RESPONDING TO SURVEY

Year Established	Years of Operation	Number of Foundations			
		Urban	Suburban	Rural	Total
1995	1	1	1	1	3
1994	2	0	1	2	3
1993	3	1	2	1	4
1992	4	0	2	3	5
1991	5	1	3	4	8
1990	6	0	0	1	1
1989	7	0	1	0	1
1988	8	0	2	2	4
1987	9	0	2	3	5
1986	10	1	4	4	9
1985	11	1	2	2	6*
1984	12	2	1	0	3
1983	13	0	0	0	0
1982	14	0	0	1	1
1981	15	0	0	1	1
Total	—	7	21	25	54
Average rev. 1994–95		$51,915	$16,915	$9,851	$17,024
Maximum		$100,000	$65,000	$36,200	$100,000
Minimum		$0	$0	$0	$0
Standard Deviation		$46,802	$15,611	$8,521	$21,489
Coefficient of Variation		0.9015	0.9229	0.8650	1.2623

* One foundation did not respond to urban/suburban/rural question.

As Figure 8.2 indicates, the formation of local education foundations accelerated during the period of 1984 through 1993, a period marked by variable growth in real per pupil revenue from traditional sources. The greatest annual increases in the number of local foundations occurred in 1988 and 1990, when real state and local per pupil revenue rose 1.1 percent and 4.4 percent, respectively. Formation of new foundations slowed in 1994, when Michigan reformed its school funding system, and accelerated again in 1997, as the constraints on traditional source revenue imposed by the reforms became binding on more local districts. The survey data summarized in Table 3 reveal that local education foundations are generally found in suburban and rural school districts. Annual foundation revenue, however, has been quite modest, averaging a mere $17,024 in 1994–95 among responding districts. Revenue levels have varied considerably across these districts, as indicated by the relatively large coefficients of variation for the district groups.

Additional data on the levels of revenue raised by local district foundations were obtained from tax records filed with the Consumer Protection Division of the Michigan Attorney General's Office. These 1997 tax year data, while incomplete, are largely consistent with the 1994–95 fiscal year survey data in revealing quite modest revenue levels. These tax data are summarized in Table 8.4.

TABLE 8.4. LOCAL EDUCATION FOUNDATION REVENUE LEVELS AS REPORTED IN 1997 FOUNDATION TAX RETURNS

	Net Assets	Annual Revenue	Annual Educational Expenditures
Minimum	$2,136	$2,365	$1,605
Maximum	936,652	198,494	66,765
Mean	142,205	44,537	14,989
Standard Deviation	196,356	42,386	12,747
Coeff. of Variation	1.3808	0.9517	0.8504

Source: Charitable Trust Section, Consumer Protection Division, Office of the Attorney General, State of Michigan

Although these data are available for only about one-fourth of all state-registered local education foundations, they reveal a modest impact on annual educational spending by local districts. Indeed, the mean annual expenditure from foundation revenue for these districts amounts to less than the operating revenue generated by three additional students through the general state aid formula for the average Michigan district.

COMPARISON OF FOUNDATION AND NON-FOUNDATION DISTRICTS

While total foundation revenues to date have been modest thus far, the presence of a local education foundation provides a potential source of supplemental revenue for and suggests a heightened community interest in local public schools. To begin testing for educationally relevant differences between foundation and non-foundation districts, one-way analysis of variance was used to compare the mean values of selected district revenue measures, household economic characteristics, district size, and measures of student achievement of each district group. The foundation districts consist of all 144 districts identified through the state databases described above, not merely the survey respondents. These mean values and associated significance levels are presented in Table 8.5 (p. 272).

As Table 8.5 indicates, local districts with educational foundations, on average, enjoy higher unrestricted public revenue per pupil, greater enrollments, higher household income and higher student achievement than their non-foundation counterparts. Foundation districts also allocate a lower proportion of their expenditures to general administration, while spending shares for instruction and school administration are roughly equal across the two district groups. The differences in the group means are statistically significant for all remaining variables except tax base per pupil and tenth grade reading achievement. Some differences are striking. For example, household incomes are more than 20 percent higher, on the average, in foundation districts as compared with their non-foundation counterparts. Foundation districts also have a lower percentage of children eligible for free and reduced price lunch under the National School Lunch Act and lower Federal Chapter 1 (now

TABLE 8.5. COMPARISON OF FOUNDATION AND NON-FOUNDATION DISTRICT MEANS OF SELECTED MEASURES OF REVENUE, EXPENDITURES, HOUSEHOLD INCOME, ENROLLMENT, AND PUPIL ACHIEVEMENT: ONE-WAY ANOVA

Variable	Foundation	Non-Foundation	P-value
Household Income	$29,336	$24,359	< .0001
% Subsidized Lunch	23%	30%	< .0001
Tax Base per Pupil	$116,937	$114,483	.7748
Math Achievement Gr. 4	64.60%	60.66%	.0023
Math Achievement Gr. 7	53.11%	48.65%	.0024
Math Achievement Gr. 10	38.72%	35.64%	.0116
Reading Achievement Gr. 4	45.18%	40.95%	.0005
Reading Achievement Gr. 7	37.40%	33.98%	.0030
Reading Achievement Gr. 10	45.11%	43.44%	.1567
Enrollment	4.267	2,605	.0421
Ch. 1 Revenue per Pupil	$109.59	$163.17	.0130
Unrestricted Public Revenue per Pupil	$5,336	$5,148	.0537
% Spending for Instruction	61.33%	61.22%	.7770
% Spending for School Administration	6.00%	5.94%	.6610
% Spending for General Administration	2.73%	3.75%	<.0001

Source: Compiled by author with published data from the Michigan Department of Education and the Michigan Department of Treasury. Data are for the 1994–95 fiscal year, except for 1993 household income.

renamed Title I) expenditures than their non-foundation counterparts. Further, the average percentage of students earning satisfactory scores on the Michigan Education Assessment Program (MEAP) is significantly higher among foundation districts on five of the six measures.

These results, while not unexpected, raise concerns regarding the equity in the distribution of educational resources across local school districts in Michigan. Michigan, along with virtually every other state, has adopted state school aid formulas designed to distribute more state aid to local districts with relatively low fiscal capacity, generally measured in terms of taxable property wealth per pupil. Further, state categorical grant programs such as special education, compensatory education and bilingual education are designed to target additional resources to local districts with relatively large concentrations of low-income children and other children who are educationally at risk. The rise of local educational foundations in relatively high-expenditure and high-income districts may offset to some degree the equity effects of the state's school aid system. Further, students enrolled in foundation districts were overwhelmingly white, with an unweighted average of 91 percent among these districts, thus raising additional equity concerns. These concerns are mitigated, however, by the relatively small financial contributions of the local educational foundations, averaging $17,024 in 1994–95 among responding school districts. These effects may be further mitigated by the relatively large foundation contributions made to urban districts. Nevertheless, the level of revenue raised by local educational foundations and booster clubs in Michigan will undoubtedly rise in the coming years and eventually could compromise some of the equity gains achieved through the state's 1994 school finance reforms.

SUMMARY AND CONCLUSIONS

Since the beginning of this decade, public schools in the United States have been faced with a dramatic slowing of per pupil revenue growth, while both school enrollments and expectations for academic achievement continue to rise. To meet community expectations, local school districts in recent years have turned increasingly to nontraditional revenue sources to supplement revenues from broad-based taxes. Such revenues are raised through donor activities, enterprise activities, and cooperative activities. Indirect donor activities are undertaken by school booster clubs and, increasingly, by means of a new form of nonprofit organization, the educational foundation. In Michigan, 153 such nonprofit organizations have been established by local districts to raise revenue for curriculum improvements, capital projects, instructional materials and enrichment activities and to strengthen links between schools and communities. This activity in Michigan is representative of activity nationwide.

While the rise of these organizations is not unexpected in light of the slowing of revenue growth and rising expectations for public schools, this development has not been viewed with universal approval. The equalization of educational opportunities for all children, regardless of the wealth of their respective local communities, has long been an important goal of education policymakers. Virtually every state allocates school aid to local districts by means of equalizing formulas designed to offset disparities in local fiscal resources. Local education foundations and other nontraditional sources of local school revenue have aroused concern that they may exacerbate the very fiscal disparities public policy seeks to reduce. Moreover, state authorities are generally unaware of the scope of revenue-raising activities of foundations and booster clubs, since such revenues are rarely included in standard school district financial reports.

The Michigan research has revealed that total foundation revenues to date have been modest. However, striking differences were found between foundation and non-foundation districts, with average household income among the former group exceeding the latter by more than 20 percent. The foundation districts also have a lower percentage of children eligible for free and reduced-price lunch under the National School Lunch Act, greater per pupil revenues from traditional tax sources, and uniformly higher measures of student achievement in reading and mathematics, as measured by the Michigan Education Assessment Program, than their non-foundation counterparts. Further, students enrolled in foundation districts were overwhelmingly white, with an unweighted average of 91 percent across these districts. Again, however, these equity concerns are mitigated somewhat by the relatively small financial contributions of the local educational foundations.

In light of these findings, it appears that the rise of local education foundations in Michigan has not measurably negated that state's efforts to reduce inter-district disparities through the reform of public funding mechanisms. This result could change, however, as the state funding reforms continue to constrain per pupil revenue growth in historically high-spending and high-income districts and such districts seek additional revenue from nontraditional sources. Moreover, such disequalizing effects may become evident in other states as local districts continue to creatively pursue new revenues and evade state fiscal controls. The point at which these local "offshore accounts" threaten state policy goals is difficult to gauge. In the meantime, states would do well to strengthen local financial reporting requirements and establish threshold levels at which local revenue growth would trigger state aid offsets in the interest of state policy goals.

REFERENCES

Addonizio, M. F. (1991). Intergovernmental grants and the demand for local educational expenditures. *Public Finance Quarterly, 19*(2), 209–232.

Addonizio, M. F., Kearney, C. P., and Prince, H. J. (1995). Michigan's high wire act. *Journal of Education Finance, 20*(3), 235–269.

Addonizio, M. F. (1998). Private funding of public schools: Local education foundations in Michigan. *Educational Considerations, 26*(1), 1–7.

Anderson, N. (1997, December 2). Going beyond the bake sale. *Los Angeles Times.*

Blair, J. (1998). Ohio district takes sports fund raising to new level. *Education Week, 18*(12), 6.

Brunner, E., and Sonstelie, J. (1997). Coping with *Serrano*: Voluntary contributions to California's local public schools. *Pro-*

ceedings: National Tax Association 89th Annual Conference, 372–381.

Chaikand, S., Danielson, L. C., and Brauen, M. L. (1993). What do we know about the costs of special education? A selected review. *Journal of Special Education, 26*(4), 344–370.

Dayton, J., and McCarthy, M. (1992). User fees in public schools: Are they legal? *Journal of Education Finance, 18*(2), 127–141.

Gold, S., Smith, D., and Lawton, S. (Eds.) (1995). *Public school finance programs of the United States and Canada, 1993–94.* Albany: The American Education Finance Association and The Nelson A. Rockefeller Institute of Government.

Governmental Accounting Standards Board (1994). *Proposed statement: The financial reporting entity—affiliated organizations; exposure draft.* Norwalk, CT: Author.

Guthrie, J. W. (1997). School finance: Fifty years of expansion. *The Future of Children, 7*(3), 24–38.

Hamm, R. W., and Crosser, S. (1991). School fees: Whatever happened to the notion of a free public education? *The American School Board Journal,* (June), 29–31.

Hanushek, E. A., and Rivkin, S. G. (1997). Understanding the twentieth-century growth in U.S. school spending. *The Journal of Human Resources, 32*(1), 35–68.

Howell, P. L., and Miller, B. B. (1997). Sources of funding for schools. *The Future of Children, 7*(3), 39–50.

Johnston, J. (1995). Channel one: The dilemma of teaching and selling. *Phi Delta Kappan,* 437–442.

Joyce, P. G., and Mullins, D. R. (1991). The changing fiscal structure of the state and local public sector: The impact of tax and expenditure limitations. *Public Administration Review, 51*(3), 240–253.

Kearney, C. P. (1994). *A primer on Michigan school finance,* 3rd ed. (Ann Arbor: Educational Studies Program, School of Education, The University of Michigan).

Maeroff, G. (1982). Schools seek private funds. *New York Times* (November 9): p. C1.

Meno, L. R. (1984). Sources of alternative revenue. In L. D. Webb and V. D. Mueller (Eds.), *Managing limited resources: New demands on public school management* (pp. 129–146). Cambridge, MA: Ballinger.

Meredith, B., and Underwood, J. (1995). Irreconcilable differences? Defining the rising conflict between regular and special education. *Journal of Law and Education, 24*(2), 195–226.

Monk, D. H., and Brent, B. O. (1997). *Raising money for education.* Thousand Oaks, CA: Corwin Press.

Mullins, D., and Cox, K. (1995). *Tax and expenditure limits on local governments.* Washington, DC: Advisory Commission on Intergovernmental Relations.

Mullins, D., and Joyce, P. (1996). Tax and expenditure limitations and state and local fiscal structure: An empirical assessment. *Public Budgeting and Finance,* Spring, 75–101.

National Center for Education Statistics. (1995). *Digest of education statistics, 1995.* Washington, DC: U. S. Department of Education.

Picus, L. O., Tetreault, D. R., and Hertert, L. (1995). The allocation and use of educational resources in California. Paper presented at the annual meeting of the American Education Finance Association, Savannah, GA.

Pijanowski, J. C., and Monk, D. H. (1996). Alternative school revenue sources: There are many fish in the sea. *School Business Affairs,* July, 4–10.

Pollack, A. (1992). With budgets cut, public officials seek private money. *NewYork Times* (May 17): L40.

Salloum, K. (1985). *Private funding for elementary and secondary public education in British Columbia.* Unpublished master's thesis, Simon Fraser University.

Siemon, C. L., and Zimet, M. J. (1992). School funding in the 1990s: Impact fees or bake sales. *Land Use Law,* July, 3–9.

Wassmer, R. W., and Fisher, R. C. (1996). An evaluation of the recent move to centralize the finance of public schools in Michigan. *Public Finance and Budgeting, 16*(3), 90–112.

Wassmer, R. W., and Fisher, R. C. (1997). *User charges and the financing of K–12 public education in the United States.* Working Paper 96–03, Graduate Program in Public Policy and Administration, California State University, Sacramento.

9

ORGANIZATIONAL BOUNDARIES, AUTHORITY, AND SCHOOL DISTRICT ORGANIZATION

Patrick Galvin
University of Utah

This chapter examines the role of the school district in the continuing negotiation of authority over control and organization of public education. Once upon a time, the organization and consolidation of school districts represented the cutting edge of reform, allegedly capturing scale economies, ensuring professional standards for teachers and curriculum, while expanding quality services to more students (Tyack 1993). During the 1950s and 1960s, the authority for educational reform resided primarily in the superintendent of the school district itself (Seashore-Louis 1989). In great contrast, the last two decades of educational reform have assumed that the school district represents a monopoly of authority, which compromises the capacity of the educational system to effectively utilize the resources necessary to produce high-quality education (Bennett 1992; Everhart 1982; Hannaway 1993). Shifting authority to the school, to parents, and to community groups is viewed, in the current era of educational reform, as a necessary strategy to foster a more efficient and productive environment (Chubb and Moe 1990; Odden and Busch 1998). Vouchers, school choice, and other market-oriented reforms are said to promote innovative practices while providing more accountability than the existing system governed by school district authority. Indeed, one of the main goals of educational reform is to de-bureaucratize schooling and make schools more responsive to the public they serve (Everhart 1982; Timar 1989).

The market ideology guiding the current wave of educational reform represents an evolution of regulatory thought in government. One of the purposes of this chapter is to place the current call for the deregulation of educational bureaucracy into a historical context. The dominant value underlying this shift from bureaucratic to market-oriented authority is efficient production. In other words, the reason educational reform is needed, according to the ideology of reform, is that bureaucratic authority has failed to produce the results expected of the system. The success of markets, however, depends upon complete information that enables consumers to make decisions that optimize their welfare. It is around the problems associated with the availability of information that a parallel line of economic thought, known as the New Institutional Economics, challenges the assumptions and conclusions of the market-oriented regulatory reforms. This line of inquiry asks, "How are exchanges governed when consumers and producers negotiate with imperfect information?" The answer derived from this theoretical perspective suggests that the structure of organization is shaped by the costs associated with governance as much as by the costs of production. Distinguishing between these two sets of costs, governance and production, helps explain the role of the school districts and their contributions to the production of educational services. This role is likely to become more important in the future, as demands for collaborative arrangements among parents, as well as among social, health, and educational agencies, will require more negotiation of purpose and coordination of efforts in order to be effective.

EDUCATIONAL REFORM,
AUTHORITY, AND THE SCHOOL DISTRICT

One striking feature of the reform literature from the last 20 years is the absence of references, with a few exceptions,[1] to the school district. This is not just my assessment of the literature; both Seashore-Louis (1989) and Firestone (1998), for example, explicitly note that relatively little research examines the role of the school district in the reform movement of the 1980s and 1990s. The reason for this absence is not subtle or mysterious; rather, it serves as the blunt instrument of reformers who see the school district, and other forms of intermediate government, as the source of bureaucratic waste and inefficiency. Murphy (1990a) makes the point sharply in his review of educational reform during the 1980s:

> For much of the last quarter-century, a general belief in the professional impotence of administrators has prevailed. The picture of the school superintendent or principal as the beleaguered professional who can exercise little influence over his or her organization, and who is only distantly connected to important educational processes and outcomes, has been widely accepted...contributing to the emerging characterization of school administrators as little more than caretakers (p 279).

William Bennett (1992), Secretary of Education during the 1980s, contributed much to this negative description of school district structures and particularly administration, which he characterized as the "administrative blob" responsible for education's productivity collapse. The criticism of school administration was taken to an extreme by Chubb and Moe (1990), who argued that not only were school administration and bureaucratic hierarchy part of the problem facing schools, but this organizational tier had nothing to contribute to the production of learning:

---

1 See, for example, Elmore (1993a), Firestone (1989), or Verstegen (1988–89).

> Because education is based on personal relationships
> and interaction, on continual feedback, and on the
> knowledge, skills and experience of teachers, most of
> the necessary technology and resources are inher-
> ently present in the school itself, and thus are at the
> bottom of the organizational hierarchy....Higher-
> level administrative units have little to contribute
> that is not already there (p. 36).

Thus, the authors argue that asking the school district to
lead reform is a little like asking the fox to guard the hen house;
that bureaucracy is not simply part of the problem, but is, rather,
the essence of the problem.

Over the last several decades two general themes emerge
from the waves of reform that have swept over education. The
first holds that states are responsible for establishing a regulatory environment, or a set of standards, by which to hold agencies providing education accountable. The reform initiatives
stemming from this tenet represent a centralization of authority
and power. The second perspective places responsibility on
school-level educators and parents for the governance and
management of educational services; this thought represents a
decentralization of authority and power. Both reform agendas
seek to divest school districts of the rights and authority vested
in their bureaucratic structures, and both contend that the creative solutions to educational problems are locked up in the bureaucratic monopoly that now governs public education.
Murphy (1990a) summarizes these points in his analysis of the
reform literature of the 1980s, in which he concludes:

> The one common thread running through the entire
> fabric of the reform movement of the 1980s is the re-
> distribution of authority. The only consistent theme
> in the reports on this topic is that district offices will
> (and should) lose power. Depending on the particu-
> lar report, one or more of the other actors in the
> schooling process—states, teachers, administrators,
> parents—should be granted more authority over ed-
> ucational issues (p. 45).

The absence of references to school district organization and bureaucracy as part of the reform of public education is no oversight. Rather, the emphasis on school-level autonomy and state regulation of standards represents a response to judgments that school district organization and bureaucracy have certainly failed to resolve, and may even have contributed indirectly to, the current collapse of educational productivity among America's public schools.

PRODUCTIVITY AND THE
HISTORY OF EDUCATIONAL REFORM

One of the great ironies of this current judgment regarding school district structures and the role of educational bureaucracy is that it stands in such sharp contrast to the history of educational thought. For most of this century, school district organization was viewed not as a pariah, but as a solution to concerns about accountability, productivity, and equity (Tyack 1993). This view of public school organization has its roots in the municipal reforms at the turn of the twentieth century (Iannaccone 1982). Partly in response to the post-Civil War corruption, municipal reform emerged as a philosophy of government that recognized a "new set of social, economic, and technological conditions in American life" (Iannaccone 1982, p. 297). Municipal reform rejected the Jacksonian individualism of the late 1800s and embraced the concept of collective action reflecting the organization of industrialization.

But these events did not, in themselves, explain the phenomenal growth of school district organization through the policy known as "consolidation." Rather, two additional events help explain this trend. First, there was widespread criticism of education at the turn of the century. Iannaccone (1982) suggests that, like the Coleman Report of the 1960s, Joseph Rice's negative assessment of public education in 1893 was shocking and profound. Callahan (1962) documents these events through his study of education and the "cult of efficiency." Public education, at this time, was viciously attacked as a veritable "cesspool" of corruption and waste. Municipal reform reflected not only a response to these forms of corruption but a move toward modernization; this movement brought social services and government under the leadership of a professional elite, and embraced the science of administration as a strategy for fixing the perceived inefficiencies of production within the existing system.

These changes may not have been possible, however, without the second event relevant to this discussion: the urbanization of America's population. This phenomenon allowed for the creation of school districts sufficiently large to warrant the hiring of a superintendent of schools, as well as professionally trained teachers and school principals. Simultaneously, state funding for public education increased significantly at this time (the 1920s), primarily in the name of school finance equity (Cubberley 1934). Why were such reforms so long in waiting before being implemented? With increased funding came a greater concern for accountability. Scientific management and school district consolidation provided the means by which to develop production efficiencies, but neither of these issues addressed the inevitable costs of implementing new budgeting strategies and monitoring the use of state resources for public education. Prior to the advent of roads, cars, and communications systems (such as the telephone), monitoring school district activity involved infrequent visits by state personnel followed by descriptive accounts of the schools and their teachers. With cars and telephones, the cost of monitoring the school district's use of state money changed, and with these changes came an increased role for state involvement in the finance of public education.

As previously noted, the proposition that concern over educational productivity underlies past reform efforts is well established by such historians as Tyack (1974) and Callahan (1962). In the next section of this chapter, I assert that the current waves of educational reform are still motivated primarily by this same concern. The second proposition in the above section is that this concern for productivity and the reforms generated in response to it are dependent upon conditions that change the relative cost of organization. Thus, the philosophies of municipal reform, introduced before the turn of the twentieth century, had to wait until the aggregation of urban populations reached the point that it warranted the hiring of professional staff. The idea of economies of scale fit well with the emergence of "scientific management," an example of the strong influence of productivity shaping educational policy. However, the critical point introduced in this section was that the state's role in financing public education depended upon changes in the cost of accountability, which was possible because of changes in transportation and communication technology. This proposition introduces a key hypothesis in the chapter that is represented by a body of literature collectively known as Institutional Economics, which suggests that institutional environments shape the cost of organizations and, hence, their history (North 1990).

This point is addressed more fully in the last sections of this chapter. First, however, I further explore the evidence suggesting that issues of productivity underlie not only historical but recent and current calls for educational reform. I then argue that these reforms reflect the evolution of regulatory reform in America (and abroad), an evolution driven by concern about the proper relationship, or boundary, between government and market activity.

SCHOOL ORGANIZATION
AND PRODUCTIVITY

Reforms are never the product of a single causal factor, but as the preceding discussion asserts, one driving force behind the educational reforms of the 1920s and 1930s was concern over both the efficient use of available resources and the quality of the educational services being provided. Mitchell and Encarnation (1984) argue that the current waves of educational reforms have their impetus from the shocks associated with the successful launch of Sputnik in 1957. This event again raised serious doubts about the quality of schooling that America's children were receiving, particularly in science and math. The concern held political power because, as was the case in the early 1980s, the failure of schools was perceived as a threat to the country's leadership among nations.

The shock of these events may have had more significance for policymakers, because at the same time (in the late 1950s), economists such as Mincer, Dennison, and Becker were developing the arguments for the human capital theory. This theory suggests that a good portion of the economic growth experienced in America during the first part of the century could be explained by improvements in the education of workers. Better-educated workers contributed to the productivity of firms in ways that made for a more efficient economic system. So persuasive were these arguments that they provided the logic necessary to support President Johnson's investments in the Great Society. Investments in social services and education, it was argued, would provide the poor with the human capital necessary to work their way out of poverty. In this context, the subsequent findings of the Coleman Report (1966) can be easily understood as a shock to both the pursuit of equity and the goals of the Great Society. The findings of the Coleman Report suggested that the relationship between the availability of educational resources and measures of outcome were not strongly correlated.

By the 1970s, after years of production function studies and the search for "effective schools," the U.S. Department of Education released findings indicating that despite significant increases in funding (even after controlling for inflation), there was little evidence of improvement in student test scores. These findings fueled the growing concerns that public education represented a monopoly that could only be fixed by breaking the bureaucratic hierarchy of school district organization (Everhart 1982). The "rising tide of mediocrity," so boldly proclaimed by the National Commission on Excellence in Education in their report *A Nation at Risk* (1983), was old, if still inflammatory, news. Indeed, some analysts, such as Brimelow (1986), took a strident view equating America's public schools with the socialist communes of the USSR. By the 1990s, the perception of the failure of schools was so popular that *Newsweek* ran a series of articles entitled "Why Schools Fail," in which the problems of bureaucracy were identified as a key factor in the failure. During this decade, calls for "reinventing" public schools in a way that allows parents to operate with more choice and requires state enforcement of standards have become common (Gerstner et al. 1994; Hill 1995).

Underlying these reform proposals is a market ideology, which holds that efficiency is achieved when the producers of goods and services are regulated by consumer preferences. The role of government, in this perspective, is not to manage the production of services but rather to establish standards that protect consumers from unfair practices. Efforts directed towards the re-establishment of proper boundaries (i.e., a balance of power) between the private and public interests are at the heart of reform proposals. This philosophy of regulation is not unique to education but, rather, reflects a general trend in regulatory theory.

REGULATORY REFORM, MARKETS, AND EDUCATION

Concerns about the balance of power between school systems and the communities they serve are hardly new. In the 1960s, the battle for community control over public education was in full force (Levin 1970) and, like the War of the Roses, had a long history of unresolved battles.[2] Gittell (1970) noted in reference to this movement, "...urban school reform through expanded community control is an attempt to achieve a new balance of power by reintroducing competition into the system... competition among groups for the resources of power generally makes for a dynamic, pluralistic system, whereas monopolies produce a static system" (p 115).

As with the issue of productivity, concern over the proper balance of authority between the district and community authorities is an ever-present negotiation in educational policy. The question, then, is why these concerns found substance in the 1980s. In other words, recognition that productivity is a fundamental issue driving educational policy does not explain why the focus shifted from organizational reforms to market-based reforms over the years. In this section, I extend the above discussion of educational productivity and reform by arguing that the current market-based reforms in education are really part of the effort to deregulate government, a reform agenda that swept through government at large during the 1970s and 1980s.

---

2 For a modern update of the issue, see collected papers edited by Ravitch (1999).

Government regulation of business began in the late 1880s with the formation of the Interstate Commerce Commission (ICC). The history of regulatory practice is grounded in the notion of market failure: that structural deficiencies inherent in the market allow industries to create a monopoly by anti-competitive, profit-maximizing practices (Daneke and Lemak 1985). Such behavior threatens the fundamental purpose of markets: to ensure that the consumer gets a good product at a fair price. Market efficiencies occur where fully informed consumers make choices about a range of products that satisfy their purposes and needs. Of course, where firms limit competition and information about alternative products, then the efficiency of the market is diminished.

The overall history of government regulation is generally divided into four distinct phases.[3] The first, in response to the monopolistic practices at the turn of the century, limited price fixing and other unethical practices in the private sector in order to protect the public welfare. These regulations were intended to ensure that all private firms played consistently by the same rules of the market.

The second phase of regulatory reform accompanied the Great Depression and represented an effort to limit destructive competition among the fledgling airline, communications, and ground transportation industries. At this point in history, the government began to recognize the existence of "natural" monopolies, where, because of economies of scale, it was deemed efficient to have only one producer serve a given market (Daneke and Lemak 1985, p. 5). The justification for the consolidation of schools rests upon this idea of a "natural" monopoly, which, if regulated by the government, could serve the public welfare better than uninhibited competition. Moreover, natural monopolies are justified where the production process is not clearly defined, making it difficult to regulate services using competition in the marketplace.

Beginning in the 1960s, the third phase of regulatory reform introduced the idea of externalities as a justification for greater

---

3 The following review of history is extracted from the work of Daneke and Lemak (1985).

government intervention and regulation of private enterprise. The term *externality* refers to the problem of how costs are distributed within a market. When producers are able to shift the cost of production to the consumer or some other private enterprise without their consent, externalities in trade exist. An obvious example of this is associated with pollution, where the production of one product negatively affects the economic interests of others. Other examples of social regulation, as this third wave of regulatory reform is known, include consumer protection and employee safety. Social regulation was justified wherever the costs of production and consumption were borne by third parties.

The fourth, and most recent, regulatory reform calls for less government intervention in the marketplace. With an increased presence of government regulation in the market, regulation itself came under mounting scrutiny. By the 1970s, there was a growing body of research suggesting that government itself was undermining the efficiency of the market. Moreover, advocates for reform argued that regulation was only one of many public policy options that can be used to promote public welfare (Daneke and Lemak 1985). Tax credits, tax reform, public ownership and subsidies all offer regulators alternative options for ensuring the welfare of the public. "Big government," with its policies of regulatory control (and especially social regulation) over business, had compromised the competitive edge of business, particularly in the global economy of the 1980s and 1990s (Button and Swann 1989). Centralized authority was not only responsible for $600 toilet seats in the military but also $50,000 janitors in education (Brimelow 1986). Competition in the marketplace is, in this view, the means by which to promote efficient production and exchange among producers and consumers, in this case the bureaucrats who control the educational system and the taxpayers who pay for it.

Once again, as in the past, a confluence of forces drives otherwise latent powers to action, in this case the move toward market-based reforms in education. Concerns about the monopolistic character of school organization are present in the policy debate early in the 1960s, as noted above. It is not, however, until the 1970s that these concerns find a political handle for reform. In the 1970s the United States, and the world at large, experienced one of the worst recessions since the Great Depression. Fears of economic and social decline were common at this time and underlie such publications as *A Nation at Risk* (1983). Government regulation was viewed in this time of adversity as a serious constraint to recovery. Deregulation, a policy sometimes associated with the Reagan administration, was first implemented by the Carter administration during the late 1970s; in other words these reforms were not necessarily the product of the "conservative revolution" but, rather, of more fundamental economic and sociological concerns. Evidence that public schools operated inefficiently made them a candidate for deregulation under the same logic as that of other regulatory reforms. The logic that recognized and supported public education as a "natural" monopoly during the 1920s and 1930s no longer seemed applicable. Rather, in the age of a global economy and new information technologies, the promise of choice as a strategy for promoting innovation and reform (with the goal of enhanced efficiency) provided direction to the shortcomings of the status quo (Friedman 1984).

By the 1980s, many economists and policy analysts were describing public education organizations as ineffective and intransigent monopolies (Everhart 1982). Suspicions about the role and influence of teacher unions in education, for example, reflect deeper concerns about the collusion of private interests in monopolistic behavior (Brimelow and Spencer 1993; Hill and Bonan 1991). Efforts to re-establish proper boundaries (i.e., a balance of power) between the private and public interests are at the heart of reform proposals.

Organizational boundaries serve, in classical economics, to define the realm of managerial discretion in response to market signals. Markets operate by price mechanisms, which are negotiated in the unfettered exchanges of suppliers and consumers. Monopolies are abhorrent to neo-classical economists because they confound the potential efficiency of the market. Proposals for decentralization, such as those advanced by Chubb and Moe (1990), embraced the neoclassical view of organization, in which boundaries are clearly defined and even essential to the efficient operation of the market.

By contrast, bureaucratic organization is predicated on a division of labor and the assignment of authority and responsibility. Bureaucratic organizations are viewed as independent of their environment and defined exclusively in terms of their internal features: specialization of role and assignment, a hierarchy of authority, and standard operating procedures (Badarocco 1991; Perrow 1986).

The classic delineation of authority as either centralized or decentralized does not fit well with the current reality facing most school organizations. This argument turns on the observation that the educational reform movement has not abandoned bureaucracy for markets but, rather, seeks a political integration of centralized authority (responsible for the establishment of standards, rules, and regulations) and decentralized authority (responsible for decisions about how to produce and deliver services). Moreover, school organizations are increasingly viewed as open, not closed, systems that are expected to coordinate activities with other social service agencies, as well as with parents (Cibulka and Kritek 1996; Pounder 1997). Such efforts blur the boundaries of traditional distinct authorities, and more to the point, leave intermediate authorities with a very different (and largely undefined) role to play.

This change in perspective is significant and reflects Badarocco's assertion that the "classic" conceptual map of the firm no longer provides good guides for the problems we need to negotiate and, hence, needs to be replaced with a better map (1991, p. 302). This new map of organization is especially relevant for the study of schools. The problem of organization from this perspective is how to minimize the cost of governance in an environment characterized by high levels of uncertainty, incomplete information, asset specificity and a peculiar ownership structure.

The argument for a new organization map draws from the work of the "New Institutional Economists,"[4] well-represented by Williamson (1996), who has been a major figure in the development of the theory. In contrast to the political theories of orga-

---

4 References to this conceptualization of the theory include Commons (1934) and Furubotn and Richter (1992).

nization, economic theories of organization focus on the cost of governance structures. The economics of organization analyzes matters of governance relative to the costs and benefits of alternative structures; the grammar of organizational governance is a matter of accounting for comparative costs. Such maps of organizational governance provide a powerful and flexible perspective on the changing boundaries of educational organizations, directing us toward new opportunities for collaborative arrangements that facilitate both centralized and decentralized polities in governance.

These significant changes in organizational theory have not received as much attention in policy circles as more classic discussions of regulatory theory grounded in the microeconomics of production. In the next section, the economic theories of organization are discussed relative to the new regulatory environment in which schools find themselves.

THE NEW INSTITUTIONAL ECONOMICS: ECONOMICS OF PRODUCTION VERSUS ECONOMICS OF GOVERNANCE

Given that the notion of "markets" is the traditional stock in trade of microeconomic theory, it is interesting that educational reformers apply so little economic thought to the subject of educational productivity and reform. This is certainly not from lack of recognition that issues of educational reform are grounded in the economics of educational productivity. Indeed, Mitchell and Encarnation (1984) argue that the current wave of reform is grounded in the nation's reaction to Sputnik and the apparent failure of America's schools to produce the science and math students needed to compete with the Russians in the race to space. The focus on educational productivity was prominent during the late 1960s and early 1970s with the microeconomic "input-output" studies (Bridges, Judd, and Moock 1979). The results of these studies, for all their statistical sophistication, did not provide conclusive evidence of the relationship between investments in education and outcomes, a fact that fueled the continued search for reform.

The current waves of reform seek efficiencies through market-oriented structures, where consumer choice promotes competition among providers. Tyack (1993) notes, however, a puzzle in these reform efforts, which he describes as the apparent disconnect between the rhetoric of reform for public education and the technology of teaching students. No matter how schools are governed, he argues, the basic technology of education has hardly changed at all. The explanation for this apparent intransigence is found in what Tyack describes as the "invisible hand of ideology." The idea is that our organizations reflect the culture and values of people (see Scott (1995) for a complete introduction to these ideas) rather than the technical assumptions of Weberian theory. The ideas are hardly new but, rather, reflect a significant change in the theory of organization. Weick (1976) helped introduce these ideas by describing schools and other complex organizations as "loosely coupled." The idea is that the structures of organizational governance are not tightly linked to the production of services, as compared, say, to a company producing aluminum, where the production function can be clearly and completely specified. Meyer and Rowan (1977) took the idea even further by describing formalized organization as "myth and ceremony." March (1991) summarizes these arguments against the rationality of bureaucracy in an article entitled "How Decisions Happen in Organizations." Tyack's puzzle is hardly news by the time he references it, nor is the move to quasi-markets as a source of reform in education.

The world of ideas is, however, wonderfully complex. At the same time that these ideas attacking the technical rationality of organizational bureaucracy are occurring, another set of theorists are developing ideas that strengthen arguments for the technical rationality of organizational hierarchy. These ideas are represented by economists under the rubric "the New Institutional Economics." The key idea underlying this line of inquiry is that formalized organization is the means by which the cost of governance is minimized among transactions that are fraught with information and ownership problems. To operate efficiently, markets require complete information and clearly defined contracts that delineate ownership. Firms (hierarchical organizations) exist where information is incomplete and ownership is unclear. Firms provide the means of reducing the cost of production as well as exchange in poorly defined markets, a condition that characterizes public education. The following text introduces these ideas and then applies them to the proposed reforms of public education. The logic of the argument concludes with the observation that the "bureaucracy" of public education contributes more to productivity than is typically assumed. Preliminary evidence for this assertion is presented in the next section.

The literature characterized as the New Institutional Economics covers a wide array of topics.[5] One place to start is with the question, "If markets are so efficient, why are transactions vertically integrated (organized) through firms?" The label "firm" refers to an organization where authority is hierarchically structured, such as schools. Indeed, this question is particularly relevant to the current debate about the reform of public education because the reform agenda seeks to decentralize authority by emphasizing market-oriented exchanges among consumers and producers via vouchers and site-based management programs.

Coase (1937) is generally recognized as having provided an answer to the above question about the existence of firms. He argued that there are costs associated with using the market, and that many of these costs can be minimized by the formation of hierarchical organizations. Such costs include the search for information, the writing of contracts, and the monitoring of activities to ensure compliance with agreed-upon contracts (the famous "post-contractual renegotiations problem"—as familiar among children on the playground as among business people). The general conclusion of this theory is that vertical organization (e.g., the firm) is an appropriate structure when the cost of transactions in the market is greater than the cost of such activities within the organizational environment of a firm. Williamson (1996) has extended this literature considerably, arguing that the structure of organizational arrangements is largely a re-

---

5 Barney and Ouchi (1986) provide an accessible introduction to these two theoretical perspectives for the non-economist.

sponse to minimizing the cost of governing activities within the boundaries of the firm.

The New Institutional Economics is largely derived from Coase's theorem. Langlois (1998) describes the issue in the following way: "The Coasean literature of the last 20 years has focused precisely on the comparative transaction costs of alternative organizational structures, including, paradigmatically, the choice between firm and markets" (p. 1). Langlois goes on to note that "this modern literature owes much to the way Coase originally formulated the problem of the boundaries of the firm…today's economics of organization bears the imprint of the economics of the 1930s and Coase's reaction to it" (p. 1).

Langlois argues that the time-dependence of Coase's work has an important consequence, which I believe is present in the conceptual mapping of today's organizational reform agenda for education. Specifically, Langlois (1995) asserts that price theory, and all its attendant assumptions, has been assigned the duty of explaining all we need to know about the production function. Such assumptions certainly underlie the arguments of Chubb and Moe (1990), as evidenced by their assertions that private markets, à la Friedman (1962, 1984), are the means by which the rigor of the market cleans up the mess of bureaucratic flab. But, as noted above, the efficiency of the market depends upon complete and perfect information as well as clearly defined ownership (boundaries).

The New Institutional Economics emerged quite separately from the studies of price theory and productivity (see Williamson 1975, 1986, and 1996 for a history of this inquiry). Indeed, Langlois (1995) notes that "…seldom do these two kingdoms converse…seldom if ever do economists in this tradition (price theory) consider that knowledge may be imperfect in the realm of production, and that institutional forms may play the role not only of constraining unproductive rent-seeking behavior but also of creating the possibilities for productive rent-seeking behavior" (p. 2).

One of the important points Langlois makes in this comment is the distinction between the economics of production and the economics of governance. Imperfect information is the reason for organizational hierarchy; bureaucracy not only serves the goal of enhancing productivity, it creates a positive environment for reducing the cost of organization. Organization provides the contacts and structure for seeking out and making use of information about possible markets, inputs, production strategies, and accountability. There is an irony in these arguments because, as Arrow (1974) argues, the aggregation of information regarding efficient forms of governance reinforces the status quo. The accumulated knowledge about how to organize and monitor the production of services tends to limit the range of alternatives for innovation. Thus, reformers seeking changes that promote efficiency in school organizations find themselves in conflict with those organizations' efforts towards the same goal.

The last point rests on a fundamental premise of the New Institutional Economics: that the form of organizational governance depends upon the idiosyncratic character of the resources to be managed in the production process (Williamson 1986, 1996). This premise suggests that there is no one best system of governance for education (or any other business or agency)—a point made powerfully by some educational historians (Tyack 1974). Rather, the organizational structure of governance mechanisms will depend upon the nature of the students, teachers, parents, and political environment in which principals and other authorities find themselves.

An example will help clarify these abstractions. It is well known that teachers have the most knowledge about the production frontiers for any given set of students within a classroom. Thus, under the banner of professionalism, it is argued that teachers should be given the authority (or discretion) to make decisions about how to organize their learning environment (Conley 1989; Darling-Hammond 1989). These are the arguments that Chubb and Moe (1990) make when they question the relevance of school district organization. The problem is that teachers do not work in isolation from other educators. Rather, the decisions of teachers regarding a particular approach to math or reading at one level have an impact on the options of teachers in other subjects and at other grade levels. For example, if two third grade math teachers use very different reading strategies (whole language vs. phonics), the effect on the fourth grade teachers is complicated; preparation will vary across students as they move from grade to grade, making the task of instruction and classroom management more difficult. Multiply this by a thousand such problems and the level of complexity and uncertainty governed by the structure of schools becomes more obvious.

The real problem for a system of education is articulating the sequence and quality of learning for students as they pass between grade levels and among teachers. In other words, devising a means by which such matters are negotiated and resolved day after day, year-in and year-out, regardless of the personalities involved, is fundamental to minimizing the cost of governance.

Of course, teachers are not the only arbiters of educational purpose and means. Parents, as consumers of the services provided by educators, have a vested interest in what and how subject matter is taught. Additionally, legislators, who through a system of taxes distribute private money to serve a public good, are sensitive to the purpose and means of education. Recognition of these negotiated environments brings the propositions of Transaction Economics well within the purview of traditional organizational and political models used to explain the behavior of school organizations (Bacharach and Mundell 1993; Barney and Ouchi 1986; Williamson 1996). The difference between political and organizational theories of behavior and economic theories of organization is the degree of attention paid to costs and their constraint on behavior.

The New Institutional Economics does not provide specific answers to the question of how schools should be organized. The framework does, however, provide an economic argument that challenges the microeconomic theories undergirding proposals for market-based reforms. Public education is characterized by a very high need for information that is associated with high transaction costs. This is true not only for parents who might seek information about whether to place their children in one classroom or another, but also for teachers, administrators and legislators—all of whom have a vested and multifaceted interest in what subject material is taught, and how.

Additionally, the technology of education is not easily, nor can it be completely, specified. The problem of incomplete contracts is that they drive the transaction costs associated with market exchanges way up, reducing the potential benefits of such arrangements. The reason this is true has to do with the need to monitor activity that cannot be specified in a contract (not that writing a contract itself is cheap).

The premise of the New Institutional Economics is that the choice between horizontal (markets) or vertical (bureaucratic) organization depends upon the relative costs of these alternative mechanisms of governance. To pronounce school organizations inefficient and call for market-based reforms proposes to replace one institutional structure with another without having taken the trouble to examine the full costs of either (Demsetz 1969). Hierarchical organization does offer the potential means by which to promote production efficiencies as well as reduce the cost of governance. Saying this does not justify hierarchical organization in itself, but it does bring into question the presumption that bureaucracy serves virtually no purpose in the organization, production, and delivery of educational services. There is countering evidence that district organizations are not simply intransigent bureaucracies unwilling to reform and, indeed, in many cases school district leaders have led the search for reform. Judging the merit of decisions about whether to undertake reform or how to achieve it requires a full appreciation of the opportunities as well as constraints facing such decision-makers. Recognition and incorporation of the economics of governance into our perspective will help better balance our sense of reality as we assess reforms being foisted upon educators.

ONCE AND FUTURE ROLE OF INTERMEDIATE TIER OF GOVERNANCE

Proposals for the reform of educational organizations, especially school districts, are grounded in the description of them as unproductive monopolies that have been neither accountable nor sensitive to the interests of the public they serve (Brimelow 1986; Everhart 1982; National Commission on Excellence in Education 1983). School district officials and teacher unions have been accused of having too much power and authority. Shifting authority to the school, to parents, and to community groups has been viewed as a necessary strategy to foster a more efficient and productive environment (Chubb and Moe 1990).

Underlying the call for school restructuring is a deep-seated suspicion that school districts (and the schools they govern) are incapable of making good use of available resources. This idea was explicit, for example, in the public's negative reaction to New Jersey's Quality Education Act (QEA) implemented in 1990, which was to increase funding for the state's very poor school districts by more than $800 million (Firestone, Goertz, and Natriello 1998). In the following statement, then-governor James Florio captures, as only a politician can, the basic elements of people's suspicion over their public school system, in an effort to save this remarkable coalition of judicial and legislative action:

> Let me make it very, very clear what this money is not for: It's not for anyone to build up flabby, lethargic bureaucracies. It's not for empire-building by administrators. It's not for business as usual in systems that have been producing poor results....It's for one thing and one thing only: our children (as quoted in Firestone 1998, p 38).

Firestone, Goertz, and Natriello (1998) detail the implementation of the QEA program in their book *From Cashbox to Classroom: The Struggle for Fiscal Reform and Educational Change in New Jersey*. Their findings indicate that the goals of the QEA were substantially realized: reduced fiscal disparity between rich and poor school districts and an expansion of educational services and opportunities for the children in New Jersey's poorest school districts. One of the important contributions of this report is that it provides details about what is accomplished with public resources in schools and schooling. Contrary to the popular perception that such investments have no effect, Firestone, Goertz, and Natriello's work reveals that the state's investment produced significant and useful progress in reform. Such well-grounded testimony is important because it provides a foundation for re-establishing trust in school organizations that are otherwise characterized in negative terms (e.g., "productivity collapse").

Trust is an important element in the economics of organization because without it, complete contracts and extensive monitoring of activity are required. Such conditions are obviously both expensive and problematic for education, where the production function is uncertain, the outcomes are shrouded in ambiguity, and paths of responsibility are difficult to delineate. Trust reduces the need for contractual monitoring of organizational activity. It minimizes the cost of governance, and, thus, enhances efficiency.

With this point in mind, I turn to the literature addressing the claims that school districts are uncompromising bureaucracies with little to contribute to the productivity of schools. On both counts, there is evidence to question these widely held opinions. What follows is a brief overview, as the topic deserves more attention than space allows.

Firestone, Fuhrman, and Kirst (1990) note in their review of the reform efforts during the 1980s that district responses to state mandates for reform were rarely characterized by resistance, and in many cases districts actually exceeded state requirements (p. 358). Indeed, they go further, to assert that much of the progress on restructuring has resulted from district initiatives (p 358). Rather than acting as recalcitrant bureaucracies, school districts appear to be leading reform efforts with innovative and experimental reforms.

In contrast to the characterization of districts as unavailable and unresponsive bureaucracies, Tyack and Hansot (1982) assert that school administrators are at the "beck and call" of every pressure group with interest in education. Assertions that school district bureaucracies are insensitive to the environment in which they are embedded ignore this history. Indeed Callahan (1962), drawing from Iannaccone's thesis that the main feature of school administrators is their vulnerability to external pressure groups, argues that the "cult of efficiency" so villainized by modern educators was actually led by educational reformists during the 1920s. He explains this irony by arguing that the uncertainty associated with how professionals use public money makes defending any practice extremely difficult.

Hence, educators are extremely vulnerable to external criticisms, which are best handled by assimilating the critics.

Drawing from past research about educational reform, Seashore-Louis (1989) concludes that while reform must focus on the school, school improvement is a multi-level process. District policies thus serve to coordinate the many actors (including parents, teachers, students, administrators, and community members, as well as representatives of other agencies related to education and social welfare) responsible for the complicated process of producing learning. In this respect, school improvement is a planned process that includes the slow implementation of and adjustment to strategies for change.

First (1992), who has long examined the role of school boards in this era of reform, comes to similar conclusions. First notes that school board authorities, like their bureaucratic counterparts in school district offices, have been bypassed in the reform movements of the 1980s. With logic similar to that of Seashore-Louis, First argues that the school board is a crucial link in the administrative fabric necessary for the successful implementation of reforms. Policies, she argues, "eliminate school district confusion in all areas and at all levels of school district management" (p 225). In other words, the policies developed by school boards become the rules of operation by which administrators operate. Clear rules simplify their job by reducing confusion, conflicting agendas, and waste. Well-written policies, she contends, foster stability and operational efficiencies in schools. These are the tools by which an enormous number of people, agencies and families coordinate their efforts to some common purpose.

The proposition that school district organizations are bureaucracies is not as important as the inference that bureaucracies are in and of themselves bad. The tendency to villainize bureaucracies is, one could say, almost second nature in American culture. Goodsell (1985), in his book *The Case for Bureaucracy: A Public Administration Polemic*, argues that the reputation of bureaucracies simply does not square with the facts. While the public attitude about bureaucracies in general suggests widespread dissatisfaction, survey results following the receipt of services delivered by "bureaucracies" reveal a surprisingly high

level of satisfaction. These findings appear similar to the assertions of most parents that, while concerned about the quality of
education in general, they are satisfied with the service and
quality of education from their own school. Moreover, the evidence of widespread policy and program reform, even before
the alleged pressure of reform agendas, is well documented by
Goodsell.

Claims that school districts are intransigent bureaucracies
full of professional autocrats resistant to and uninterested in
change may be overstated. Nonetheless, the search for new
forms of governance structures is central to the reform agenda
of the 1990s (Murphy 1990b). Odden and Busch's (1998) proposals for financing high-performance schools are good examples
of this search. While this reform focuses on the role and rights of
school-level personnel in managing the production process, the
authors recognize the significance of the district role in reform.
Indeed, Odden and Busch note, "Contrary to popular understanding, districts remain important even when many management functions are decentralized to schools" (p. 187). Specifically, the authors argue that the district-school relationship
should be "based on school-specific performance agreements
that stipulate the results schools are to produce, allowing each
school to select the strategy to produce those results" (p. 188).
The role of the school board and central office staff is to write
performance-based agreements with every school, as well as
manage the negotiations associated with the implementation
and monitoring of those contracts. These authors argue that district leadership is crucial in the coordination of efforts among
these quasi-independent agencies—schools.

With regard to the contribution of school districts to learning, the literature is much thinner. Galvin (forthcoming Developments in School Finance series edited by William Fowler,
NCES) found evidence that about 30 percent of the variance in
school-level performance scores could be attributed to school
district organization. This study used statewide assessment
scores for fifth, eighth, and eleventh graders, which were aggregated to give an indication of school performance. School scores
ranged from a minimum average score of 10 to over 280 on the
test scale. Because schools are nested within school districts, cre-

ating significant intra-class correlations, the analysis used a Hierarchical Linear Random ANOVA (see Bryk 1992 for details) to get the results. This method provides a powerful, and statistically accurate, means of partitioning the variance across hierarchically nested organizational environments. To ensure that these results were not unique, data sets for five years were constructed and examined using the identical analysis (1990–91 to 1994–95, all fifth and eighth grade schools; N = 505). The results confirmed the initial finding, that about 30 percent of the variance (plus or minus 4 percentage points), can be accounted for by district-level factors.

A second study examined a nine-year time series of school level performance scores. Utah's Statewide Testing Program was first implemented during the 1990–91 school year. Thus, most schools had nine scores over time. These time-series data are analyzed using the repeat measure analysis available in HLM (see Bryk and Raudenbush 1993, Chap. 6). The results of the unconditioned ANOVA in this analysis, which partitions the variance of test scores between school-level and district-level factors, indicate that about 25 percent of the variance in test scores is accounted for by district-level factors.

These findings are significant because they challenge Chubb and Moe's (1990) assertion that district-level organization has nothing to contribute to the efficient production of educational outcomes. Indeed, in a field of study where explaining 10 percent of variance is considered an achievement (Bridge, Judd, and Moock 1979), accounting for 30 percent of the variance is clearly noteworthy.

CONCLUSION

While calls for the reform of school district organizations are based on the belief that they have little to contribute to the production of quality educational services, the evidence that actually examines the school district's role in reform paints a different picture. This apparent inconsistency was what originally propelled my inquiry into the logic and source of proposals for regulatory reform and market ideologies that now guide the current waves of reform in education. The evolution of regulatory reform and its application to concerns about educational productivity fail, however, to recognize the rapidly changing context for educational organizations and the multiple problems related to governing a quasi-public institution characterized by uncertain technologies, ambiguously defined outcome measures, and multiple owners—all problems that confound the efficient operation of markets. The New Institutional Economics theory provides a way of thinking about these complicated issues and, moreover, recognizes the positive role of bureaucracy as a mechanism for governing complex organizations as well as enhancing productivity.

The current debate over the organization of schools is foundering in a simple dichotomy that pits centralized authority against decentralized governance. The balance of power and authority among constituent members resembles, in this perspective, a World War I front, where the battle for authority and autonomy is clearly demarcated between opposing parties. Economic theories of organization and governance, as introduced above, suggest an alternative image, where the negotiation of authority, responsibility, and governance is structured around the specific details of a category of exchanges.

In their review of the current debate involving centralized versus decentralized governance, both Tyack (1993) and Elmore (1993b) come to the conclusion that the issue is not either/or but rather what and at whose benefit or cost. These authors make two general observations relevant to this discussion. First, this debate over centralization versus decentralization is cyclic. To quote Tyack on the topic, "One period's common sense becomes a delusion in the next" (p. 1). In the past, consolidation and centralization efforts were viewed as the means by which to ensure accountability and efficiency in the delivery of educational services. Current literature regularly blames these same strategies for the failure to achieve accountability and efficiency in schools today. Second, that school reform proposals grounded in the ideology of decentralization reflect, as Tyack describes it, an "imagined past" or, as Elmore describes it, a "democratic ideal," free from bureaucratic meddling and intervention.

The traditional "maps" that have guided the way we think about the organizational terrain of schools and schooling are no longer useful. The "geo-politics" of these traditional maps, which defined the boundaries of roles and responsibilities within an organization, are changing. New alliances, new technologies, and new purposes are reshaping the organizational environment that houses the time-honored business of educators: that of teaching. Successful negotiation of these new alliances and boundaries is central to the establishment of trust among educators and the public they serve—an ingredient that is notably missing in the reform agendas of the 1980s and 1990s. Without trust, and the grace that accompanies it, education may well balkanize into a competitive market that poorly serves the interests of parents, children, and society. The alternative is the creation of cooperative markets that exploit the potential of the emerging boundaries by which authority for schooling in America is defined and distributed.

REFERENCES

Arrow, K. J. (1974). *The limits of organization.* New York: W. W. Norton & Company.

Bacharach, S. B., and Mundell, B. L. (1993). Organizational politics in schools: Micro, macro, and logics of action. *Educational Administration Quarterly, 29*(4), 423–452.

Badarocco, J. L., Jr. (1991). The boundaries of the firm. In A. Etzioni and P. R. Lawrence (Eds.), *Socio-economics: Toward a new synthesis* (pp. 293–327). Armonk, NY: M. E. Sharpe.

Barney, J., and Ouchi, W. G. (Eds.) (1986). *Organizational economics.* San Francisco: Jossey-Bass Inc.

Bennett, W. J. (1992). *The de-valuing of American: The fight for our culture and our children.* New York: Summit Books.

Bridge, R. G., Judd, C. M., and Moock, P. R. (1979). *The determinants of educational outcomes: The impact of families, peers, teachers, and schools.* Cambridge, MA: Ballinger.

Brimelow, P. (1986). Are we spending too much on education? *Forbes,* (December 29), 72–76.

Brimelow, P., and Spencer, L. (1993). The national extortion association? *Forbes,* (June 7), 72–84.

Bryk, A. S., and Raudenbush, S. W. (1992). *Hierarchical linear models: Applications and data analysis methods.* Newbury Park, CA: Sage.

Button, K., and Swann, D. (Eds.) (1989). *The age of regulatory reform.* Oxford, UK: Clarendon.

Callahan, R. E. (1962). *Education and the cult of efficiency.* Chicago: The University of Chicago Press.

Chubb, J. E., and Moe, T. M. (1990). *Politics, markets, and America's schools.* Washington, DC: Brookings Institution.

Cibulka, J. G., and Kritek, W. J. (1996). *Coordination among schools, families, and communities.* London: Falmer Press.

Coase, R. H. (1937). The nature of the firm. *Economica, 4,* 386–405.

Coleman, J. S., Campbell, E. Q., Hobson, C. J., McPartland, J., Mood, A. M., Weinfeld, F. D., and York, R. L. (1966). *Equality of educational opportunity.* Washington, DC: Department of Health, Education and Welfare, U.S. Government Printing Office.

Commons, J. R. (1934). *Institutional economics: Its place in political economy.* New York: MacMillan.

Conley, S. C. (1989). "Who's on first?" School reform, teacher participation, and the decision-making process. *Education and Urban Society, 21*(4), 366–379.

Cubberley, E. P. (1934). *Public education in the United States.* Boston: Houghton Mifflin.

Daneke, G. A., and Lemak, D. J. (Eds.) (1985). *Regulatory reform reconsidered.* Boulder, CO: Westview Press.

Darling-Hammond, L. (1989). Accountability for professional practice. *Teachers College Record, 91,* 59–80.

Demsetz, H. (1969). Information and efficiency: Another viewpoint. *Journal of Law and Economics, 12,* 1–22.

Elmore, R. F. (1993a). The role of the local school districts in instructional improvement. In S. H. Fuhrman (Ed.), *Designing coherent education policy: Improving the system* (pp. 96–124). San Francisco: Jossey-Bass.

Elmore, R. F. (1993b). School decentralization: Who gains? Who loses? In J. Hannaway and M. Carnoy (Eds.), *Decentralization and school improvement: Can we fulfill the promise?* (pp. 33–54). San Francisco: Jossey-Bass.

Everhart, R. B. (Ed.) (1982). *The public school monopoly: A critical analysis of education and the state in American society.* Cambridge, MA: Ballinger.

Firestone, W., Fuhrman, S., and Kirst, M. (1990). An overview of education reform since 1983. In J. Murphy (Ed.), *The educational reform movement of the 1980s: Perspectives and cases* (pp. 349–364). Berkeley, CA: McCutchan.

Firestone, W., Goertz, M., and Natriello, G. (1998). *From cashbox to classroom: The struggle for fiscal reform and educational change in New Jersey.* New York: Teachers College.

Firestone, W. A. (1989). Using reform: Conceptualizing district initiative. *Educational Evaluation and Policy Analysis, 11*(2), 151–164.

Firestone, W. A., and Fairman, J. C. (1998). *The district role in state assessment policy: An exploratory study.* San Diego, CA: American Educational Research Association.

First, P. F. (1992). *Educational policy for school administrators.* Boston: Allyn and Bacon.

Friedman, M., and Friedman, R. (1980). What's wrong with our school? *Free to choose.* New York: Harcourt, Brace, Jovanovich.

Furubotn, E. G., and Richter, R. (Eds.) (1992). *The new institutional economics.* College Station, TX: Texas A&M University Press.

Gerstner, L. V. J., Semerad, R. D., Doyle, D. P., and Johnston, W. B. (1994). *Reinventing education: Entrepreneurship in America's public schools.* New York, NY: Dutton.

Gittell, M. (1970). The balance of power and the community school. In H. M. Levin (Ed.), *Community control of schools* (pp. 115–137). Washington, DC: Brookings Institution.

Goodsell, C. T. (1985). *The case for bureaucracy: A public administration polemic.* Chatham, NJ: Chatham House Publishers, Inc.

Hill, P. T. (1995). *Reinventing public education.* Santa Monica, CA: Rand.

Hill, P. T., and Bonan, J. (1991). *Decentralization and accountability in public education*. Santa Monica, CA: Rand.

Iannaccone, L. (1982). Changing political patterns and governmental regulation. In R. B. Everhart (Ed.), *The public school monopoly: A critical analysis of education and the state in American society* (pp. 295–324). Cambridge, MA: Ballinger.

Langlois, R. N. (1998). Transaction costs, production costs, and the passage of time. In S. G. Medema (Ed.), *Coasean economics: Law and economics and the new institutional economics* (pp. 1–21). Boston, MA: Kluwer Academic.

Langlois, R. N., and Robertson, P. L. (1995). *Firms, markets and economic change: A dynamic theory of business institutions*. New York: Routledge.

Levin, H. M. (Ed.) (1970). *Community control of schools*. Washington, DC: Brookings Institution.

Madaus, G. F. (1985). Testing as an administrative mechanism in educational policy: What does the future hold? *Educational Horizons*, 34–39.

March, J. G. (1991). How decisions happen in organizations. *Human Computer Interaction, 6*, 99–117.

Medema, S. G. (Ed.) (1998). *Coasean economics: Law and economics and the new institutional economics*. Boston: Kluwer Academic.

Meyer, J. W., and Rowan, B. (1977). Institutionalized organizations: Formal structure as myth and ceremony. *American Journal of Sociology, 83*, 340–363.

Mitchell, D. E., and Encarnation, D. J. (1984, May). Alternative state policy mechanisms for influencing school performance. *Educational Researcher*, 4–11.

Murphy, J. (Ed.) (1990a). *The educational reform movement of the 1980s: Perspectives and cases*. Berkeley, CA: McCutchan.

Murphy, J. (1990b). The reform of school administration: Pressures and calls for change. In J. Murphy (Ed.), *The educational reform movement of the 1980s: Perspectives and cases* (pp. 277–303). Berkeley, CA: McCutchan.

National Commission on Excellence in Education. (1983). *A nation at risk: The imperative for education reform*. Washington, DC: United States Department of Education.

North, D. C. (1990). *Institutions, institutional change and economic performance*. Cambridge, UK: Cambridge University Press.

Odden, A., and Busch, C. (1998). *Financing schools for high performance: Strategies for improving the use of educational resources*. San Francisco: Jossey-Bass.

Perrow, C. (1986). *Complex organizations: A critical essay*. New York: McGraw-Hill.

Pounder, D. G. (Ed.) (1997). *Restructuring schools for collaboration: Promises and pitfalls*. Albany, NY: State University of New York Press.

Ranson, S., and Tomlinson, J. (Eds.) (1994). *School co-operation: New forms of local governance*. Essex, UK: Longman.

Ravitch, D. (Ed.) (1999). *Brookings papers on education policy*. Washington, DC: Brookings Institution.

Scott, W. R. (1995). *Institutions and organizations*. Thousand Oaks, CA: Sage.

Seashore-Louis, K. (1989). The role of the school district in school improvement. In M. Homes, K. A. Leithwood, and D. F. Musella (Eds.), *Educational policy for effective schools* (pp. 145–167). Ontario, Canada: OISE Press.

Timar, T. (1989). The politics of school restructuring. *Phi Delta Kappan*, 265–275.

Tyack, D. (1993). School governance in the United States: Historical puzzles and anomalies. In J. Hannaway and M. Carnoy (Eds.), *Decentralization and school improvement: Can we fulfill the promise?* (pp. 1–32). San Francisco: Jossey-Bass.

Tyack, D., and Hansot, E. (1982). *Managers of virtue*. New York: Basic Books.

Tyack, D. D. (1974). *The one best system*. Cambridge, MA: Harvard University Press.

Verstegen, D. (1988–1989). Assessment and reform: The local district response to state mandated changes. *National Forum for Educational Administration and Supervision*, 7(3), 78–105.

Weick, K. E. (1976). Educational organizations as loosely coupled systems. *Educational Administration Quarterly, 21*(4), 1– 19.

Williamson, O. E. (1975). *Markets and hierarchies: Analysis and antitrust implications.* New York: Free Press.

Williamson, O. E. (1986). *Economic organization: Firms, markets and policy control.* New York: New York University Press.

Williamson, O. E. (1996). *The mechanisms of governance.* New York: Oxford University Press.

PART V

CONCLUSION

10

Achieving a "Just Balance" Between Local Control of Schools and State Responsibility for K-12 Education: Summary Observations and Research Agendas[1]

Betty Malen,
Neil Theobald,
and
Jeffrey Bardzell

1 We thank Sharon Conley, Tim Mazzoni, Donna Muncey, Robert Michael, and Jennifer King Rice for their feedback on an earlier version of this chapter.

Reflecting this Yearbook's intent—to examine and to interpret changes in state-local relationships—we try, in this closing chapter, to highlight several cross-cutting themes and their implications for work in the interrelated fields of education finance and governance. Recognizing that a single volume cannot deal with all important aspects of a topic, we acknowledge some of the Yearbook's omissions and limitations that could be accommodated in subsequent treatments of this topic.

Our aims are modest. We do not assume the heady responsibility of advocating a new model of governance nor compare alternative models of intergovernmental relations, although examples of such treatises are certainly evident in academic literatures, policy papers, and popular press writings on education reform.[2] Rather, we set forth, in broad strokes, several observations about state and local roles, responsibilities, and relationships. In so doing, we seek to direct attention to some of the issues that warrant further consideration as we work to understand more fully and to address more explicitly the ever-present tensions and value-laden dilemmas embodied in education proposals, policies, and practices generally, and in education funding patterns more specifically.

SUMMARY OBSERVATIONS

Four general observations about state-local relationships capture many of the common themes found in this Yearbook. These observations provide a prelude to the discussion of future research agendas.

---

2   See, for example, Bull (Chap. 2, this volume), Smith and O'Day's writings on systemic reform (Smith and O'Day 1991), McDermott's recommendations for redefining governance that grew out of her study of local districts in Connecticut (McDermott 1999), the report of the Education Commission of the States' National Commission on Governing America's Schools entitled *Governing America's Schools: Changing the Rules,* and the array of governance proposals disseminated in *Education Week* and other popular press venues. For recent examples, see McAdams and Urbanski (1999) and Wang and Walberg (1999).

GOVERNMENTAL RELATIONSHIPS AS
CONTINUALLY CONTESTED TERRAIN

This volume reminds us that a "just balance" between state authority and local autonomy is continually contested terrain. As the opening section of this Yearbook demonstrates, whether viewed philosophically, historically, legally, or politically, competing conceptions of "appropriate balance" resurface directly as part of governance debates and judicial interpretations, or indirectly through policy disputes about the related or residual effects various education policies and practices may have on state and local powers and prerogatives.

Bull's critique of the normative assumptions embedded in proposals for systemic reform, Beadie's analysis of proposals for greater state control and pleas for greater local control of public education, along with Dayton's review of recent education finance litigation—all demonstrate the controversial nature and value-laden character of the divergent and recurrent efforts to determine how state authority and local autonomy may be defined and distributed (Bull; Beadie; Dayton; Chaps. 2, 3, and 4, respectively, this volume). And, as the subsequent chapters by Fowler, Mazzoni, Malen and Muncey, and Galvin (Chapters 5, 6, 7, and 9, respectively, this volume) illustrate, conflicts about how governmental responsibilities are to be divided are implicitly, if not explicitly, a fundamental feature of the more recent rounds of education reform legislation and litigation.

Such ongoing contention is to be expected (a) when core societal values, or more precisely, diverse conceptions of core values such as liberty, equity, efficiency, and excellence are at stake; (b) when public education matters become the medium for reappraising the manner in which these and other major values may be affirmed, altered, or realigned; (c) when neither state nor local government has a clear claim on virtue; and, (d) when policy actors realize that governance arrangements not only affect the distribution of power and authority, but also the distribution of credit and blame.[3] As the Bull (Chap. 2), Beadie (Chap. 3), and Galvin (Chap. 9) chapters demonstrate, popular presumptions about which levels of government hold the comparative advantage in promoting or protecting particular values are not dependable propositions. These authors show that both state and local units have been sources of initiative and seats of inaction; both have worked to extend educational opportunities and perpetuate ingrained inequities; both have a place in the press for efficiency; and both have worked to protect and restrict individual and institutional freedom.

We add and underscore that neither state governments nor local units have mobilized on behalf of policies that might tackle some of the underlying causes of educational problems as well as grapple with how states and localities construct their respective roles. For example, efforts to redistribute wealth, expand the scope of promising interventions, or otherwise confront the life conditions, as well as the learning opportunities, of children are few and far between (e.g., Anyon 1997; Edelman 1987; Schorr 1988; Tyack and Cuban 1995). Thus, neither state governments nor local units can assemble a policy history that makes an irrefutable case for a particular division of duties.

STATE GOVERNMENT AS ASCENDING POWER

Although state-local relationships have undergone repeated, arguably cyclical iterations, the current configuration reflects a shift from governance arrangements that favored the district to governance arrangements that favor the state. As several chapters demonstrate, the shift from a local to a state advantage in the balance of power is both noticeable and consequential.

Despite the continuous expansion of state power and occasional federal intervention, the traditional pattern of power tended to favor the local district (Theobald and Bardzell; Bull;

---

3 For elaborations of the first two points, see, for example, Frohock (1979), Mazzoni (1991), and Mazzoni (Chap. 6, this volume). To be sure, there are other reasons for the contention, but these factors appear to be especially potent explanators.

Beadie; Fowler; Galvin; Chaps. 1, 2, 3, 5, 9, respectively, this volume). In this traditional pattern, districts had considerable latitude in terms of the educational revenues they could raise and the particular programs and priorities they could pursue. Districts were accountable to their local constituents in that they recognized the importance of cultivating positive sentiments toward and public confidence in public schools. Although scholars regularly questioned whether local districts and individual schools were really open to lay influence and whether they operated as responsibly and efficiently as proponents of "district-centered" governance models suggested, this arrangement prevailed in many states (e.g., Boyd 1976; Burlingame 1987, 1988; First and Walberg 1992; McDermott 1999; Ziegler and Jennings 1974).

To be sure, tensions between districts and schools were ever-present during the decades of more "district-centered" governance, and became evident when issues such as school autonomy, and, at times, issues regarding educational quality, equity, and efficiency became part and parcel of proposals to decentralize and/or revitalize school districts (Fager 1993; Gittell 1973; Mann 1979; Burlingame 1987). Moreover, tensions between local schools and the broader system were also apparent. Federal and state interventions of various sorts were introduced in, and, at times imposed on, school districts. Working primarily through persuasion or exhortation, states and the federal government intermittently adopted a reformist stance. At times, these broader units coupled exhortation with regulation to address particular issues, such as parent involvement in school governance, fair funding practices, and equitable educational opportunities for students with particular "disabilities" or "disadvantages" (Burlingame 1987; Campbell, Cunningham, and McPhee 1965; Davies 1978; Mann 1979). And, at times, the courts became directive around particular issues, such as school desegregation and state finance equalization. Still, legislative and, in some instances, judicial efforts to "intrude" on local prerogatives were constrained by many forces, including the presumption that state and federal governments ought not tarnish the cherished tradition of local control.

With the onset of extensive state activism, the dynamics changed markedly. Districts were not just "the forgotten player on the education reform team" (Danzberger, Carol, Cunningham, Kirst, McCloud, and Usdan 1987). Districts became the maligned players (Galvin, Chap. 9, this volume). A convenient, if not always deserving recipient of criticism and blame, local districts, and the professional educators employed by them lost favor. But the tendency to ignore or indict local districts was just one of many indications that the balance of power was shifting, that traditions of local control were being challenged in dramatic, if not unprecedented fashion (Mazzoni; Malen and Muncey; Galvin; Chaps. 6, 7, and 9, respectively, this volume).

Relying primarily on their regulatory and their purse-string authority to craft mandates and incentives, state governments adopted a more aggressive and intrusive stance. Their education initiatives tended to be both more directive in tone and more comprehensive in scope. As Bull summarizes it, states have become more prescriptive about both "the purposes for which the school funds available to localities are to be used and the education means by which those purposes are to be pursued" (Bull, Chap. 2, this volume). Relying primarily on what Jung and Kirst (1986) termed the "bully pulpit" strategy, the federal government endorsed regulatory policies and "results-based" initiatives that added a layer of legitimacy to actions states were taking.

Although considerable variance across the states is evident, the state-local control equation now favors the state. The state holds the comparative power advantage in part, as Fowler's chapter (Chap. 5) points out, because states are using the "legal foundations" that have always existed. The state also holds the comparative power advantage in part because, as other chapters point out, states are focusing their actions in ways that extend their regulatory reach and amplify their influence on districts and sites (Mazzoni; Malen and Muncey; Galvin; Chaps. 6, 7, and 9, respectively, this volume). While there will always be discrepancies between states' formal authority over school systems and their actual influence on school developments, while there will always be some slippage as policies made at higher levels of the system filter through other parts of the education enterprise, it seems that the balance of power has shifted substantially.

EFFICIENCY AS DOMINANT SOCIAL VALUE

Changes in governance often affect as well as reflect changes in the core values that are emphasized in the larger society and the policy strategies that are deployed in the public sector. This tendency is apparent here.

The multidimensional shifts in governance, values, and strategy include, as Galvin (Chap. 9, this volume) notes, state policy actions that begin with a general recognition of and reliance on local, often district, initiative and move to a heady array of regulatory strategies, including greater reliance on market rather than bureaucratic mechanisms to encourage efficiency. The transition from what Galvin terms "trust" agreements to regulatory arrangements, including attempts to subject public school systems to the cleansing power of market forces, may not only redistribute organizational power and authority in highly consequential ways (Malen and Muncey; Galvin; Chaps. 7 and 9, respectively, this volume), but also realign social values in important ways.

For example, states intensified their use of bureaucratic controls through the imposition of academic standards, "high stakes" testing programs, school report cards, and other publicly disseminated indicators of organizational performance. As these and other accountability-driven, efficiency-oriented reforms took center stage in state, and at times federal arenas, other social values, notably equity and autonomy received less attention. Issues of excellence and economic growth often superseded issues of equity and local autonomy in state and federal arenas (Boyd 1988; Howe 1991). Through exhortations, mandates, and inducements at the state level and "bully pulpit" pronouncements at the federal level (Jung and Kirst 1986), both levels of government seemed to be seeking dramatic and inexpensive ways to foster efficiency even if the mechanisms they employed were ignoring, jeopardizing or, in some cases trumping, efforts to foster equity and protect autonomy (Clark and Astuto 1986; Howe 1991).

Further, the states' willingness to entertain seriously, if not enact formally, policies that might break up public education's "natural monopoly" (Galvin, Chap. 9, this volume), augmented by the federal government's endorsement of choice experiments, challenged the status of public schools and signaled a change in the values emphasized and the mechanisms used to deliver educational programs and services.[4] Some of the multiple school-choice plans and charter school proposals tried to preempt equity concerns in the rhetoric, if not the design, of their initiatives. Nonetheless, the primary appeal appeared to be that the dynamics inherent in the free market will provide parents with more choices about where to send their children and, as a result, will force public schools to become more efficient in the production of services and more responsive to the interests of their targeted constituencies.

These and other indicators suggest that states have emphasized efficiency. Although states have continued to consider fiscal equity, at times because new rounds of litigation required them to do so, states emphasized efficiency-oriented policies (Theobald and Bull, in press). Reflecting this emphasis, states enacted an array of requirements, incentives, and sanctions that simultaneously increase the demands on districts and schools, reduce their discretion, and hold them ever more responsible for performance. States also used their funding systems to leverage marked changes in governance as well as to focus attention on desired changes in performance. For instance, states have withheld funds, pending adjustments in local governance and/or the negotiation of "state-local partnerships" that substantially alter governmental roles and relationships in select urban areas (Henig, Hula, Orr, and Pedescleaux 1999; Orr 1999). And, in many regions, they have put the focus on financial (as well as reputational) incentives and sanctions rather than fiscal and programmatic entitlements. While these and other financial manifestations of changes in the locus of power receive much less attention than we intended to give them, the broad trends

---

4 Natural monopolies occur when economies of scale require only a single provider of a service for maximum efficiency. The case of power companies is often used as an example of a natural monopoly.

noted here highlight the nature of the policy and value shifts associated with the governance changes we are witnessing.

STATE ACTIVISM AS ENDURING PHENOMENON

Although governmental actions at any level of the system defy precise prediction, it seems that state activism in education may well be here to stay. Fowler and Mazzoni (Chaps. 5 and 6, respectively, this volume) discuss the multiple factors that have converged to increase significantly, and at times dramatically, the scope and intensity of state involvement in school reform. Major changes in state capacity, as well as in state opportunities and incentives, have contributed to the evolution and expansion of the states' role in education. As Mazzoni demonstrates, the signs and seeds of intensive and extensive state involvement were evident long before the oft-cited *Nation at Risk* report was released. Indeed, state activism in education policy has a longer, stronger history than treatments of the more recent "waves" of reform acknowledge (Mazzoni, Chap. 6, this volume; Wirt 1977). Although Mazzoni's nuanced analysis of state activism calls attention to the differences as well as the similarities across states, his analysis supports Fowler's "cautious prediction" about continued state activism.

We concur. The states' long-term record of involvement, along with the high-valence economic and educational stakes now vividly and vehemently attached to school reform suggest that states are likely to continue their quest for improvements in the performance and productivity of schools. Given the challenge of producing meaningful improvements, the difficulty of demonstrating significant gains on test-based accountability measures, the frustration that comes with reports of "flat" or "declining" scores, the embarrassment that accompanies exposes on various schemes devised to artificially and dishonestly increase test scores, and the impatience that smolders as policy elites await the results they seek, state governments may become more desperate, more aggressive, more prescriptive, or more punitive. It is not likely, however, that they will become less insistent on discernible and substantial indications of school improvement.

RESEARCH AGENDAS

If the preceding observations are valid, we have a great deal of important work to do. Our knowledge of the changes in state-local relationships and the consequences of those changes is limited. As authors of chapters in this Yearbook indicate, we may have "tip of the iceberg" understandings of extraordinarily complex developments, because the empirical base for analyzing and interpreting these developments is fragile and fragmented. In some cases, the conceptual groundings may be underdeveloped or misguided. While each chapter contains its own implications for future research and theoretical development, the set of chapters suggests streams of work that might help us understand more fully changes in the state-local relationship as well as examine more comprehensively the consequences of shifts in value emphasis and policy strategy. While empirical research and theoretical advancements can not answer the normative questions embedded in efforts to define a "just balance" between state responsibility for and local control of education, they can inform the public debate on those matters. Thus, we turn to lines of research that may be particularly helpful as we work to unpack the issues, weigh the evidence, and contribute to the debates.

ACTORS AND ARENAS

Both the Fowler and Mazzoni chapters (Chaps. 5 and 6) underscore the importance of continuously tracking political dynamics at the state level and systematically arraying the complex web of actors, interests, powers, and pressures that combine to shape education policy choices. In addition to providing fairly comprehensive accounts of the congestion and competition that characterizes state arenas, research might also focus on the contextual forces and the national and international networks that are operating to standardize state initiatives (Mazzoni, Chap. 6, this volume). Such analyses might yield important insights about whose interests are being served by the education reform proposals and about how various contextual forces (global, national, and regional) and actor alignments interact to produce policy choices that affect and reflect how social values become redefined and realigned.

Both the Malen and Muncey and Galvin chapters (Chaps. 7 and 9) underscore the importance of carefully mapping the political dynamics in district and school arenas as well. Knowledge of these dynamics can help us understand how district and school actors are responding to state initiatives and how state policies may be permeating districts and schools in subtle but important ways. Knowledge of these dynamics could also help us see how clusters of local actors might be able to influence the formulation as well as the implementation of state education policy choices. When coupled with studies of state education policymaking processes, attention to the politics in local arenas could provide the basis for multilevel analyses that reveal how levels and units of the education policy system interact to shape policy choices and policy outcomes (Malen and Muncey, Chap. 7, this volume; see also Malen and Hart 1987, and Spillane 1999).

Studies that seek to describe the sets of actors that do not clearly cluster around the notions of "local" and "central" arenas are certainly in order. To illustrate, the emphasis on market mechanisms is encouraging new actors (e.g., management corporations, contracting firms, organizers of public, for-profit schools) into state and local arenas (Walsh 1999). These actors are, in many ways, creations of the market and are neither "local" nor "central." How these and other new, and in some instances returning, players seek to influence education policy could reveal a great deal about the interests served and the values promulgated through market as opposed to bureaucratic mechanisms of control.

COSTS AND CONSEQUENCES

Among the most fundamental lines of research are ongoing studies that investigate the costs and consequences of this latest round of education reforms. Unfortunately, the fiscal dimensions of changes in state-local relationships get short shrift in this Yearbook. But this limitation does not diminish the importance of tracking (a) the actual investments in, and the opportunity costs of, various education reforms, as well as (b) the anticipated and unanticipated effects of these policies.

Because education reforms carry a human as well as a financial toll, studies that seek to delineate costs, broadly conceived, could be particularly useful additions to the literature (King 1994; Rice 1997). Such analyses not only provide a more complete account of the visible and hidden costs of reform, they also yield information about what resources are allocated to support various reforms and what resources may be required for different reforms to operate. Thus, research on costs, broadly conceived, could enhance the ability of state and local policy actors to more effectively align reform options with resource requirements and to more readily detect, and more reliably provide, the kinds of resources (e.g., money, expertise, time, personnel) that may be needed for particular reforms to achieve their stated aims (see, for example, King 1994).

It is also helpful to map how costs are borne and how they are accommodated (Rice 1997). For example, we could lay out the financial contours of state education reforms, not only in terms of the allocations made to districts and sites, but also in terms of the dislocations that may occur as localities respond to and cope with state directives (see, for example, Spillane 1999). As Addonizio (Chap. 8, this volume) illustrates, districts may cope with state funding restrictions by engaging in a host of entrepreneurial activities to generate discretionary funds. Such activities may affect fiscal equity and organizational efficiency, particularly if they continue over a long period of time.

Other work indicates that, largely in response to state testing pressures, districts and sites may redirect fiscal, human, and instructional resources, including time, to those students who need the least assistance in order to make the largest gains on official tests, while students who arguably have the greatest need for supplemental services may receive less, and at times, no additional attention.[5] There is also evidence that both state and local testing requirements consume considerable instructional time (Malen and Muncey, Chap. 7, this volume; see also Malen, Croninger, Redmond, and Muncey 1999). Yet these and other trade-offs embedded in diverse approaches to reform are not often arrayed and compared in ways that clarify the trade-offs.

Beyond addressing the complex issues associated with identifying and gauging the multiple costs of education reforms, research that extends our understanding of the anticipated and unanticipated consequences is also necessary. Chapters in this Yearbook demonstrate the importance of examining the consequences of state policies, and local responses to them, on a host of dimensions including the appropriate role of school districts in school reform (Galvin, Chap. 9, this volume), the multiple ways state policies may be permeating schools and engendering changes in the underlying conceptions of school improvement possibilities as well as in the daily decisions about organizational operations (Malen and Muncey, Chap. 7, this volume), and the inefficiencies that may result from reduction of the school district role (Galvin, Chap. 9, this volume). Critical issues raised by, but not examined in, this Yearbook include the effects of state pressures on professional educators' work environments and occupational choices and the impact of various organizational accommodations on the availability and quality of learning experiences in schools.

Given actual and imminent changes in the regulatory environment, research that focuses on various regulatory strategies is especially salient. As earlier noted, states have intensified their use of a broad range of bureaucratic controls. As part of the press for improved performance, states have intervened, or threatened to intervene in a variety of ways, including "take-

---

5 Several in-progress case studies and one unpublished case study of district and site responses to state accountability pressures suggest that local units may be inclined to, and at times directed to, steer resources (in the form of tutorials, after-school programs, and summer school programs) to students who may be able to pass the state tests with this assistance. In some instances, students who are farther from the "minimum standard" may not have access to these or other relevant supports (Malen 1999).

overs" and "partnerships" between state and local actors. Because these interventions are punitive as well as a corrective in tone and design, they can have especially powerful effects on the ability of state and local authorities to cooperate and collaborate. Moreover, these state interventions can have significant effects on the ability of local communities to develop what Stone (1989) terms "civic capacity," the social, fiscal, and intellectual capital required to bring about major improvements in public service institutions writ large and public school systems per se.

A recently published analysis of the Baltimore city-state partnership for school improvement illustrates the point (Orr 1999). According to Orr's analysis, this city-state partnership was forged, in part, to avert even more intrusive legislative and judicial prescriptions and in part, to access funds the state was withholding until new governance arrangements were put in place. The "partnership" helped "free" state funds for investment in the city's schools, though the amount of state money allotted was less than half that recommended by a state-commissioned study of the city's school system. But the partnership also altered the local infrastructure, intensified racial strains and otherwise signaled that the interactions between "external actors," such as state and federal governments and local cultures may have multiple and mixed effects on both the willingness and ability of state and local actors to develop the stable, broad-based coalitions required for substantial and enduring improvements (Orr, 1999; see also, Henig, Hula, Orr, and Pedescleaux 1999).

Because the regulatory environment is also characterized by a willingness to use market mechanisms to improve schools, it seems prudent to focus research on the consequences of a transition from natural monopoly to free market in urban, metropolitan, and rural settings. Drawing on evidence from various experiments with market models in U.S. settings and in other countries, scholars are starting to inspect the assumptions, "test" the propositions embedded in various choice plans, and discuss the impact of various choice arrangements on key aspects of core social values, notably equity, efficiency, and liberty (see, for example, Fowler 1992a, 1992b; Goldhaber 1999; Handler 1996; Lauder and Hughes 1999; Levin 1989). Scholars have also started to gather data on charter schools (see, for example,

Berman, Nelson, Ericson, Perry, and Silverman 1998; Wells and Associates 1999). Such efforts provide a basis for future inquiry that seeks to determine whether and how various market mechanisms actually affect the efficiency of organizational operations and the quality and distribution of educational services in various contexts.

BENEFITS AND BURDENS

The preceding sections identify lines of research that, taken together, might provide more fine-grained responses to the "Who Benefits" and "Who Pays" questions that undergird much of the literature in the education finance field and the parallel "Who Wins" and "Who Loses" questions that undergird much of the literature in education governance. Carefully aggregated and integrated studies, such as those highlighted here, could detail in what ways and to what degrees various actors benefit from and pay for education reform. Answers to these questions will not be formulated easily or accepted uniformly (see, for example, Elmore 1993). But carefully qualified, even-handed efforts to address these overarching questions can tell us a great deal about how the benefits and burdens are distributed and aligned.

Moreover, these patterns reveal a great deal about how society is currently defining liberty, efficiency, equity, and quality and how education policies may be affirming, neglecting, or ignoring critical dimensions of these core values. Consequently, these lines of work could enable us to develop well-reasoned and well-informed judgments about how education policy choices affect key social values. With that foundation more firm, we will be better equipped to bring principles of fairness to the fore and to strike a just balance among the fundamental values we advance through the sets of education policies we endorse.

REFERENCES

Addonizio, M. F. (2000). Salvaging fiscal control: New sources of local revenue for public schools. In N. D. Theobald and B. Malen (Eds.), *Balancing local control and state responsibility for K-12 education*, Chap. 8. Larchmont, NY: Eye on Education.

Anyon, J. (1977). *Ghetto schooling: A political economy of urban educational reform.* New York: Teachers College Press.

Beadie, N. (2000). The limits of standardization and the importance of constituencies: Historical tensions in the relationship between state authority and local control. In N. D. Theobald and B. Malen (Eds.), *Balancing local control and state responsibility for K–12 education*, Chap. 3. Larchmont, NY: Eye on Education.

Berman, P., Nelson, B., Ericson, J., Perry, R., and Silverman, D. (1998). *A national study of charter schools: Second-year report.* Washington, DC: Office of Educational Research and Improvement.

Boyd, W. L. (1976). The public, the professionals and education policymaking: Who governs? *Teachers College Record, 77,* 539–577.

Boyd, W. L. (1988). How to reform schools without half trying: Secrets of the Reagan Administration. *Educational Administration Quarterly, 24,* 299–309.

Bull, B. (2000). Political philosophy and the state-local power balance. In N. D. Theobald and B. Malen (Eds.), *Balancing local control and state responsibility for K–12 education*, Chap. 2. Larchmont, NY: Eye on Education.

Burlingame, M. (1987). The shambles of local politics. *PEA Bulletin, 13,* 3–8.

Burlingame, M. (1988). The politics of education and educational policy: The local level. In N. Boyan (Ed.), *The handbook of research on educational administration.* New York: Longman.

Campbell, R. F., Cunningham, L. L., and McPhee, R. F. (1965). *The organization and control of American schools.* Columbus, OH: C. E. Merrill.

Clark, D. and Astuto, T. (1986). The significance and permanence of changes in federal education policy. *Educational Researcher, 15*(7), 4–13.

Davies. D. (1978). *Federal and state impact on citizen participation in the schools.* Boston: Institute for Responsive Education.

Danzberger, J. P., Carol, L. N., Cunningham, L. L., Kirst, M. W., McCloud, B. A., and Usdan, M. D. (1987). School boards: The forgotten player on the education team. *Phi Delta Kappan, 69,* 53–59.

Dayton, J. (2000). Recent litigation and its impact on the state-local power balance: Liberty and equity in governance, litigation, and the school finance policy debate. In N. D. Theobald and B. Malen (Eds.), *Balancing local control and state responsibility for K-12 education,* Chap. 4. Larchmont, NY: Eye on Education.

Edelman, M. W. (1987). *Families in peril: An agenda for social change.* Cambridge, MA: Harvard University Press.

Education Commission of the States. (1999). *Governing America's schools: Changing the rules.* Report of the Education Commission of the States' National Commission on Governing America's Schools, available from the Education Commission of the States, Denver, CO.

Elmore, R. F. (1993). School decentralization: Who gains? Who loses? In J. Hannaway and M. Carnoy (Eds.), *Decentralization and school improvement: Can we fulfill the promise?* San Francisco: Jossey-Bass.

Fager, J. (1993). *The "rules" still rule: The failure of school-based management/shared decision-making in the New York City Public School System.* New York: Parents Coalition for Education in NYC.

First, P. and Walberg, H. (Eds.). (1992). *School boards: Changing local control.* Berkeley, CA: McCutchan.

Fowler, F. C. (1992a). American theory and French practice: A theoretical rationale for regulating school choice. *Educational Administration Quarterly, 28,* 452–472.

Fowler, F. C. (1992b). Challenging the assumption that choice is all that freedom means. In F. C. Wendel (Ed.), *Reforms in empowerment, choice, and adult learning.* University Park, PA: University Council for Educational Administration.

Fowler, F. C. (2000). Converging forces: Understanding the growth of state authority over education. In N. D. Theobald and B. Malen (Eds.), *Balancing local control and state responsibility for K-12 education,* Chap. 5. Larchmont, NY: Eye on Education.

Frohock, F. (1979). *Public policy, scope and logic.* Englewood Cliffs, NJ: Prentice-Hall.

Galvin, P. (2000). Organizational boundaries, authority, and school district organization. In N. D. Theobald and B. Malen (Eds.), *Balancing local control and state responsibility for K-12 education,* Chap. 9. Larchmont, NY: Eye on Education.

Gittell, M. (1973). *School boards and school policy: An evaluation of decentralization in New York.* New York: Praeger.

Goldhaber, D. (1999). School choice: An examination of the empirical evidence on achievement, parental decision making, and equity. *Educational Researcher, 28*(9), 16–25.

Handler, J. F. (1996). *Down from bureaucracy: The ambiguity of privatization and empowerment.* Princeton, NJ: Princeton University Press.

Henig, J. R., Hula, R. C., Orr, M., and Pedescleaux, D. S. (1999). *The color of school reform: Race, politics and the challenge of urban education.* Princeton, NJ: Princeton University Press.

Howe, H. III (1991). America 2000: A bumpy ride on four trains. *Phi Delta Kappan, 73*(3), 192–203.

Jung, R., and Kirst, M. (1986). Beyond mutual adaptation, into the bully pulpit: Recent research on the federal role in education. *Educational Administration Quarterly, 22*(1), 80–109.

King, J. A. (1994). Meeting the educational needs of at-risk students: A cost analysis of three models. *Educational Evaluation and Policy Analysis, 16,* 1–19.

Lauder, H. and Hughes, D. (1999). *Trading in futures: Why markets in education don't work.* Philadelphia, PA: Open University Press.

Levin, H. (1989). *The theory of choice applied to education.* Stanford, CA: Center for Educational Research at Stanford.

McAdams, D. R., and Urbanski, A. (1999, November 24). Governing well: Two approaches from a national commission for honing the enterprise to support better schools. *Education Week,* pp. 32–33, 44.

McDermott, K. A. (1999). *Controlling public education: Localism versus equity.* Lawrence, KS: University Press.

Malen, B. (1999). [District and site responses to state accountability pressures]. Unpublished case study.

Malen, B., Croninger, R., Redmond, D. and Muncey, D. (1999). *Uncovering the potential contradictions in reconstitution reforms.* A paper presented at the annual conference of the University Council for Educational Administration, Minneapolis, October, 1999.

Malen, B., and Hart, A. W. (1987). Career ladder reform: A multi-level analysis of initial effects. *Educational Evaluation and Policy Analysis, 9,* 9–24.

Malen, B., and Muncie, D. (2000). Creating "a new set of givens"? The impact of state activism on school autonomy. In N. D. Theobald and B. Malen (Eds.), *Balancing local control and state responsibility for K-12 education,* Chap. 7. Larchmont, NY: Eye on Education.

Mann, D. (1979). Political representation and urban school advisory councils. *Teachers College Record, 75,* 251–170.

Mazzoni, T. L. (1991). Analyzing state school policymaking: An arena model. *Educational Evaluation and Policy Analysis, 13,* 115–138.

Mazzoni, T. L. (2000). State politics and school reform: The first decade of the "education excellence" movement. In N. D. Theobald and B. Malen (Eds.), *Balancing local control and state responsibility for K-12 education,* Chap. 6. Larchmont, NY: Eye on Education.

Orr, M. (1999). *Black social capital: The politics of school-reform in Baltimore, 1986-1998.* Lawrence, KS: University Press.

Rice, J. K. (1997). Cost analysis in education: Paradox and possibility. *Educational Evaluation and Policy Analysis, 19,* 309–317.

Schorr, L. B. (1988). *Within our reach: Breaking the cycle of disadvantage.* New York: Anchor Press.

Smith, M. S., and O'Day, J. A. (1991). Systemic school reform. In S. Fuhrman and B. Malen (Eds.), *The politics of curriculum and testing* (pp. 233–268). Bristol, PA: Falmer Press.

Spillane, J. P. (1999). State and local government relations in an era of standards-based reform: Standards, state policy instruments, and local instructional policy making. *Educational Policy, 13*, 546–572.

Stone, C. N. (1989). *Regime politics: Governing Atlanta, 1946–1988.* Lawrence, KS: University Press.

Theobald, N. D., and Bardzell, J. (2000). Introduction and overview: Balancing local control and state responsibility for K–12 education. In N. D. Theobald and B. Malen (Eds.), *Balancing local control and state responsibility for K-12 education,* Chap. 1. Larchmont, NY: Eye on Education.

Theobald, N. D., and Bull, B. (in press). *Objective measures for informing policy debate and action around school funding issues.* Oak Brook, IL: North Central Regional Educational Laboratory.

Tyack, D. and Cuban, L. (1995). *Tinkering toward utopia.* Cambridge, MA: Harvard University Press.

Walsh, M. (1999, December 15). Report card on for-profit industry still incomplete. *Education Week,* pp. 1, 18.

Wang, M. C., and Walberg, H. J. (1999, December 1). Decentralize or "disintermediate"? Trapped between top-down and bottom-up expectations, schools need a governance system attuned to both accountability and entrepreneurship. *Education Week,* pp. 36, 52.

Wells, A. S., and Associates. (1998). Charter school reform in California: Does it meet expectations? *Phi Delta Kappan, 80*(4), 305–312.

Wirt, F. M. (1977). State policy culture and state decentralization. In J. Scribner (Ed.), *Politics of education* (pp. 164–187). Chicago: National Society for the Study of Education.

Ziegler, H., and Jennings, M. K. (1974). *Governing American schools.* Scituate, MA: Duxbury Press.

INDEX